"Give me your coat," Dina said, standing just behind Rosemary.

For Rosemary that was not possible. The slow, low-flamed need of six years, the moments that collected to hours of standing next, turning toward, only to be offered something, something else—a courtesy—turned her now slowly into Dina's arms, face offered up to face that had hovered over her in a thousand fantasies, serene-eyed always. Rosemary's hands cupped Dina's head and drew her down to the slow, seeking appetite of her own mouth which could discover against all the barriers of clothes what Dina wanted or could be made to want.

Against the Season

by
Jane Rule

the NAIAD PRESS inc.
1984

Printed in the United States of America

First Naiad Press Edition   1984

Cover design by Tee A. Corinne

For my *mother* and *father*

Other Works by Jane Rule

1964 Desert of the Heart*
1970 This Is Not for You*
1971 Against the Season*
1975 Lesbian Images
1975 Theme for Diverse Instruments
1977 The Young in One Another's Arms**
1980 Contract with the World*

*Available from THE NAIAD PRESS
**Available from THE NAIAD PRESS (Fall, 1984)

I

AGAINST THE SEASON, which was spring, and against the day, iris limp and azaleas sodden in rain, Amelia Larson was in a burning mood.

"Not the right spirit for the kitchen," she said to Kathy, the maid she'd soon lose to the unwed mothers' home. "Just leave Cole's place set. I'll wake him when I go up. I think it's a morning for the attic."

The girl nodded, a great emotional distance from what was being said to her, but serene there. Amelia's educated eye estimated another three weeks to a month. Friends were beginning to be critical, under the guise of concern: "Now that Cole's staying with you, wouldn't it be better to have permanent help?" or "Don't you think by now other people could take on this sort of thing?" They implied, of course, that Amelia was too old, too much out of touch, and perhaps always had been too much of an amateur to deal with these girls. The morality of it had, for thirty years or more, threatened propriety; but while Amelia's sister lived and there were only the two of them, no one could say just why a string of pregnant girls in the house didn't seem right. Now Cole Westaway, a cousin's son who was to be with her for his college years, was a new fact, corrupting or corruptible, Amelia wasn't sure which her friends thought. She must, within the next month, get to know her own mind, which was not as positively made up as she claimed.

Her second cup of coffee finished, Amelia hoisted herself out of her father's large, carved chair and let her considerable weight down on her lame side. Then in a slow, strong rocking-chair movement, checking the pockets of her smock for scissors, pad and pencil, magnifying glass as she went, Amelia left the large dining room, crossed the hall, and seated herself in the chair lift, installed five years ago, not for her but for her sister, after the first stroke. Amelia had used it since in order not to waste it, she said. Having been born lame, she had never been allowed nor had she allowed herself to be pampered. Still, she was glad not to spend the energy on those stairs any longer, and she liked the ride, sidesaddle, past the mottoes cross-stitched by three generations of Larson women, a stop at the landing to look through the stained-glass window onto her mother's rose garden, the first blooms heavy-headed in the rain this morning, then on up to the second floor.

"It would be as good as a London tube escalator if you'd put up some ads," Cole said, standing at the top of the stairs, a little thin and sharp-faced to be handsome, his fair hair soft over one eyebrow, a child's hair. He looked younger than twenty. "Say, some ladies' underwear or suntan oil or . . ."

"Put up anything you like," Amelia said and then added, pleased with herself, "as long as it's uplifting."

Cole laughed. He did not offer to help her up, having been given the simple instruction when he moved in: "When I want help, I'll ask for it." He stood, looking past her to the mottoes.

"When you've finished your breakfast, bring me some boxes from the back porch up to the attic. I'm going to burn things today."

"What kinds of things?" Cole asked.

"I don't know yet, but the rain's put me in a destructive mood— or rebellious, maybe. Sister never let me touch a thing up there, and there must be some old valentines or May Day cards from seventy-five years ago that we could live without."

"Do you think so, Cousin A? A lot of that stuff may be historically valuable by now. Cousin B used to say . . ."

"I know . . . that every old photograph and letter should go to the city archives. I'll be careful, and anything to do with your side of the family you can look at again yourself if you want to."

"I just meant . . ."

Amelia was by now at the door to the attic stairs, and she left Cole to just mean whatever he had, if he had. Sister, if she had been on her way up in front of Amelia, would have said: "One: that remark about 'uplifting' was uncalled for. Two: you should take your leave of people not when they have no more to say but when they have stopped the actual noise of conversation." And Amelia would have had to listen very carefully through the heaviness of her own progress to catch the tone in her sister's voice, for she might be scolding or teasing or approving. Beatrice Larson, five years older than Amelia, formidable even before she was an old lady, prided herself on her own irreproachable social behavior and despaired with great good humor of her sister's directness. "One day, as a result of you, something is going to happen to us," she would say, and that, too, could be offered as reprimand or commendation. Whatever the moral tone, there was always hope in it. And love in it.

"Memory isn't the same," Amelia said aloud as she labored up the narrow stairs, though in a sense she was speaking to Beatrice still, four or five steps ahead of her, there where she had always been.

Amelia had not told Cole the exact truth about her work in the attic. One of these days she must, in fact, begin to clear out a ballroom full of family history, unsorted since the year after her mother died and then with Beatrice's sense, not her own. Today, however, she was not after old valentines and photographs and letters. She was fulfilling a promise she had made to her sister six months ago, the day before she died.

"Burn my diaries."

Amelia had no reluctance. She would have gone to the attic the day after the funeral to carry out this last request if she had been free to believe it. But Beatrice no more wanted those diaries burned unread than she wanted anything else destroyed that had been executed by the human hand. Only she had been afraid that one day someone other than Amelia might find them. Or was it, rather, that she knew Amelia would want to burn them and not be able to without the request? Had she been sparing Amelia even then? Or was it that the order to burn them was calculated to arouse Amelia's curiosity sufficiently to ensure a reading of them before they were burned? Beatrice's tone had always been the clue, but on that day her impaired speech made it impossible to judge. Not knowing what to do, Amelia had done nothing for six months.

At the top of the stairs, she rested. Then she opened the door to the enormous space that had, in her father's youth, been a ball-room. She suspected that its gradual deterioration into a storage area had to do not only with "the times" but with her lameness. In her memory, there had never been dancing in the house. First only one corner had been walled off for trunks that mildewed in the basement, but gradually furniture and boxes spilled out onto the dance floor; a cardboard cupboard was partnered with the grand piano, a large bird cage with a commode, a chest with a dress dummy, and these unlikely matings gradually produced clustered families of boxes and parcels. It was not exactly hap-hazard. There were winding paths and categories of sorts, and always a wide space was left to the raised turret corner where on a hard and dusty seat generations of women had sat, watching the harbor for a ship to arrive or leave. When relatives and lovers no longer traveled in this manner, it was still a place in the house for solitude. Amelia had never used it, obviously because the stairs were a chore but also because she was not of a tempera-ment for solitude. It was first her mother's place, then her sister's. Amelia rocked her way over to it, pulled herself up and onto the seat. The rain had closed in the view of the sea and all but the gray line of larger buildings by the old docks. But she could look over the ten-foot-high hedges of her own acre of garden into the neighborhood, which was no longer elegant, more boarding houses than family homes by now. There was talk of buying up the old houses, restoring them, turning them into elegant clubs, exclusive rest homes. But the town—city—was really not that sort yet, and it seemed unlikely that it would ever be. Amelia was interested in the town, its strong but stunted life, and she could have turned her mind to it, but she had come to find the diaries, many pages of which had been written in this very place, though probably with few entries about this view or neighborhood or town. She must find sixty-nine of them, one for each year since Beatrice was six and had learned to write. They were not all carefully stored in several boxes. They were, Amelia believed, in "year boxes," one book in among all the things Beatrice saved in a year.

Up again with the violent decisiveness that was part of any

physical moving, Amelia started down the most likely trail, her magnifying glass out to read the labels, and soon she found "B, 1967," a box that had brought cat food into the house. She snipped the string, lifted out carefully ribboned packets of letters and postcards, a stack of graduation and wedding photographs, receipts, canceled checks, an appointment calendar, and finally the familiar English diary, the size of a Gideon Bible and always in the drawer by her sister's bed. She had given up the sort with a flap and key years before, perhaps in her early thirties, either for want of secrets or want of anyone to hide them from, though she had always kept the diary in her sewing bag on Thursdays when the cleaning woman came. Amelia did not turn the pages. She simply set the book aside, replacing the other contents, and wrote BURN in dark letters across the top of the box. She was at the year 1954 when Cole arrived with several empty boxes.

"Those thirteen should go to the basement by the incinerator," Amelia directed, and to his again uncertain look she explained, "They're all Sister's private papers; she asked to have them burned."

He took three at a time and moved quickly, with unconscious impatience. Amelia knew he had nothing to do that morning, with three days free now before his last exam, which he claimed he couldn't study for. He always rushed at anything he was asked to do or set himself to do, as if the only pleasure were in having done with a game of tennis, a book, or a chore. But he didn't enjoy empty time when he arrived at it. He occupied himself then with nervous habits, smoking, biting his left thumbnail, starting conversations he wasn't interested in about things no one else was interested in either. After his third trip to the basement, Amelia told him to sit and rest for a bit. He folded himself up on the turret bench and stared out the window.

"I wonder if it will rain all day," he said.

Amelia put the 1951 diary into the box and then turned round to look at Cole. "You're not a happy boy," she said.

"Why?" he asked, without turning to her.

"I don't know," she said. "What are you going to do with yourself this summer?"

"Work at the mill," he said, bewildered by so obvious a question.

"Would you rather not?"

"I have to. I mean, I have to have my fees."

"If I paid your fees, what would you do?"

"I couldn't let you do that, Cousin A. You already . . ."

"There's the money. Why don't I send you to Europe again?"

"No," he said. "No, thank you. I'm really not ready for that again. I don't mean I didn't enjoy it very much, but it was pretty overwhelming, you know, when you've never been anywhere before. All those people."

"All right, but you don't have to work at the mill."

"I don't mind it," Cole said quickly. "I'm used to it. It's something to do."

"Something to do," Amelia repeated and then turned her back on him.

"What are those things?"

"Sister's diaries."

He put a hand on one, a new interest in his face.

"To be burned, too, but later."

"Are you going to read them?" he asked.

"I'm not sure," Amelia said. "There's nothing in them I don't already know, unless I shouldn't know it."

"It's better not to know."

"At your age?"

"At any age, I think," Cole said.

Amelia could not find the boxes for the years 1933 through 1935, nor those from 1913 through 1915. Mislaid? She doubted it. Destroyed? Perhaps. But if they were around anywhere, hidden, those were the years Sister would want burned, read or unread. Amelia was tired, too tired to imagine where else she might begin to look. She told Cole to carry the sixty-three books she had found down to her room.

"And, Cole, do you see that little chest there? I think Harriet would like that. If you'll take that down to the front hall, I'll show it to her. If she does, I'll call Dina to mend it."

She followed Cole down the stairs for a rest before lunch. The boxes of diaries, on the floor by her desk, troubled her. Or was it really that she could hear Beatrice say, "Are you going to put Harriet Jameson in your debt? If so, why?" "Oh, why not, Sister, why not? They're only things, after all." And if anyone was in debt to anyone, it was Amelia to Harriet, who, Amelia thought with pleasure, would be here tonight for dinner, along with Peter Fallidon.

8

May, 1899: Sister falls down and Mama cries. I hurt my own leg and Papa laughs at me.

or

May, 1906: Sister climbed the apple tree again today and shouted across the hedge, "If I can't walk, I'll learn to fly." Papa spoke to us about thinking and showing off, the good and the bad. "Beatrice fails at the first, and Amelia succeeds at the second." When he is a hard teacher, I cry. Sister never cries.

or

May, 1912: Am I the only one in the world who cannot bear roses?

or

May, 1917: Papa would have loved this day full of gulls.

or

May, 1940: Sister has argued for the last time about this war. She has such a good nature, I don't understand her international irritabilities. We don't read the same books. A pity.

or

May, 1955: I have grown up and grown old here, hating roses.

✳

Cole opened the door to Harriet Jameson, awkward with umbrella and an armload of library books.

"This rain," she said.

"I'll take the books," Cole offered. "Any for me this week?"

"One. I don't think you'll like it much. It looks like a morality tale simply disguised as science fiction. But I thought you'd be studying for exams anyway."

"Do you want to go upstairs, or shall I take your coat?"

"Thanks. I won't bother."

There was a hall mirror, before which Harriet could appraise herself quickly, knowing she was always neat, even in a high wind, never really groomed, which was for horses and women of other sorts of ambition. She resettled her jacket over thin shoulders, long thin arms, and made sure the rather tastelessly old-fashioned pin was fastened and straight. There were specks of rain on her rimless glasses. Whatever prettiness she had was of the sort admired by old ladies—a healthy, shining head of nevertheless very ordinary hair, a clear complexion, really blue eyes, some refinement of feature, not quite sharp. She looked what she was: a thirty-six-year-old spinster librarian.

"Cousin A wanted you to look at this chest," Cole said, occupying himself with Harriet's coat and umbrella. "She's going to get Dina to mend it and wondered if you'd like it."

"But it's beautiful," Harriet said, an opinion she had without discrimination of everything in this house.

They both heard the heavy sound of Amelia coming toward them from somewhere at the back of the house, probably from where she had been speaking to Kathy about dinner.

"So here you are," Amelia said, in the soft folds of black she had worn since Beatrice died, holding out both strong, old hands, which Harriet took as she leaned forward to kiss Amelia's cheek. "Isn't Peter with you?"

"It seemed silly since we're on opposite sides of town. Anyway, he was afraid of being late at the bank."

"Did Cole show you the chest?"

"Yes, and it's beautiful, but . . ."

"Good, I'll call Dina in the morning."

Amelia had released only one of Harriet's hands. Leading her by the other, not for steadiness but for happy possession, Amelia jarred them off toward the library. There, in the room the sisters always used in preference to the larger drawing room, Harriet still felt the absence of Beatrice, with whom she had never been as much at ease as with Amelia but whom she had loved with uncritical admiration: the image of grand age which no one would ever reach again. The force in Amelia was different, without her sister's faint, ironic haughtiness, nobility of head, command. Amelia took nothing from the setting, simply inhabited it in abrupt, forthright generosity.

"Kathy's forgotten the ice," Amelia said.

"I'll get it," Cole volunteered.

"He's a good boy," Harriet commented as he left the room.

"And it's too bad in a way, isn't it?" Amelia said. "For him, I mean. It's nice for the rest of us, of course."

"You probably would have said that of me at his age," Harriet decided.

"No, even then you would have been brighter than you were prissy."

"I was very prissy," Harriet laughed.

"Do you keep a diary?"

"A diary? Not exactly," Harriet said. "I did when I was younger."

"Why?"

"I'm not sure. Literary pretensions maybe, or a way to declare I was lonely in a very noisy world. Being the odd one of five children."

"The odd one?"

"Otherwise there would have been four children," Harriet said. "Why do you ask?"

"Sister kept a diary religiously from the time she was six years old."

"Have you got them?"

"Yes."

"What are you going to do with them?"

"Burn them."

"Should you?"

"Yes, I should. Do I have to read them first?"

"Don't you want to?"

"I loved my sister," Amelia said. "I don't know whether I can."

"Do you want someone else . . . do you want me . . .?"

"What would anyone be looking for, Harriet?"

"In a diary? Well, greater understanding, maybe, or information or simple curiosity."

"Would you be curious?"

"If I were you?"

"Yes."

"Maybe not," Harriet said.

"I'm not frightened. It isn't that," Amelia said.

"What kind of diaries are they? Would they have historical importance? I should think they would. Simply the people who came in and out of this house."

"She asked me to burn them."

"Oh."

"I looked at a few of them this afternoon, just glancing at seasons. She turned a nice phrase often."

"She certainly did," Harriet said.

The front doorbell sounded, and Cole, just turning in with the ice bucket, ducked out again to answer it, but he paused a moment before the mirror to brush his soft, falling hair off his temple and to see if the jumping nerve in his cheek was as irritating to look at as it was to feel. Then, guilty of the delay, he wrenched the door open and greeted Peter Fallidon with embarrassingly loud cheerfulness.

"You're in good spirits tonight," Peter said, offering to shake hands.

"Trying to beat the weather," Cole said, who never knew quite how to take hold or when to let go.

Peter, for Cole's sake, wanted to teach him just such simple protections so that the boy wouldn't suffer the ordinary as much as he did now. But he was aware that Cole was embarrassed in a kind of pleasure, too. It was, therefore, necessary to be casual with him as well as instructive.

"How did the math go?"

"I still have it to write," Cole said.

"Are you going to be finished by next Thursday?"

"Yes . . . Monday."

"Somebody gave me a couple of tickets to the stock car races Thursday night," Peter said. "I can't go, but I thought maybe you'd like them."

"Great!" Cole said.

"Here, they're in my coat pocket."

Peter Fallidon, who had not been a friend to the household until after Beatrice was ill, sensed her absence only in Amelia, when he sensed it at all. His concern, from the beginning, was for her. Coming from out of town to be manager of the bank old Mr. Larson had founded, Peter had first called to win the confidence of the Misses Larson. Beatrice well would have required just that of him. Amelia hadn't either that kind of patience or shrewdness. She had looked at him, then taken his hand in both of hers and said, "Thank God you've come, Mr. Fallidon. I need you." It had been a surprise to Peter and also an unexpected relief to be so immediately welcomed. He knew that he was somehow a little too good-looking, too solid in stature, too un-solicitous, to be most people's image of a bank manager. In his dark face, his jade and jaded eyes could easily be mistrusted. What he did not know was that the expression in them was one that often moved people—widows in particular. They looked not hurt or sorrowing so much as capable of those emotions, as if he might have been born to be a widower. In the eighteen months he had been in town, it was decided that he was a widower. Then someone suggested that his wife had died in childbirth. The fact that, at forty-three, he hadn't married simply didn't suit him. Because he was not in the habit of speaking about his personal life, people accepted the rumor that became him. Even Amelia might have offered it if someone had asked directly about Peter's life, though his personal history, because it did not seem to interest him, was of no interest to her either. She had liked his eyes, yes, but she had liked even better his confidence. After having been at the mercy of the cretinous incompetence of Peter's predecessor, a hand-rubbing, how-are-we-today local, she chose to trust what other people—even perhaps Beatrice—would have called arrogance.

She looked up with pleasure now as Peter came into the library and offered up her hands to him, which he had learned to take, just as Harriet had. Then he turned to Harriet, nodded and smiled.

"Are some of those books in the hall for me?" he asked.

"No," she said. "I left yours in the back of my car."

"Peter's got me tickets to the stock car races next Thursday," Cole said, holding them up.

"I have a couple of tickets to the chamber music concert next Friday night as well," Peter said. "Could you use one?"

"Lovely," Harriet said.

"And for you, Miss Larson, a briefcase full of papers to sign, which I didn't bring tonight—selfishly. Could I bring them round tomorrow afternoon?"

"Of course," Amelia said.

"Sherry, Cousin A?"

"Gin and tonic for you, Harriet?" Peter asked, moving over to the drink tray with Cole.

It was a game like bridge, the four of them choosing and changing partners through the half an hour before dinner was served. In the last six months they had met to play it at least once every ten days, sometimes oftener. Peter and Harriet had first met nearly a year ago as if by accident one afternoon when she was on her way out of the Larson house and he on his way in. She had, with quickly controlled embarrassment, agreed to stay for a drink. Soon after that Amelia had asked them both for dinner, but it had been a business meeting, to do with Amelia's concern about the new wing of the town library and ways of financing it. Still Harriet and Peter understood that they were being encouraged to take an interest in each other. When Peter telephoned to ask Harriet to a concert, she had said, "That's kind of you, Peter, but I . . ." He interrupted to ask if he could come round for coffee at once. Then he made the speech that he had made to a number of women before. He was neither interested in nor capable of marriage. He did not want an affair. If "no intention" could be considered honorable, he would like to take Harriet out occasionally, but, particularly at their age, it might be misinterpreted by other people as a courtship. That would, if anything, be a convenience for him, but it might be a limitation for her.

"I'm no more interested than you are," Harriet said.

"Then could I be some sort of relief to you?" he asked. "You would be for me."

Harriet considered objecting to it and saw no real reason to. Only, increasingly, she would have liked to say to Amelia, "Peter and I have no interest in each other," and did not know how. For to say so was to give some importance to what she intended to deny. Only by their behavior—usually arriving and leaving separately and speaking to each other as if they had not, as indeed they often hadn't, talked with each other recently—they tried to indicate to Amelia how casual a relationship it was. But, if Amelia noticed such things, she received them as facts rather than social messages.

"Dinner's served," Kathy said, large in the doorway of the library.

"How are you tonight, Kathy?" Harriet asked.

"Fine, Miss Jameson."

"There are some books for you in the front hall."

"Thank you."

Because of the peculiar domestic arrangements, food at the Larson house was, at stretches, either very good or very bad. Amelia did supervise, but the four months she had a girl were not a time for demanding standards. Amelia had to identify the standard she could expect and then accept it. Kathy, a country girl, was a good cook for anyone who did not suffer from gall bladder attacks. And, fortunately, none of these four did. Amelia's older friends, after one experience, suggested evenings of bridge after dinner until Kathy was delivered. Tonight there was rich cream of chicken soup before the pork roast, and there would be cream again for dessert, which would cover the biscuits they had been eating throughout the meal with sweet butter.

Amelia was gradually aware that, during these meals with Peter and Harriet, conversation shifted from the light gossip and sharp wit Beatrice had always sponsored and encouraged to sets of earnest topics of the sort their father had required: local politics, agricultural information, the war, computerized business. If it was a bit heavy, like the food, she couldn't help it. Harriet, argumentative, could prime Peter into sharp assertions. Cole's interest flickered, brightened, died again.

"But, if what turns a town into a city is greed and vanity, then . . ." Harriet began to protest.

"Ah, but what keeps a town a town is also greed and vanity," Peter said.

"Does a place have to grow or die?" Cole asked.

"First one, then the other," Amelia said. "Here, at any rate. The growth was very fast; the dying very slow. Giving us time to pay for our sins, my father would have said. His father helped to figure out how to drive out all the cheap Chinese labor, not just from the town, from the whole county. To this day, we have no Orientals, no blacks, no race problems."

"Which could be made very attractive to industry," Peter said.

"Where's the work force?" Amelia asked.

"It would come. The town doesn't have to die."

"We've survived crucial failures," Amelia agreed, "but we've refused to develop the docks or the dead center of parking lots. This is probably the only town of this size in North America without a parking problem. We haven't supported education . . ."

"There's still wealth here," Peter said.

"But why have a parking problem?" Cole asked. "Why fill the bay with freighters? I wouldn't want to go to a huge university—I probably couldn't even get in. And I don't want to major in the industrial-military complex and race riots."

"That's one answer," Harriet said. "The people who stay here stay because it isn't a city, nor even threatening to be a city."

"Is that why you've stayed?" Peter asked.

"In part," Harriet said.

"And why you won't, for long," Amelia said to Peter.

"I'm not sure," Peter said. "It may be Harriet and Cole who have to move."

"You should have been my generation. We were all girls or remittance men."

"The two necessities for building North America," Peter said, smiling.

"You talk this way," Harriet said, "but you came here to get away from the city, not to build one."

"Only in a way," Peter said. "With planning, we could come into the seventies and eighties with responsible industry, a balanced population. Oh, with problems of course, but healthy problems, not the terminal disease of either big cities now or this town now."

Cole fidgeted with pieces of silver he had forgotten to use.

"Are you going out tonight?" Amelia asked him.

"Some of us were thinking of meeting at Nick's for a while, but no special time," he said.

"Let's go to coffee. Kathy shouldn't be on her feet too long. Cole, you run along."

Amelia was never sure whether he went away because he wanted to or because he felt he should. His nervous boredom was no measure. She knew he took that with him to Nick's or the movies or his room. But, though Peter was good for him and Harriet affectionate with him, it was probably better that he spend time with his own friends. And Amelia, tonight, had things on her mind that she could not discuss in front of Cole.

They had finished coffee and Kathy had come in for the last time to get the tray before Amelia took the random conversation up into her hands and stopped it.

"Kathy won't be here more than another three weeks," Amelia said. "My old and dear friends think it's time for me to have permanent help. They seem to feel, among other things, that the moral influence on Cole couldn't be a good one. I don't seem to be able to settle my own mind about it."

"Unmarried, pregnant girls," Peter said with measured seriousness, "are probably the best moral influence a young man could have."

"If he needed a moral influence," Harriet added.

"Now that's a question I hadn't put to myself," Amelia said. "Maybe Kathy is a real discouragement to Cole."

"Do they have much to do with each other?" Peter asked.

"Not a great deal," Amelia said. "But we've had other girls who would have been much harder to ignore. There have been vixens and charmers."

"But very pregnant," Peter said.

"Yes," Amelia agreed.

"Still, I suppose he could want to make an honest woman of

someone," Harriet said.

"Cole doesn't seem to me that romantic," Peter said. "Or to have that kind of confidence in himself."

"And, if he did," Amelia said, "if he could get that involved . . ."

"You wouldn't find anything to object to," Harriet finished.

"Is that rather naïve of me?"

"I don't suppose his mother would like it," Peter said.

"No," Amelia agreed, but in a tone that suggested what Cole's mother thought was of no great moment to him or anyone else.

"But it's all very theoretical," Peter said, "and unlikely."

"There's something else," Amelia said. "It's not often a girl needs as little as Kathy in the way of company or instruction. Am I getting too old? Friends my age don't hesitate to say, 'Yes, you are.' Be frank with me. Are they right?"

"No," Harriet said, "not unless you're tired of it, not unless it does begin to seem too much to you."

"I've never been much of a psychologist," Amelia said.

"That's probably why you've been such a help to so many people," Peter said.

"Is that flattery?"

"No," Peter said, "no, I mean it. I'm with Harriet. If you still want to do it, you should do it. I can't see that it's any real problem to Cole. And you know that Mrs. Montgomery, whatever she says, would be disappointed to lose any point of moral speculation."

Amelia smiled at him. Beatrice would have learned to like him.

Harriet was the first to say she must go. Peter, remembering the books she had in the back of the car, got up to leave with her.

"Don't see us to the door," Harriet said.

But Amelia did. ("This is not to be a house of people letting themselves in and out"—Beatrice, on Ida Setworth's once delivering a present, unannounced, in the kitchen.)

When she had shut the door behind them, Amelia put a hand on the small chest she intended to give to Harriet. Then she turned herself to the chair lift. Cole would deal with the lights when he got in. Once in her bedroom at the front of the house, Amelia could still hear Peter's and Harriet's voices faintly in the drive. It must have stopped raining. A moment more and the first car door slammed—Harriet's Volkswagen, then the second, Peter's, heavier, quieter.

✳

May 1, 1942: The bulk and vulgarity of our latest charge make us accept dinner invitations more readily than usual. "What I can't stand most," she complained at breakfast, "is the way I smell." "Similar to sweet fish," Sister said. How I wish I could be protected either from or by her impervious accuracy. To Ida tonight, who has the sense to live among the odorless dead.

May 2, 1942: We played Mah-Jongg last night. Ida has been archaic since she was seven years old and has that effect on all of us. Sister seemed to me uncomfortable. If she would ever complain, I would not have to be so sensitive—a complaint I must remember to pass on to her if she's had a troubled night.

May 3, 1942: We knit for illegitimate children, soldiers, and plant a victory garden. If Sister mentions a cow, I will be gravely disapproving.

May 4, 1942: There is nothing in the world to do about May but live through it. Today Ida's nephew is missing in action. She seems to have expected it. There is never any comfort for Ida.

May 5, 1942: Since Mother died, the morning sounds of this house have been unnatural. Sister, who used to sit at her desk, pursues them all, as a way, I suppose, of hearing none of them. She walks deaf, and we shout at her.

May 6, 1942: There have been no letters to answer in days. I write to myself without interest.

May 7, 1942:

II

DINA PYROS RAN SOMETHING between an antique and a junk shop called simply George's, wedged in between Charlie Ries's drugstore and Cater's Ice Cream on F Street, which cut wide and uncertainly commercial across the whole of the uncertain city. Dina's better customers, like Ann and Charlie Ries from next door, Harriet Jameson, the librarian, and Ida Setworth, one of the town's finest antiques herself, complained about the space she took up with the empty beer bottles and old paperbacks she bought. But her best customers, like Rosemary Hopwood, who was a social worker, and Peter Fallidon, the bank manager, liked the paperbacks as much as they did the stripped-down and refinished tables and chests. Dina's friends, like Sal and Dolly who ran the corset shop down the block, wouldn't have an excuse to visit during business hours unless they could bring the bottles Dina had helped to empty over the weekend. Even more important, those people who weren't exactly friends and certainly not customers could always collect a dozen empties or a handful of old mysteries and have an excuse to pass half an hour or an afternoon by Dina's old stove with the cats and the radio. They got in the way sometimes and left sometimes with things more valuable than what they had brought in, though they rarely had either the skill or initiative to carry out furniture. Charlie Ries said they all but ruined Dina's business and too often spilled over into his drugstore. But Dina imagined Rosemary Hopwood sometimes came in because of them, and Dina's friends didn't mind as long as there was some place to sit down and a little air coming in from the back door. For Dina herself, the people around the stove were as important as the old pieces of furniture she brought in, collected from fire sales, real junk shops, old ladies' attics, sometimes even the dump. She knew good wood and good lines. She had an eye for grain and bone structure in a face as well. Not many phonies of any kind came into the shop and stayed. Anyone who asked, "Who's George?" or, worse, "Where's George?" didn't stay long or come back. Nor did anybody who called Dina "George." Whether the Rieses or Ida Setworth approved of the tone or not, there was one—a kind of hum that came from power tools even after they had been turned off or the old tubes in the radio or the cats—some sort of constant that made the shop seem at the same time drowsy and alive.

Something dangerous, or dangerously comfortable, about George's or the young woman who ran it, so Rosemary Hopwood had thought when she first discovered it six years ago just after she'd come back to town. The line of an old rocker had clipped her vision at thirty miles an hour so that she slowed, drove round the block, and parked her rather too expensive car for the price she intended to pay right at the front door. Dina Pyros was alone in the shop that morning, crouched at the bottom drawer of an old chest, fixing the last of the brass handles. She went on working while she exchanged looks of appraisal with her customer. Rosemary Hopwood had time, therefore, to consider that face and the price tag on the rocker before she had to speak. There wasn't, she was interested to discover, much margin for bargaining in either the price or the face, which she regretted briefly, knowing no other way to have a conversation.

"I'd like the rocker," she said.

Dina stood up, squarely built, solidly balanced, in a heavy, dark sweater, other uncountable layers of clothing visible at the neck, lined jeans, and boots. She must have said something, but Rosemary's memory of the transaction was that it was nearly wordless. She had the right change. Dina put the rocker in her car. That was all. The radio had been playing, surely. It always was.

The shop had never been empty again when Rosemary came in, once every two or three months, sometimes honestly looking for a piece of furniture, more often simply lingering at the paperbacks, accepting a cigarette or a cup of coffee, strong and bitter, boiled with its grounds in an old tin pot. Occasionally she met someone she knew: old Ida Setworth or Cole Westaway, the boy who had come to live with Amelia Larson. And the faces of those she didn't know, collected around the stove, became familiar to her. For her, there was no conversation ever, just the hum of the shop, voices somewhere in it, from the radio or the people by the stove, and the owner's square, drowsy courtesy. Rosemary would stay a little longer than made sense and go before she was ready to.

At first Dina had been no more than surprised by Rosemary Hopwood, who was not a woman one could reasonably expect to drop in at George's or, for that matter, anywhere else in this by-passed, sea-sided town. That first day she was still dressing as she had in some other world, in black, with something bright and soft at her throat. Her hair was black—and her eyes—and she had a slow, very white smile. Dina was not so much aware of how little had been said as she was of Rosemary's voice, low, with breakings in it. When Dolly asked Dina to describe Rosemary Hopwood, Dina could only say, "Around forty, about to age." And Rosemary had aged in those six years, for Dina nearly at once when she discovered Rosemary's name, which was as old as any name in town, then again when Dina discovered that she was a social worker.

"What if she's looking for grass?" Dina asked Dolly.

"It's not as if you were pushing it," Dolly said.

"No, but you know . . . the kids."

"So? They're better by your stove than down on the docks."

"Still, you can smell it."

"Maybe she's your type, is she?" Dolly asked.

Dina shrugged, as if to say *she* wasn't particular.

"Sal wonders, are you coming over tonight?"

"Don't know," Dina said.

It would depend, as Dolly knew, on whether or not Dina got involved with a piece of furniture or a woman. If a woman, she might bring her along, but if a piece of furniture, she was lost to them. Dina never really planned her involvements, as long as they were in something of a constant rhythm, which somehow usually happened without her ever directly initiating anything.

So, for six years, Rosemary Hopwood had been coming into the shop, along with a number of other people, and Dina had got used to her, though never quite to the sound of her voice. Dina sold her a table or made her a cup of coffee or offered her a cigarette, that was all.

Sal, in the shop just a couple of months ago, saw Rosemary for the first time and said, when she had gone, "I wonder where she buys her underwear."

Dina turned on the sander.

"I don't believe a word you say," Sal shouted uselessly. "You gray-eyed Greek!"

It was not a hard exercise in cynicism, since Dina spoke so few, ever.

Saturday morning was always a bad one for Dina because she drank every Friday night at Nick's, partly out of family loyalty to her cousin Nick, partly out of immigrant loneliness for a country she didn't remember, partly out of dull habit. It was a rest at the time, the place full of young men: college students and sailors off the few freighters that still did come in to port here. But she always drank too much. Dolly and Sal didn't know why she opened up on Saturday, except to provide a place by the stove for the drifting kids. That was why. She seemed to herself, on Saturday morning, one of them. Often she did no work at all, sat on the back step with a bottle of beer, and stared at weed patches in the concrete. Even addressed, she might not respond, but George's was open. The radio was on. The cats came in and out, over and around her.

"Shall I get the phone?" someone asked.

Dina didn't answer.

"It's Miss A, Dina," the same voice said. "She wants to talk to you, if that's all right."

Dina put the bottle of beer down carefully between her feet, got up, and backed away from it. To anyone else, if she had bothered to take the call, she would have said, "I don't *repair* furniture," but to Miss A, Dina would say yes to whatever request. It was not that she had her eye on pieces of furniture in the house, though there were some she would have loved to buy. Neither Miss B nor Miss A would ever sell anything. It wasn't, either, that the old Larson ladies were people no one refused, though that was true. Dina liked old people generally, particularly antiques like Ida Setworth. Still, she could say no to Ida Setworth. Miss A was, Dina tried to explain, "one of a kind." Not her lameness, no, not that. And Dina had seen better faces. Miss A's tended to pudding when she was tired. She was open and closed, open to know and still complete in herself. What she asked for was all that she ever wanted.

"Yes," Dina said, "tonight as soon as I've closed the shop. . . . No, not for supper, thanks, Miss A, but I'll have a sherry with you before I go."

The effort of that kept Dina from getting all the way back to the door. She settled in her old chair instead, a seat left vacant for her even when the shop was crowded. It turned partly away from the stove and the couch, not quite toward a remarkably orderly desk. From it, she could seem to turn her back and still watch the front area of the shop. And she could hear, without getting involved in, the arguments about baseball scores or narcs or how much it didn't cost to get to Mexico, usually quietly going on under the sounds of the radio.

The street door opened and Grace Hill walked into the shop, a long-boned, expensive woman with migraine eyes and an unalterable mouth. She started a look toward Dina and then veered away. She was too nervous to browse with books. Instead she got very aggressive with chairs, shaking them, turning them upside down, even lifting one or two off the wall where Dina had hung several sets.

"How much are these?" she finally called.

"Price is on the bottom," Dina replied, without looking over or moving.

"I'd like to be shown," Grace Hill said.

The others by the stove watched Dina for the moment before she moved, knowing it was a contest. Dina got up, walked over, and lifted half a dozen chairs off the wall.

"I don't really want chairs," Grace Hill said.

Dina yawned through her ears.

"Couldn't you come and have a drink?"

"Don't close the shop until six."

"Perhaps I'll come back."

Dina did not respond one way or the other. Grace Hill waited, then turned and walked out.

"Tight ass," one of the boys commented.

"Don't be mouthy about her broads," another said.

"What's mouthy?"

"Tight ass," Dina agreed, and she reached out to pour herself and the others coffee.

If Grace Hill did come back at six, Dina was not there to know

23

it. She had locked up at five-thirty in order to get to Miss A's to pick up the chest and drink a glass of sherry.

Since Dina had wrecked her sports car two years ago and spent three months in the hospital in traction, she had not owned a car. She drove instead her ancient junk truck, a reliable traffic hazard, built before automobiles became the first self-destruct art object. Sometimes it was reluctant to start, but there was nowhere in town that Dina couldn't get a push from a gang of kids or a bank manager. And, if she missed the light at M Street and therefore didn't get a run on the hill, she could always turn the truck around and back up, a sight familiar to local drivers and accepted by the police. This evening she was lucky and arrived at the crest of P Street at a sturdy ten miles an hour, only five or six patient cars behind her. Because of the high hedges around the Larson house, Dina did not see Rosemary Hopwood's car until she had turned into the drive. She sat in the high seat of her truck for a moment, leaning on the steering wheel. Then she cupped her ears in her hands, incidentally flattening the wings of her dark, strong hair.

"Hi, Dina," Cole called, coming across the drive from the side garden.

She gave him a minimal salute.

"I came about the chest."

"It's in the front hall. I'll help you carry it out," Cole said. "Then Cousin A says you'll stay for sherry."

"She's got company," Dina said.

"Just Miss Hopwood about Kathy."

"What's the matter with Kathy?"

"Well, you know, it's about time . . ." Cole said.

She followed him to the house, and together they carried out the chest either of them could have managed quite easily alone, but because Cole had nothing but goodwill invested in the gesture, Dina accepted it. She felt, with a dim kindness, sorry for Cole Westaway. He let so little out but goodwill. "The kind of guy to grow up to be everybody's left-hand man," her cousin Nick said, with some impatience, which Dina couldn't feel. She swung up on the truck deck and let Cole hand the chest up to her. He waited while she roped it down.

"It's a nice piece," she said.

"It's to be a present for Harriet Jameson."

Cole consciously did not offer his hand as she came down off the truck, just as he consciously did not offer a hand to Cousin A in any of her gettings up and gettings down. But knowing what not to do only left him doing nothing nervously. He would have liked to make Dina a friend of his, but he saw no clear way of going about it. He dropped in at the shop occasionally. He saw her often at Nick's, but he felt the distance she kept around herself from everyone, the kids in the shop, the women she drank with.

"Are you going to Nick's tonight?" Dina asked, making a rare effort at a question.

"Probably. Are you?"

"Don't know. Probably. There's a Greek ship in."

Dina wore nothing Cole could offer to take from her; so he led her at once down the hall to the library. She stood stolidly in the doorway for a moment, like the gardener or plumber; then she moved to the hands Miss A offered up to her.

"Dina," Amelia said. "Do you know Miss Hopwood?"

"Yes, we know each other," Rosemary said, offering only her very white smile. "How are you, Dina?"

"Well enough for Saturday," Dina said.

"Did Cole show you the chest?" Amelia asked.

"Yes, I can have it done for you in about a week. Do you want me to bring it back here or take it over to Miss Jameson's?"

"Well, yes, that's a sensible suggestion."

Cole was pouring her a glass of sherry, protecting himself from the silence in the room. Amelia listened to it as easily as if it were conversation. Rosemary was less comfortable in it, but what occurred to her to say, tested quickly in her head, seemed either false or forward. She reached for her purse and a cigarette, which signaled Dina to produce a pack from somewhere inside the layers of clothes she seemed to wear in all seasons.

"Thank you," Rosemary said. "I always seem to be smoking yours."

Dina shrugged, waited, and lighted the cigarette. Then she turned to Cole and her sherry.

"We've been talking about what to do when Kathy goes," Amelia said. "Apparently there are more girls than places just now."

"Grace Hill was thinking of taking a girl," Dina said.

"Do you know her?" Rosemary asked. "Well enough, I mean, to know how it would be for a girl in her household?"

25

"A house full of boys," Dina said. "A lot of work, probably."

"She has come to see me," Rosemary admitted. "She seemed . . ."

"I don't think it would be a good idea," Dina said flatly, to close the conversation.

But Amelia couldn't accept that, in concern of her own. "Why?"

"Do you know Mrs. Hill?" Rosemary asked.

"No," Amelia said. "I know who her husband is, of course, but I don't know her."

Dina had taken a seat across from Rosemary, her booted feet separately planted on the floor, her glass in a hand between her knees.

"Why, Dina?" Amelia asked again.

"She wants more than she asks for," Dina said. "These kids . . . you need to be willing to take less . . . like you."

"She said she'd had some training in social work," Rosemary said.

Dina looked over at Rosemary.

"She's an awfully nervous person," Cole said suddenly. "I don't really know her. I've just seen her in the shop a couple of times. But, if I were pregnant . . ." he stopped, half-amused, half-embarrassed.

Dina's laugh was like the bark of a deep-throated dog. "I'm with you, Cole," she said. "But you're already in the best house for pregnant girls in town."

For Amelia the conversation was both distressing and reassuring. Dina Pyros was no fool, and she was both young enough herself—probably not much over thirty—and in tune enough with young people to make such a judgment sensibly. Still, Amelia now was not the Amelia of six months or a year ago. She was older and heavier with grief. She was alone, with only the mirror of her sister's diaries to look into, where before she had been able to look into her sister's face. Other faces did not do in the same way and never would, much as she liked the two now turned toward her, the shrewd, gray-eyed Greek with her broad-planed face and the bred beauty of Rosemary Hopwood, as nerve-sharp as Dina was willfully bland.

"I don't know," Amelia said. "I just don't know."

"I don't have to send Agate to you," Rosemary said. "There are two other girls. . . ."

"Agate?" Cole asked.

"A bright and angry twenty-year-old from downstate," Rosemary said. "You'd like her well enough, but she's obviously going to be a handful at times. And maybe . . ." She turned to Amelia.

"Let me think about it," Amelia said. "Kathy has another three weeks probably."

"The doctor today said maybe just another week," Rosemary said and added, because of the surprise on Amelia's face, "There's a family history of complications."

Dina stood up and put her glass on the table. "Thanks for the sherry."

"Will you call me or Miss Jameson?" Amelia asked.

"Just as you like."

"Call her," Amelia decided.

"Good-bye, Dina," Rosemary said. "I'll have to stop in and see you one day soon. I'm looking for a bedside table."

"Any time," Dina said. "See you tonight, Cole."

"Yes," he said. "I'll see you to the door."

Dina went to Miss A, leaned down, and kissed her, not on the cheek, on the side of her brow, where the old, fine veins made a pattern.

"I like that young woman," Amelia said, when she and Cole had left the room. "Do you?"

"Why, yes. Why would you ask?" Rosemary said.

"You seemed to have some distaste for her boots," Amelia said, smiling.

"Sometimes you want me, just for a minute, to be Beatrice," Rosemary said.

"Yes, it's the shape of your head, I suppose."

"But I like Dina's boots. I like Dina. I confess that for some time I even tried to make friends with her, after I first got back."

"Did you really? And couldn't?"

"No more than you see," Rosemary said.

"She hasn't much talent for friendship. Cole tries, too. She doesn't talk long enough."

"No, though today she said more than I've ever heard her say before."

"You want me to take Agate," Amelia said.

"Yes, Amelia, I do, but I don't want to force her on you."

"What if I can't handle her?"

"I don't know," Rosemary said. "You won't have to if you can't, of course."

"Is Kathy going to have a difficult time?"

"I don't think so. It's just a precaution," Rosemary said. "And, by the way, something I think you *are* getting too old for is the waiting room."

"Nonsense. It's the one thing I don't feel too old for. And don't you misjudge Kathy. She asks very little, but she's going to need somebody there, and I'll do. I always have."

"Think about Agate. I'll stop in again later in the week."

"There's plenty of dinner," Amelia said.

"I know . . . with Kathy there always is, but I must go along."

Dina and Cole were still in the driveway when Rosemary came out of the house.

"Anything the matter?" she called.

"A flat," Dina said, "and I've left the spare at the shop."

"Do you want me to drive you down to get it?"

"I can, Miss Hopwood," Cole said.

"I think Kathy's already waiting dinner. I'm in no hurry. Come on, Dina."

"Thanks then. Thanks anyway, Cole. You go on in and have your dinner. I won't come right back."

As Dina got into Rosemary's car, Rosemary said, "I can bring you right back. I really am in no hurry."

"Neither am I. If you drop me at the shop, I can get Cole to bring me out tonight. He's coming down anyway, to Nick's."

They didn't say anything else to each other until Rosemary parked in front of George's.

"Thanks," Dina said, her hand on the door handle, but she had turned to look at Rosemary. "Are you coming in?"

"Shall I?"

"Up to you," Dina said, turning away.

It was as much of an invitation as and the only one Rosemary would ever get from Dina. She was not about to refuse it. She followed Dina to the door of the shop and waited while she unlocked it. Then she followed Dina in through the near darkness, cool with scents of wood and cosmetic oils and ashes, into the workshop where stairs led to the second floor. Not until Dina opened the door into her living room did she turn on a light. It was not at all what Rosemary had imagined, this white-walled space, rich with textures and deep colors that came from books and rugs and shawls thrown over tables and chairs. On the windowsill there were fresh daffodils.

"Will you stay for dinner?" Dina asked.

"Yes, thanks."

Dina went to the kitchen, got things out of a large refrigerator, and turned on the oven.

"Can I help?"

"Nothing much to do," Dina said. "Nick's cook sends things over." She was reading typed instructions, to do with temperatures and times, on several packages, wrapped professionally in foil. "Do you want a drink?"

"Thank you."

Dina opened a cupboard of bottles and displayed it to Rosemary. "Ouzo?"

"You like ouzo?"

"Yes," Rosemary said.

Dina poured a generous two jiggers into the bottom of each of two glasses, then filled a small jug with water, and put all three on a tray.

"Take these in."

Rosemary put the tray on a table by the couch, looked at half a dozen formally framed snapshots, one of Nick Pyros much younger, one of an old woman in a black shawl who might have been Dina's mother. Group pictures: one a large peasant family probably in Greece, another a large family dressed in city clothes, on a city street, Chicago, perhaps? New York?

"Give me your coat," Dina said, standing just behind Rosemary.

For Rosemary that was not possible. The slow, low-flamed need of six years, the moments that collected to hours of standing next, turning toward, only to be offered something, something else—a courtesy—turned her now slowly into Dina's arms, face offered up to the face that had hovered over her in a thousand fantasies, serene-eyed always. Rosemary's hands cupped Dina's head and drew her down to the slow, seeking appetite of her own mouth which could discover against all the barriers of clothes what Dina wanted or could be made to want. But Dina's mouth, so reluctant in speech, and her body, so solid and stolid in a weight of soft, carefully undefining armor, answered not quickly, no, but with an accepting authority, tongue delicate, then deep, a thrusting entrance into desire, hands lifting and spreading buttocks so that Rosemary must open and cling, her whole weight held into Dina. When she finally felt herself released, she wasn't sure she could stand. She tried, but kept her arms about Dina's neck, resting her head on Dina's shoulder.

"I've loved you for six years," Rosemary said.

Dina moved then, turned Rosemary so that she could take her coat, laid it casually and yet carefully over the arm of a chair, poured a small bit of water into each of the glasses of ouzo, watching the clear liquid swirl gently into milk. She handed one to Rosemary, sat down on the couch, and took Rosemary with her, onto her lap. She gave them time for two sips of the drink, then set the glasses aside.

Rosemary did not know finally how she had become naked. Dina's hands did not acknowledge or tear at cloth. She touched through it, defining the shapes of breast, belly, thigh, all undoing then without urgency, sexual in itself, hand through nylon, heavy, sure, then on the soft skin of the belly, the hip, the buttocks, gently parted, probed, left quiet for a moment, gradual nakedness, gradual openings everywhere to the hands, the mouth, until Rosemary came to her beyond any fantasy or experience she had ever had. Dina held her gently, as if she were a child, stroked her hair, kissed her temple until she was quiet. Then she held the ouzo for Rosemary to drink from the glass.

"I must get your dinner," Dina said.

"Darling . . ."

"Don't dress. There's a thing on the hook on the back of the bathroom door . . . through there."

Rosemary got up, went through the bedroom where she noticed only a large bed and the sense of other furniture. She sat on the toilet and shook, again like a child, taken to the bathroom in the middle of the night. She had no idea what time it was. Should she take a shower? She didn't want one. Wash at least. She encountered the mirror before she could wish she hadn't, but the face she had gradually grown uncertain of was not there. The curling, tangled hair, the dark, desiring eyes, the full, so beautifully used mouth belonged to a younger face, one she had not seen since she had come home, defeated, six years ago. There was no vanity in her pleasure, simply wonder. The robe was red silk. Rosemary put it on without thinking about it, without wondering who had worn it the night before, or the night before that.

When she got back into the living room, she found her clothes very neatly arranged on the chair with her coat, and the table was set. Dina was in the kitchen, still in her boots, lined jeans, and large, obscuring sweater.

"Do you like retsina?" she called.

"Yes."

To drink what had the faint flavor of resin was to feel uncertain of the nature and needs of the body, slight metaphor for the confusion of wood and flesh, of cloth and skin. Rosemary ate with Dina's silence.

"Now," she said, "I want to go to bed with you. I want . . ."

"I have to get the truck," Dina said. "Then I drink at Nick's."

"But I want you like that," Rosemary said. "Don't you want me?"

"A Greek, to marry well, must be a virgin," Dina said.

It was a joke the more pompous and preposterous for Dina's serious face, and Rosemary laughed with the same low breakings that were in her speaking.

"Do you want to go drinking?" Dina asked.

"I couldn't. I couldn't possibly."

Only as they were driving silently back to the truck did Rosemary begin to feel uneasy. There was nothing to say, and Dina made no gesture or suggestion as she got out of the car. Cole came down the front steps, as if he had been waiting for her.

"Dina?" Rosemary asked.

"Good night," Dina said, as she reached for the tire in the back seat.

"I began to think you weren't coming back," Rosemary heard Cole say.

"We had dinner."

Rosemary drove off without speaking to Cole, feeling both older and more foolish than she could quite believe she was. A piece of furniture.

III

THERE HAD ALWAYS BEEN a foursome for games. When they were children, the four were the family. After Mr. Larson died, Ida Setworth took his place, not so inappropriate a substitution as it might appear since, as Beatrice had observed, Ida was archaic and without sympathy from the beginning. When Mrs. Larson died, Maud Montgomery joined them, a luxury she would allow herself away from her invalid husband because she was going to a household of even graver sorrows. Then last year, when Beatrice was finally too ill to sit at the table, Carl Hollinger, widower of a good wife and no children, semiretired minister of God, accepted the fourth position. They were not serious bridge players. Often they played coon hollow instead, a nearly mindless rummy. If they met on Sundays they played Mah-Jongg, in forgotten deference to that once holy and cardless day.

Kathy had brought Amelia a bowl of milk and a rag for cleaning the pagan ivories, backed in bamboo, the winds and dragons, the dots and characters and bamboos, white, bright teeth of the wall of China to be built, opened, and destroyed that evening by the remnant four: Amelia, Maud, Ida, and Carl.

"It's what I'd like for my supper, too," Amelia said. "A bowl of milk."

"There's a chicken in the oven," Kathy said.

"So there is, and I'll enjoy it."

"So that I can make chicken sandwiches for later."

"Yes, I remember."

"The doctor said, yesterday, maybe I'd go next week," Kathy said.

"I know," Amelia said.

"I don't want it born."

"Well, you can't go around eight months' pregnant for the rest of your life."

"You're lame," Kathy said, as if that cast doubt on Amelia's statement.

"You'll be glad once it's over."

"I won't. I'll have to give it away, and then I'll have to go home, empty."

"That's all right."

"It isn't. I don't want to go. Couldn't I just come back here? Couldn't I just go on working for you?"

"You haven't even finished school."

"I don't care about that. I never did. Anyway, they'll all say things, they'll . . ."

"Kathy," Amelia said, quietly.

"Miss Hopwood said I shouldn't ask you."

"*Shouldn't* isn't ever very strong against *needing to*. Miss Hopwood understands that," Amelia said, both to comfort and to end the conversation.

"She's pretty, and she's not really strict, but she's not kind the way Miss Jameson is. I hope Miss Jameson's going to marry Mr. Fallidon."

"Do you?"

"Oh yes, don't you?"

"If they'd like to," Amelia said. "Now go along and get the table set."

Was it something lacking in her nature, Amelia wondered, that she did not speculate about such matters? The only thing she ever tried to look ahead to was trouble, and even that was an alien exercise which she took on now simply because Sister was not there to do it for her. Beatrice, reader of horoscopes and weather reports, was, just the same, often surprised about what finally did happen. Amelia rarely was. Without expectations to contradict, she could usually see how whatever it was had come about, motives and clues stored for after-the-fact. She was never as well prepared as Beatrice to accept responsibility, though better prepared simply to accept: love, death, a hot day. And Agate? As

Rosemary pointed out, whether Amelia was going to be good or bad for Agate wasn't the issue; there was no one else to take her. That was not, of course, what Amelia would say to Maud Montgomery tonight.

"I've taken Rosemary Hopwood's advice," Amelia said.

"I don't believe Rosemary Hopwood is a real social worker. I never have," Maud said, trying to find the die she had just cast in one of the two lower areas of her trifocals.

"It's a two, Maud," Ida said, without aid.

"Just turning up like that," Maud said, "*after* her mother died."

"She has a master's degree in social work," Carl said.

"I'm not talking about degrees. I'm talking about the *feel* of a thing. Anyone who would advise Amelia to take another of these girls is simply not competent."

"Well," Carl said, "we're all too old to be doing what we're doing, but we go on doing it."

"If you're suggesting that I should hire a nurse for Arthur . . ."

"Not at all," Carl said. "What would you do with yourself if you did?"

"It's Arthur I'm thinking about, not myself. He simply couldn't stand someone he didn't know doing the things I do for him."

"He'd have to if you got sick," Ida said.

"I don't intend to get sick."

"Six, Carl," Ida said. "So, double East, pick up your luck."

"Thank you," Carl said, putting the die on his rack. Mah-Jongg was a relatively new game to him, and he often forgot the ritual gestures, which were more important at this table than any concentration on the game itself. This attitude, in his profession, should have suited him well enough, but he never had been able to accept it easily—in church or at the gaming table.

"The way some of these young women behave," Maud said. "They don't even seem to think they have to get married any more. Harriet Jameson, for instance. She apparently believes she can be anywhere with Peter Fallidon, even in his apartment, as long as she takes her own car. He trails her around the city, following her little Volkswagen as if he were a private detective instead of a bank manager. I think it's disgraceful."

Ida smiled, opening her part of the wall. Peter and Harriet driving around after each other all over town did not interest her so much as having seen Rosemary's car parked in front of George's last night after the shop was closed. Rosemary interested Ida.

She found Harriet frankly dull and was sure that, however silly the arrangement with Peter Fallidon might be, it was perfectly innocent.

". . . perfectly innocent," Amelia was saying.

"Oh, Amelia, every girl in this house is treated as if she were victim of the immaculate conception. Sorry, Carl."

"Quite all right, Maud. I don't believe in it myself as anything but a metaphor, though it's an accurate one."

"Do you know anything about the new girl?" Ida asked.

"Not a great deal," Amelia answered. "Her name is Agate."

"Agate?" Maud repeated.

"Short for Agatha, I suppose."

A peculiarity of the arrangement was that none of these girls was ever given a last name, except in the records.

"Pung," Ida said, picking up Carl's discard. "What color are her eyes going to be?"

"What an odd thing to wonder," Maud said.

"Dark gray?" Carl suggested.

"They must catch the light anyway," Ida said.

She had no further help, and Amelia regretted it, but she had nothing in her of Beatrice's whimsy, which could always encourage Ida in her own.

"Kong," Maud said.

Amelia drew from the wall, paused, and said, "Mah-Jongg."

Carl never liked the moment of counting because he could not remember the doubling intricacies of flowers and winds, kongs of dragons. He did not mind being helped, but he was always reminded, by Maud, that technically any help disqualified him. She liked disqualifying people so that she could then be generously forgiving. Carl had promised himself for months that he would read and memorize the scoring, but, once away from the table, he could not feel defensive enough to bother.

"I know I pay everybody double," he said hopefully.

"And with a count of fifty, you'll be paying everybody," Ida said.

Maud glared with a slowly raising head so that she could register disapproval in all three ranges of vision. Ida smiled at her, offering her ivory counters, held out in her frail, ivory hand. Payments made, it was time to build the wall again.

"Their ancient, glittering eyes were gay," Ida said.

"Yeats?" Carl suggested.

"Yeats," she said. "About some Chinamen on a mountain."

"I· don't want to talk about the war," Maud said, "or anything related to it."

"Hysterical women," Ida thought, still in the poem and staying there.

"Pung," Carl said, resisting a boyish temptation to shout "bonsai!" instead. It was a burden of age to feel more often childish than adolescent. To deal with it, he added, "Old Tom Berger died last Wednesday."

The other three nodded. They had read the death notices. All four had one thing in common: Ida at seventy-eight, Maud at seventy-five, Amelia at seventy-two, and Carl at seventy did not wonder which one of them would be next. Each one, in relative health and commitment, imagined into at least another five years. It made them, for all their other differences, comfortable companions. They would see each other through a number of other deaths first, as they were still, to some extent, seeing Amelia through Beatrice's.

"Was that a chest of yours I saw on Dina's truck today?" Ida asked.

"Yes," Amelia said. "I'm giving it to Harriet."

"To Harriet? What for?" Maud asked.

"She liked it," Amelia said.

"Oh."

"Is she going to marry Peter Fallidon?" Ida asked.

"I don't know," Amelia said.

"I don't think he's the marrying kind," Carl said.

"How do you judge that?" Maud wanted to know. "He's already a widower."

"You know, he's nearly convinced me that this town may still turn into a city," Amelia said.

"So he doesn't want you to sell the F Street property?" Maud asked.

"Yes, that," Amelia said.

Kathy was at the door with the chicken sandwiches.

"Is it that time already?" Amelia asked.

"Ten-thirty, Miss A."

On a Saturday night they often played whatever they were playing until midnight. On Sunday, though none of them had any reason to consider Monday the beginning of anything, they were careful to stop early. And they could stop in the middle of a

36

rubber or round, in the middle of a hand, since there was never anything at stake, not even their interest. So now they pushed away from the table, variously adapting to their frailties, except for Ida who seemed to have none aside from being frail. Kathy left the sandwiches and came back with thin, hot, nearly bitter chocolate, the only thing Amelia insistently taught all her girls to make, for it was a specialty of the Larson house. Her guests could trust it, no matter who had made it. They were not so confident about the sandwiches, but they ate briefly against the alarms of both butter and mayonnaise, knowing remedies.

"A week from Friday?" Amelia suggested, as she stood with her guests at the door.

They agreed, soft, old lips against the soft, old cheek, careful of dentures. There was only one car in the drive, Carl's. He helped both his passengers in.

Maud needed to be driven simply round the block.

"Love to Arthur," Ida said. "I'll call in during the week."

"Do that," Maud said. "He's always better for a visit. Don't bother, Carl."

But Carl had already opened his door. He would see Maud to her house, as he always did, courtesy relieving his small guilt at being glad to be rid of her once again.

"What will she do when Arthur dies?" Ida asked, as Carl got back into the car.

"Perhaps he won't be that unkind," Carl said.

Ida sat with that, interested in the unkind dead, who had always been as much her companions as the living. There were so many more of them, and they were her neighbors, which was Ida's most important comic fact. She lived on the top of a hill in a little white house, overlooking the graveyard. She had lived there since she was seven, orphaned by a fire and taken by her aunt, the "first" or "original" Miss Setworth, who said, "The dead are friendly, peaceful companions, and I would sooner recommend a man to their company than to a good many of the livelier worlds I've known." But her aunt was neither sinister nor cynical. She had been a loving guardian and a loving friend, teaching Ida truths that did not seem hard at the time: fearlessness, horticulture, poetry, and self-discipline. It was one of the marks of a stagnant town that no one had ever thought to suggest that, once old Miss Setworth was dead, Ida should move into town. No one would ever suggest to Amelia that she should move out of the house she had grown up in, either. When anyone had to move, there was sympathy. But before that, there were ways of adapting large houses to reduced numbers and circumstances, ways of limiting isolation and loneliness. It would never have occurred to Ida to apologize to Carl or Cole or Rosemary Hopwood or any of the others who so often drove the five miles out of town to pick her up or take her home. She was too old to drive herself and too careful to spend much on taxis, even though the flat rate to Ida's had been fixed at $1 years ago and had never gone up. It was a pleasant trip on a back road, past a dairy farm, then along the rising slope of graves, through an old prune orchard to her own dirt drive.

"Are you going to ask me in for a brandy?" Carl asked.

"Do you need one?"

"Yes," Carl said.

The flowered summer slipcovers were already on the old couch and the armchairs by the fire, and only the African violets and Christmas cactus remained on the plant stand in the window. The others had been put out in the gentle weather. It was not a cluttered room, perhaps because the two Misses Setworth had been domestically related to no one but each other and had shared a taste for serene space. The quiet seascape over the fireplace mirrored in miniature the view from the front windows and the terrace, over the town to the sea.

"How many years have you lived alone now?" Carl asked, standing while Ida got the brandy and, he was interested to see, two glasses from the cupboard.

"Nearly thirty," Ida said.

"A long time."

"Not as long, I imagine, as the last two years have been for you."

"It's obvious I do it badly, isn't it?"

"Not badly," Ida said, offering him the job of pouring the drinks. "You keep yourself clean and cheerful and busy. You just don't enjoy it. Why don't you marry again?"

"I'd like to."

"Then you should go about it," Ida said. "Stop hiding with A and Maud and me. You never will learn to play Mah-Jongg, you know, and you'd like a serious bridge partner."

"I'd like to marry you, Ida," Carl said.

She did not reply except with the unguarded surprise in her finely set, light eyes.

"Does that seem ridiculous to you?" he asked, smiling an apology.

"Yes," she admitted.

"I suppose it is ridiculous then," he said, taking his brandy like medicine but immediately pouring himself another—"for you."

"Why would such a thing occur to you?"

"Well," Carl said, "I think we're companionable. I think it might make financial sense. I don't like living alone. And—if it doesn't sound foolish—I love you."

"You *love* me?"

"Yes, Ida, I do," Carl said, and again he smiled.

"I'm seventy-eight years old," Ida announced. "I have not been domestically intimate with anyone for thirty years. In my life I have never been affectionately intimate with anyone."

"You've never loved anyone?"

"No," Ida said, sharply.

"A word both too sacred and too profane for your critical use," Carl said.

"Is that a reprimand?"

"I suppose it is. Forgive me. The natural bad habit of a minister. 'Love' is an easy word for me. I mean by it all kinds of very ordinary needs and pleasures. I mean by it admiration and affection."

"I don't know anything about ordinary needs and pleasures," Ida said, finishing her own brandy.

"Another?"

"Thank you."

"I think you know more about them than most people. How else could you have lived alone so contentedly?"

"I'm not always content," Ida said. "My aunt once said to me, 'The only way I could ever be sure of having my own way was to live alone.' She said she was of too amiable a nature to get along with people in a way that would suit her for very long."

"She got along with you to suit her well enough."

"I was a child," Ida said. "A well-behaved child.'

"But not *too* amiable," Carl said.

"No, I suppose not. Carl, if you want a wife, you must find

someone who knows something about the job and someone young enough to . . ." She gestured to end that sentence. "Not a virgin, eight years your ancient. That is simply absurd."

"Put that way, probably. But I don't really want 'a wife.' I'd like for whatever years we have left to share as much with you as we can. And, for heaven's sake, Ida, I'm not talking about sex."

"How should I know what you're talking about?" Ida demanded in embarrassed irritation.

"By listening to me. By considering what might be a perfectly practical, sensible proposal." Carl was also feeling irritable.

Quite suddenly Ida burst into tears.

"My dear," he said gently and went to her where she sat on the couch, her face in her hands.

"I shouldn't have taken that second brandy," she said, as she recovered.

They sat side by side, Carl's arm around her, stiff and awkward in their bodies but somehow easier with each other. Then Carl reached for the bottle.

"How are you going to drive home?" Ida demanded.

"Maybe I'm not going to," Carl said. "Will you have another?"

"I have also never been drunk in my life," Ida said. "And this is no time to begin. You must go home, Carl."

"Must I? Why?"

"I don't know," Ida said.

"Will you marry me?"

"I don't know."

He put the bottle down without having poured another drink. Then he kissed her on the cheek and got up.

"I'll phone you in the morning," he said.

"I won't know in the morning."

"I know," he said. "But one of these mornings you may."

When he had gone, Ida did pour herself another drink, and, as she drank it, she cried again, a frankly drunken crying, though it was true that she had never been drunk in her life. When she had finished those tears, she went into her bedroom and carefully took off all her clothes. Then she stared at her hairless nakedness, the soft folds and puckers of skin that had been her breasts so long ago she had forgotten their shapes, and at her ancient face, bluish and stained now with confusion as well as age.

"Oh, Beatrice, where is your sharp tongue now?" she demanded theatrically. "We are such old fools because the ones who laugh best die first. I can't love Carl Hollinger. I don't even know what it means."

Then she took from the hook on her closet door a pink flannel nightgown and a robe. In the bathroom, she did not look into the mirror after her teeth were out. She never had. And this was certainly no time to begin.

＊

May 20, 1936: Ida called today to say they wouldn't be able to come for the evening because Aunt Setworth is ill again—the same digestive complaint. Mama is more irritable about other people's ailments than she is about her own. She is disappointed, of course. Sister offers double solitaire, a game which might have been invented for Ida and Aunt S. How can we all be so resigned?

May 21, 1936: Met Ida for lunch today. She doesn't look well herself but was as full of whimsy as ever. She never gossips the way I do. She imagines people just as they are not. The way she turned Maud into a scheming nurse after a rich man's money still makes me laugh. What I said was simply that she does *make* Arthur sick, which is an exaggeration. At least Ida's interested. Sister has odd gaps of humor or some lack of malice. It isn't loyalty in her. It's a lack.

May 22, 1936: When Maud told us today that Arthur was suffering from slow deterioration, Mama had a real lapse of tact and said, "It's really everyone's disease." Sister does get that from Mama, though Sister's really much worse. Maud was quite put out though she tried not to show it.

May 23, 1936: Doing nothing but trying to love friends and relatives makes a bitter, frivolous life. Not for Sister. Will I never outgrow envying her deformity? Being in some dark way in love with it, wanting it for myself. But for me, it would be simply another excuse, a way to rest in self-pity. She is so placidly grotesque. With my body, she would have escaped without effort and without guilt.

IV

AT THE SEA END of F Street, on the corner of Main, among a waste
of used-car lots and low warehouses was an old, twenty-five-room
hotel which had been bought and was maintained by the Protes-
tant churches in town as an unwed mothers' home. In an in-
formal, reciprocal arrangement with churches in other towns and
cities, most local girls were sent away and out-of-town girls accepted. The isolation of the hotel from stores, coffee shops, and
movie theaters as well as from the residential areas of the town
was a natural and welcome barrier for those who wanted to practice charity without moral confusion. Since the F Street bus
hadn't gone all the way out to Main for twenty years, and since
the girls usually knew no one in town to come to pick them up,
chaperoned excursions were their only means of seeing what
there was to see. Aside from the embarrassment of being chaperoned there was the humiliation of being herded into a movie or
shop along with a half a dozen others as huge with guilt. Therefore, except for those who had very recently arrived, most of the
girls did not take advantage of what the town did offer but occupied the hotel as if they were under house arrest or siege, playing cards, watching television, writing letters they usually didn't
mail, telling each other comforting or terrifying lies. They were
given some few chores to do, encouraged to sew and read, and
everyone who was feeling up to it took a daily walk along the
seawall, a sight funny and forlorn and also beautiful, as so many

animal groupings are against the largeness of ocean and sky.

"Awful," Rosemary Hopwood said aloud, the first time she saw them like that, a straggling single line of swelling females, awkward over the awkward terrain. Thank heaven there was not a collie. "Awful," but she went on watching until she began to smile.

Homes of this sort were, of course, not sane solutions to the problem. They were a dangerous breeding ground for things more difficult and less lovable than babies. Any hope that the Pill or more liberal abortion laws would finally phase out these places as TB sanatoriums had been phased out twenty years before had collapsed. No scientific or legal advance could move beyond community morality, which still required a life sentence for children conceived on beaches and in back seats. Ten years ago there were often empty beds at the hotel. Now there was always a waiting list, even though Rosemary worked hard to find jobs for the girls and to persuade them to move out into the community. The two sorts of girl she wanted to get out as soon as possible were the simple country girls like Kathy and the potential troublemakers like Agate. The Kathys were easy enough since they were shy and ashamed and used to work. The troublemakers were just that.

Agate had been at the home only a week, and already the staff was complaining of a new market in pills and pot and pornography, late-night parties, hysterical episodes. Rosemary had to get Agate out before she was thrown out.

"I think I've found you a job, Agate," Rosemary said, sitting behind the office desk and looking down at papers.

"What do I want with a job?" Agate asked.

"For one thing," Rosemary said, "you have to have some place to go when you're thrown out of here."

"Who's going to throw me out?" Agate asked, amused.

"Ultimately, I am."

"Why?"

Rosemary watched Agate, who lounged back in a wooden chair, one sneakered foot pressing against the center panel of the desk so that Rosemary, on the other side, could feel the pressure. She was a good-looking girl with, as Ida Setworth had supposed, remarkable eyes, which could be a kind of tawny yellow or spring green, tropical, light-struck, but rarely warm. She was long-thighed, deep-breasted, entirely generous-bodied, more the sort of girl fantasy would put here than the sort that usually arrived.

"What kind of an answer would you like?" Rosemary asked finally in return. "I could simply say you're a troublemaker, and we could play the game of 'prove it.' Or I could describe to you how you'll feel if you stay here for another month with the novelty of trouble wearing thin. I could entertain you with attempts at reform. What would you like?"

"I think you've got the wrong impression entirely," Agate said, tipping forward with a jolt. "I've done nothing but work at raising the morale of this place ever since I arrived. You should be thanking me. You probably should even be paying me for the job I'm doing here."

"I was under the impression that you *had* been making money at it," Rosemary said.

"Well... nothing but what you might call commissions for certain services," Agate said.

"Some drugs, Agate, are particularly dangerous for pregnant women, and nearly all drugs are dangerous for these particular pregnant women, you included," Rosemary said carefully and watched Agate's face close. "Why didn't you get an abortion in the first place?"

"It's illegal," Agate said with a broad, bright smile.

"Not in Mexico. Not in Japan."

"I wasn't in the mood for that kind of trip."

"You felt more like four months in a church-run hostel. Or maybe you're interested in participating in the experiment to see if LSD really does change the chromosomal balance."

"There isn't any of that stuff around here," Agate said sharply.

"My point is that there shouldn't be any kind of any stuff around here, and that's why I'm going to throw you out unless you give me your word that there won't be any more of it."

"My 'word'? You're a real girl scout, you know that?"

"How good is your cooking?"

Agate didn't answer.

"I said, how good ..."

"I refuse to answer on the ground that it might incriminate me."

"A good cook," Rosemary said. "How good are you at dealing with old people?"

"Old people?"

"A lame old woman, physically independent, as bright—brighter—than you are, kind. She's willing to take you. Room and board, a hundred dollars a month, for cooking for her and her young cousin, Cole Westaway. And she has a good many people for dinner, particularly if your cooking is good."

"What did you tell her about me?"

"That you'd like each other, that you needed her, that you wouldn't last here."

"That I needed her?" Agate repeated.

"Yes, Agate," Rosemary said. "Will you come out with me and meet her anyway?"

"Do I have any choice?"

"Yes, you have a lot to lose if you don't," Rosemary said, and she smiled.

"All right," Agate said. "When do we go?"

"Sometime in the week. I'll let you know. Meanwhile, I suggest you clean your room—thoroughly."

"The books, too?"

"The books, too," Rosemary said.

When Agate had left, Rosemary packed up her briefcase and purse. She had a meeting with two other social workers and a psychiatrist in half an hour on the other side of town. The quickest way was straight across on F Street, and it was ridiculous of her to consider any other route; therefore, driving past George's would have to become part of the discipline she was designing for herself, just as not driving past George's had been part of the discipline for the last three days.

Rosemary had known, from the moment she left Dina with Cole, that there would be no telephone calls unless Rosemary made them, that there would be no further encounters unless Rosemary presented herself for that purpose. And, even if she did, she was not sure that Dina would be so hospitable again. Why had Rosemary told Dina she loved her? If she hadn't said that, or if she hadn't said later, "I want you like that," if she had been as silent as Dina herself, she could make some sense of what she might do now.

"I don't love her," Rosemary said aloud, driving steadily along F Street. "I don't even particularly want her . . . like that."

That wasn't exactly true. Rosemary simply didn't imagine making love to Dina or couldn't imagine it and, with that limitation, believed she could survive without it. But not without Dina, whose sexual authority obsessed her in a way that falling in love had never done. The gentle fantasies, harmful only in that they had prepared her for the real encounter, were as remote to her now as her adolescence. Now she simply relived what Dina had done to her, not only in the privacy of her own night or early morning but without defense in the middle of the working day as she was filling out forms, even as she was talking on the phone.

"Having a hot flash?" her even more aging secretary had asked in a kindly tone. "I'll open a window."

It was bitterly funny and a relief to know that such sweating, shaking appetite could be ordinarily diagnosed. Glands. And suddenly every memory of a well-padded or bone-brittle woman—a teacher she had had in college, Maud Montgomery at her mother's bridge table, her cleaning woman, even the haughty Beatrice at the dinner table, quickly reaching for a handkerchief, more urgent and embarrassed than in any need to sneeze—became transformed for Rosemary into horrified hilarity. Menopause as pure lechery. No wonder then the sudden hysterics, the glooming depressions, the paranoid jealousies if the terrible truth was that each of these ludicrous bodies was suffering its first, and only, experience of pure appetite, obsessed by who knew what object: everything from the proverbial milkman (egg lady?) to the unprepared and certainly unwilling husband (best friend at the church bazaar? sister?). A kept secret only because for most it was too preposterous to accept and act upon? For most the body was already chained and shamed by childbearing or operations, by years of intimately indifferent companions or singleness, by a morality that could hide all vanity? Or did Maud Montgomery suddenly present herself to her slowly deteriorating husband, Beatrice to her lumbering, beloved sister, her mother to ... heaven knew whom?

"I am out of my mind," Rosemary said, the sweat beginning, and she violently turned off F Street just two blocks before she would have to pass George's.

She therefore did not see the sign that occasionally hung at the door, saying OUT TO LUNCH. And she would not have recognized Grace Hill's car parked indiscreetly in front of Ries's drugstore.

Instead she was saying to herself, "I've got to keep myself busy, very busy." For she only wished that she could not imagine herself, having said what she had said, phoning Dina, going to Dina, pounding down the door to say, "I don't love you. I don't even know you. I don't care how little interest you have in me. I don't care how aloof you stay from me. Just take me." Rosemary Hop-

46

wood, who had always been pursued, who had always been circumspect, "socially and emotionally impeccable!" a lover had once shouted against her pride and self-control, had to stop imagining herself capable of what she had already done.

She was very grateful to know that she would be having dinner with Ida that evening, for, if anyone could have a calming effect on her, it was Ida, who had served Rosemary as a model of self-sufficiency all her life.

The drive out to Ida's was always peaceful, and now in late May it was light enough to see the deepening green fields through fences tangled with wild climbing roses. But the graves were not, this evening, like grazing sheep, not the Setworths' easy companions, not the finally silenced rancor of dead parents, not even the mortality Rosemary might be said to be struggling against or toward. Dull punctuation, that was all, but that would have to be distraction enough for now. At the top of the hill would be the positive relief of Ida, who had never at any age or any season been troubled by the bitter comedies of flesh that visited everyone else.

If Rosemary had not been a more than normally tactful person, she would have commented on Ida's appearance at once. She looked, in ways hard to account for together, dreadful. Her eyes had faded to nearly no color, as if the blue had drained into her cheeks, and she was wearing a gash of lipstick which, instead of brightening her face, made it the more cadaverous. Ida usually wore the kinds of clothes no one noticed beyond the impression of neat, soft freshness, like her voice in ordinary conversation. This evening she had on a strong, busy print, splotched with red.

"Is that a new dress?" Rosemary asked, intending kindness.

"I suppose it is," Ida said, looking down at it as if to make sure.

There was no slur in her speech, and she moved about the room with characteristic frail efficiency, but Rosemary couldn't dismiss the fear that Ida had had a small stroke.

"Do you think I'm getting too old to live out here by myself?" Ida suddenly asked.

"Do you think so?"

"No," Ida said.

"Then who does? Haven't you been feeling well?"

"Well enough for seventy-eight," Ida said.

"I suppose it must feel isolated sometimes," Rosemary offered carefully.

"I'm used to that. More often than not I like it."

"Yes, I've always thought you did."

"But you think it would be sensible if I moved into town, at my age," Ida said, in a tone that implied it was Rosemary's suggestion in the first place.

"If you want to," Rosemary said. "If you'd be more comfortable."

"I can't imagine that I would be. I've lived in this house for seventy-one years."

"Then why are you thinking about it, Ida? What's worrying you?"

"Am I worried?"

"Well, I don't know," Rosemary said.

"I miss Beatrice," Ida said.

"Yes, I'm sure you do. In ways it must be as hard for you as it is for Amelia," Rosemary said. "Were you thinking that, perhaps, you might go to Amelia?"

"To Amelia? Heavens no. I can't talk to Amelia. I don't even want to. Do you mean to live?"

"I just wondered . . ."

"With Amelia and Cole and a light-struck girl? What an idea, Rosemary!"

"I didn't mean to say I thought it was a good one."

"I must put on the vegetables," Ida said.

Rosemary picked up the volume of Yeats that was always by Ida's chair and opened it to:

> But Love has pitched his mansion in
> The place of excrement;

turned pages quickly and saw:

> Only the dead can be forgiven;
> But when I think of that my tongue's a stone.

glanced down the page to:

> What matter if I live it all once more?
> Endure that toil of growing up;
> The ignominy of boyhood; the distress
> Of boyhood changing into man;
> The unfinished man and his pain
> Brought face to face with his own clumsiness;

and stopped.

"I don't know how you go on reading him, year after year," she said to Ida as she came back into the room.

"He's an honest companion," Ida said.

"Give me a happy liar then."

"The remarkable thing about poetry is that you always think you understand it until you understand it differently and realize you didn't."

"What do you mean?" Rosemary asked.

"I suppose simply that a good poem tells you what you need to know at the time, or what you can take. Aunt Setworth used to say no one under seventy could have any idea what Yeats meant, but I thought I did."

"And didn't you?"

"No better than you do," Ida said. "If you want another drink, you had better fix it for yourself. Dinner's nearly ready."

"I think I won't, thanks."

"You look tired," Ida said.

"I suppose I am. I probably ought to think about taking a vacation."

"Did you have dinner with Dina Pyros last Saturday?"

"Yes, I did," Rosemary answered, trying to sound unguarded.

"That must have pleased her."

"Why do you say that?"

"She seems to me an intelligent young woman. She must get bored with the number of young delinquents who take up her time . . . and the neurotics like Grace Hill."

"Do you know Grace Hill?"

"Only enough to know she makes a nuisance of herself. Feller Hill would have gone a long way in politics by now if he hadn't been tied to her."

"Where did he find her anyway?"

"In the wicked city," Ida said. "Some people haven't the sense not to bring them home."

"That sounds more like Beatrice than it does like you."

"It is Beatrice," Ida said. "What is most tiresome about the dead is having to keep up both sides of the conversation. Is that what's the matter with me, I wonder."

"What is the matter, Ida?"

"I'm too old to be struck by lightning," Ida said. "Come. Let's have our supper."

They ate and then tidied the kitchen together in quiet amiability of the sort they had shared for a number of years rather like mother and daughter but much more like friends. Settled again in the living room, Ida was looking better, and Rosemary had relaxed.

"If you don't want to go on living alone," Rosemary said. "Why don't you come and live with me?"

"You sensibly escaped your own mother's old age. There's no reason for you to deal with mine."

"I didn't love my mother," Rosemary said. "You know, it might be a very happy arrangement for both of us."

"Why is it suddenly that everyone wants me to move into town?" Ida demanded.

"Everyone?"

"Rosemary, how old are you?"

"Forty-six."

"Do you think you're too old to marry?"

"Of course," Rosemary said, "and not in the least interested in the idea. I never have been."

"Neither have I," Ida said. "But at the age of seventy-eight, I'm considering it. Please laugh."

Rosemary did not. She sat, widely darked-eyed, and waited.

"I may marry Carl Hollinger."

"Carl Hollinger?"

"He's lonely. He's a good man. He suggested the idea as sensible. I don't think it is. In fact, I can't imagine it, but I find, as the days pass, that I'm trying to."

"Do you want to, Ida? Do you love him?"

"I'm upset by the absurdity of it."

"What's absurd about it?" Rosemary asked.

"Beatrice could have told you."

"Beatrice is dead," Rosemary said. "And I never really did like her sense of humor."

"I depended on it," Ida said. "If you've had to be, all your life, a quaint little bag of bones in a graveyard, the best sort of friend is one who thinks it's funny."

"Oh, Ida . . ."

"She also knew her kind of beauty—and yours—were bad jokes."

"Beatrice Larson was a bitter old woman," Rosemary said.

"Yes," Ida agreed. "But she knew how to laugh."

"Marry him," Rosemary said.

"I don't know," Ida said. "I don't know."

V

AMELIA WAS AT HER DESK late Friday afternoon, waiting for Rosemary and Agate to arrive. Below her in the side garden Cole, in a pair of modest trunks, lay stricken in the sun for vanity rather than pleasure. If she had thought he would stay there long, she might have suggested that he move, though she doubted that the pale-bodied boy would excite any interest in the drug-peddling, angry young mother-to-be she was about to interview. Amelia was not apprehensive. She was distracted and heavy with the diaries she had been reading. Her first method, reading through sixty-three Mays, had been arbitrary and frivolous, giving her little of Sister but her hatred of roses and chronic spring envies. So Amelia had started again at the beginning. Those first years, like the first years of any life, passed quickly, but now she was in distended adolescence, and she began to realize what a long life Sister had had of roses and relatives. It depressed her, but she felt, by now, committed to the task, as she had been committed to living with Beatrice through all those years the first time. Why? She couldn't explain it to herself except as moral perversity: love.

"Miss A?" she heard Kathy call, though she hadn't heard the bell. "Miss A?"

"Are they here?" Amelia answered.

"Miss A?" The calling was urgent.

Amelia hoisted herself up from her desk and turned on her good leg. "What is it, Kathy?"

"Miss A?"

Amelia could not hurry. She had to move at the same pace to dinner or disaster. As she crossed the hall, she knew Kathy had stopped calling because she could hear Amelia coming toward the kitchen. There Kathy stood, leaning on the kitchen table, water streaming down her legs.

"It's all right, child," Amelia said. "The sac's broken, that's all."

"What will I do?"

"Sit down."

"I can't. I . . ."

"Yes you can."

"I have to clean it up. I have to clean myself up."

"You have to sit down," Amelia said, reaching her and steering her to a wooden chair. "There's nothing wrong, except it's time."

"It's not supposed to do that," Kathy said.

"It's just one of the ways, one of nature's ways," Amelia said. "Now you stay there, and I'll call Cole."

"No, no, don't call Cole!"

"He'll get the car," Amelia said. "By that time you'll be fine. We'll just get some towels. You'll be fine."

"It's not supposed to do that," Kathy repeated, tears of fear and embarrassment beginning to brighten her eyes.

"Yes it is," Amelia said. "The sac has to break some time. This is one of the times. Now just sit there."

Amelia crossed the hall again and went to the study window. "Cole? Pull on some trousers and a shirt and get the car. It's time to take Kathy to the hospital."

The abruptness of his response belied the relaxation of his pose. He was out of the lawn chair like something released and nearly collided with Amelia as she crossed the hall again.

"What shall I do?" he asked.

"Just what I said," Amelia said. "Quietly and calmly."

"Is she all right?"

"Yes, she's all right. The sac's broken, and that's a little uncomfortable. That's all. When you've got some clothes on, get a bathmat and some towels and put them on the back seat of the car before you bring it round."

Back in the kitchen, Amelia found Kathy trying to clean up the floor.

"Kathy, I told you to sit down. Now don't be silly."

Amelia went to the phone and called the hospital. Then she

tried to reach Rosemary at the unwed mothers' home, but she and Agate had already left; so Amelia took a piece of kitchen notepaper and wrote a message to be left on the front door. Kathy sat, a fist in her mouth to keep herself quiet.

"Can I put on another skirt?"

"Of course."

Cole brought the car right to the bottom of the front steps and opened both the back and front doors. Then he stopped to tie his tennis shoes, his hands shaking, the tic in his cheek leaping. He was surprised to see Kathy coming through the front door the shape he'd grown accustomed to. He had half imagined that there in the kitchen she was slowly going down like a balloon while he tore on clothes and floundered downstairs in danger of his flying laces. He could see that she had been crying, and he suddenly felt sorry for her in a way that hadn't occurred to him before in her gentle, slow-moving dullness. She must be frightened much more importantly than he was, who was only concerned about his own clumsiness. Without deciding to, he went up the stairs, put an arm around her waist, the other under her arm, helped her down the stairs and into the back seat, strewn with ill-matching towels. Amelia was tacking a note to Rosemary on the door. Cole returned for her, waiting two steps down for her hand on his shoulder. As soon as he felt that weight, he took a slow step down, then another, teetering a little as he always did when he couldn't move at the pace his own balance dictated, but behind him Amelia was as steady as she was unbalancing. Once at the car, she helped herself in.

"All right now?" she asked over her shoulder.

"Yes, it's stopped, I think," Kathy said.

"Now, once you're there and they admit you, I'll go on up to the waiting room, and, as soon as you're settled, I'll be right there."

"Oh, Miss A, you don't have to. . . ."

"I'll be right there."

"But you're expecting Miss Hopwood and the new girl. You're..."

"I've left them a note. They can come any day."

"But who's going to cook supper?"

"There probably won't be anyone home to eat it," Amelia said.

"I can cook," Cole offered. "I make great scrambled eggs."

He was a careful, sometimes even slightly nervous driver for all that he loved the stock car races, and now that his intense moment of pity for Kathy had passed, he was aware of the pulsing nausea

53

in his guts. He braked too hard at the edge of the street, and then the car stuttered slightly into the turn.

"We're not in any desperate hurry, Cole," Amelia said, to reassure him. "There's plenty of time."

"Is the baby all right in there without the water?" Kathy asked.

"Oh yes," Amelia said. "Just beginning to learn to live on dry \ land."

Dry land: but Cole saw it like something trapped in a collapsed balloon, a fish flipping, snapping itself in two, dashing itself against the rocky of pelvis. His own stomach lurched, and he remembered reading in anthropology about a tribe in which the men lay in bed, writhing in sympathetic labor, while the women delivered their babies squatting in the fields. And he felt stupidly frightened, ignorant of all the simple facts of life. Was Cousin A telling the truth? Was it all right? Or was it like a fish, dying in there, as he drove, on the fleshy shores of her womb? The images had the quality of hallucination: he was running down the pink and blood-pooled shore toward a baby, flipping and twisting itself, and he must get to it quickly, pick it up, and hurl it back into the sea. Or he was pulling to get the creature out, out of the cavern of her flesh, and how could it come, wedged there, without the tearing of limbs, the crushing of head?

"Take F Street," Amelia suggested unnecessarily.

"It feels sort of funny, Miss A."

"I know. It will now, but it's all right. Look, there's Dina, putting Harriet's chest on the trunk. Give her a honk, Cole."

Dina looked up, saw the Larson car, saw Kathy in the back, and waved. She stood on the deck of the truck and watched the car out of sight, her hand moving from her hip to her belly, where she could feel the gathering of her own wasted blood. Then she turned back to the rope in her hand and tied the chest down. Harriet Jameson had said she could be home at five thirty to receive it. When Dina looked up again, Rosemary Hopwood was driving by with a remarkably good-looking girl sitting beside her. Neither of them looked up, but Rosemary must have seen Dina, who wanted to call out some greeting or at least make some gesture, though she was in the habit of making no first move. It had been a very long week since she had poured those glasses of ouzo, Grace Hill only making it longer. Answering a need in women had for years seemed to Dina simply a way of answering a minor need of her own, a quieting of the guilt she felt about a mother and sisters who worked the fields their men had died in through serial wars with the Andartes. She did not remember any of them, nor had she ever learned the language they spoke. It would have done no good to write to them anyway, since they could not read. She gave money to Nick, who mailed a check every month to the Greek head of the family, their shared grandmother.

So what did it matter whether Rosemary Hopwood came back or not? If she needed to, she would. If not, there was no point. But, surely, if a woman needed that once, she needed it more than once.

"You take her, Dina," Sal had said only an hour after Dina had taken her, "and you'll get more than you bargained for. A woman like that."

Less, Dina would have said now if she did say anything about it. Rosemary had not even telephoned. But Dina did not really talk with anyone. It was not her way. Less.

She got down off the truck and went back into the shop.

"I'm closing up," she said. "I have to make a delivery."

Three of the kids got up at once, and, seeing that the fourth was not going to move without encouragement, they pulled him to his feet and led him away, floating vaguely after them like an uncertain kite. Dina shook her head after them. A little grass never hurt anyone, but that kid was on other things. Too bad. Pain around here—what grew and broke in a kid—could be deadly dull.

Harriet Jameson lived in one of the old houses that had been converted into apartments. Her partitioned-off drawing room was as close as she could get to the serene security the Larson house had always represented for her. And gradually she was furnishing it with pieces Dina found for her. Now for the first time she would have something that had actually come from the Larson house. Dina knew how much that meant to Harriet, and she had taken pains with her mending and refinishing.

"It's nice of you to have done it so quickly," Harriet said as she let Dina in.

The wall she had chosen for it made no comfortable sense, forcing a line-up of couch and chairs, but it was the only honoring wall where the chest could be displayed.

"Do you think that's right, Dina? Do you think that's where it should go?"

"Looks fine," Dina said, stepping back.

"Isn't it beautiful?"

"A nice piece," Dina agreed.

"Will you have a drink with me?" Harriet asked. "I feel as if I should celebrate in some way."

"Thanks," Dina said.

"Maybe I should phone Miss A first, just to tell her it's here."

"She's not home," Dina said. "She and Cole have taken Kathy to the hospital."

"So soon? Is Kathy all right?"

"I don't know. I just saw them driving past as I was loading the truck."

"I wonder if I should phone the hospital."

Dina made no suggestion.

"Well, let's have a drink first."

There was always something a little nervous about Harriet in her own apartment, as if, though she had actually lived there for some five years, it was all new to her: the space, the furniture, the hospitable rituals. It was remarkable to Dina that Peter Fallidon would come here, sit in this old maid's parlor as she sat, and not only endure but apparently enjoy Harriet's slightly ungainly fluttering. Dina liked Harriet, approved of her genuine and ordinary kindness, the pleasures she took in what other people might hardly notice, her earnest cheerfulness. But there was also a sexless prissiness about her which made it hard for Dina to enjoy her company for long or to imagine any man in it at all, particularly a man like Peter Fallidon, who, though carefully formal, gave the impression of being firmly in check rather than cold. He couldn't relax here surely. But Dina often did not understand the pairing of people, as she did not understand her own singleness going on so long, while she waited for a mythical Greek to come and claim her and her dowry. Out of a land of widows and children, she expected still that at least one had not been slain in those fields, would come down out of the mountains, perhaps, to cross the sea, and he would not be unlike Peter Fallidon in arrogance and formality, in dark good looks. But he would be Greek. No Greek would choose a bony butterfly like Harriet Jameson.

"I'm sorry, there's only gin," Harriet said.

"That's fine," Dina said, though for her it was like drinking perfume. It would not do to refuse. "Thank you."

"I wonder if that is the right wall for it," Harriet said, standing away and then going over to the chest. "You've done beautiful work on it, Dina. Whatever made you decide to get into your kind of business?"

"I took shop in school," Dina said.

"Shop?"

"I already knew how to cook, as much as I wanted to. I didn't want to sew. So I asked to take shop."

"How good that they let you," Harriet said. "You must have to know a lot about accounting as well, don't you?"

"Numbers come easy to me," Dina said.

"So many people—women—never do find anything they like to do. Or anyway they don't make a career of it. Miss Setworth should have been an English teacher. But it's easier for us, in our generation, I guess."

"A woman should marry," Dina said.

"Really? All women?" Harriet asked, surprised.

"Any woman."

"Easier said than done," Harriet answered, immediately embarrassed by what she had said.

"Anything is," Dina said. She had finished her drink. She stood up.

"Thank you again, Dina."

"Thank Miss A."

"Oh, I will. I'll call the hospital now."

But when Dina had gone, Harriet decided instead to go to the hospital, where she knew Amelia would be until the baby had been delivered. Perhaps Harriet could spell her while she got some supper, or go out and bring something back to her if Cole wasn't there. Enough for the boy to drive them down. The maternity waiting room was no place for him. But on her way to the hospital, Harriet did not think of Cole or Amelia or even Kathy. Her mind was on Dina Pyros. If she really wanted to marry, why on earth did she go around dressed the way she did? For the work she did it was all right, of course, but Dina went everywhere in those boots and trousers and sweat shirts, even drinking at Nick's. Harriet had seen her when she and Peter occasionally stopped in after a movie or concert. And she was never with any men. She always sat with those two peculiar women who ran the corset shop. Once Harriet had seen Dina dance, but she danced by herself the way Greek sailors did. She danced well but with a nearly masculine grace, controlled, sharp, strong. Under that bulk of clothes and manner, it was hard to believe that there might be a quite ordinary woman, dreaming of a husband and children. Harriet could no more understand why Dina wouldn't let the world know than Dina could understand why Harriet dressed to look as much like a librarian as she did and kept her own yearnings as far from sight as Dina did—farther, because Harriet Jameson no longer really admitted them even to herself. She was, at thirty-six, beyond all that.

Harriet found Amelia comfortably settled with a book in the chair by the waiting room door. She was alone in the room.

"Harriet!"

"Dina told me you'd brought Kathy down. I thought I'd phone, and then I thought I'd just come down to see if there was anything I could do."

"That's dear of you," Amelia said. "But you needn't have."

"How's Kathy?"

"We don't know yet. The doctor's just come in. The sac broke."

"It's early," Harriet said.

"Yes. I suppose they'll induce labor."

"Poor girl. Is she frightened?"

"Yes," Amelia said simply.

"I don't know how you go through this with them time after time," Harriet said.

" 'Time after time' is the way," Amelia said. "I'm used to it. And they know so much more now than they used to. There isn't the danger there used to be."

"Even so, it's not a happy thing," Harriet said.

"For someone it will be. And I think Kathy's going to have a fine, placid, healthy baby."

"Dina brought the chest over," Harriet said. "It's just beautiful."

"Did she mend it well?"

"Beautifully. She does, of course."

"I'm glad you like it. High time it came out of the attic," Amelia said.

The doctor came in.

"This may be a fairly long wait, Miss Larson. Would you like someone to take you home? I can have you called nearer the time."

"Thank you, no, Gerry," Amelia answered, smiling at him. "Once I'm here, it's really easier for me to stay, and it's good for Kathy to know I'm around."

"But we may not be delivering until morning," the doctor said.

"Well, I sleep nearly as well in a chair as I do in a bed. Sometimes I think even better."

Knowing Miss Larson, the doctor didn't try to change her mind, but Harriet was distressed.

"Surely you're not going to stay all night!"

"I often have before," Amelia said. "And it's true, I'm perfectly comfortable. People come in and out. It's quite interesting, and sometimes the young fathers need an old lady like me to talk to."

"Well, at least let me take you out for some supper, or, if you'd like me to stay while you go or bring you something . . ."

"You know, the thought of not having supper is a real pleasure to me," Amelia said. "The only thing I'm not going to miss about Kathy is the pounds of biscuits I've eaten in the last four months."

Down the corridor there was a sudden yelp of pain.

"Is that . . . Kathy?"

"No," Amelia said.

"It must be a bit hard on the fathers to be able to hear . . ."

"Yes," Amelia said, "but over the years one of the things that's impressed me is the change in men's attitudes about birth. This generation is better informed, I suppose. Lots of these young men stay right with their wives until they're taken in for delivery. If they've come out of the labor room for a cigarette, they want to be within earshot. Last time I was here, one woman let out a real scream, and one of the young men said to the other, 'Relax, that's mine. She never does let me finish a cigarette.' And back he went. I think it must be more the way it was when children were born at home and women had nothing to pull on but their husbands' belts. It's not a bad thing, not for most."

Perhaps not, Harriet thought, if you were involved and hopeful. Or as amazingly accepting of what happened as Amelia. But what about Kathy, obviously in for a long labor? What difference did it make to her whether the baby was placid or colicky? She'd never know.

"Should I go down to see her?" Harriet asked.

"Probably better to come see her in a day or two," Amelia said. "She's a little embarrassed just now."

There was another cry.

"Is that girl's husband already with her?" Harriet asked.

"It's another of the girls from the home," Amelia said. "You know, if I am going to spend the night, it would be a good idea for me to have a bit of fruit and a package of cookies. And then, maybe, if it wouldn't be too much trouble, I could give you my key and you could go in and feed the cat. I somehow think Cole won't remember."

Harriet knew Miss A was giving her something to do to get her out of there, and she could only be grateful. As the door of the elevator closed, there was a genuine scream, followed by "I want my mother. I want my mother. I want my mother." And Harriet knew that in the waiting room Amelia Larson was hoisting herself out of her chair, not because it was Kathy's voice but because it was a child who needed her, the lame, old spinster who knew more about motherhood than anyone else in town.

VI

PETER FALLIDON ARRIVED for the concert in a mood he hoped Haydn and Harriet Jameson would change. It had been a week of irritations and disappointments which he had grown accustomed but not resigned to. In this town people lived on coupons and deteriorating real estate and could not or would not see that repairing a roof or investing in new business was finally to their own advantage. In the year and a half he had been here, he had found only a few allies in his campaign against the decay. Miss Larson was important, both because she had the money to spend and the influence to encourage others. And Feller Hill was increasingly interested in Peter's proposals for the reconstruction of the downtown area. If he could be made enthusiastic, a number of other businessmen might be persuaded to move beyond complaining into some kinds of positive action. Peter had been particularly depressed, therefore, by the interview he had had with Mrs. Hill just before he left the bank this afternoon.

"I'd like to help you in any way I can, Mrs. Hill," he had said in a tone of cooperative reluctance, "but I can't give you a loan without your husband's signature unless you have securities in your own name."

"A married woman doesn't have her own name, Mr. Fallidon."

"I mean any security you don't hold jointly with your husband," he explained, ignoring her sarcasm.

"But I don't want him to know. It's none of his damned business."

"I'm sorry. There's no way to arrange a loan for ten thousand dollars without securities. You don't have an income of your own, a salary."

"No, Feller sees to that. It's incredible, isn't it, in this day and age that a woman is still simply a domestic animal? You men don't need to farm anymore. You can still make a cow and a horse and a dog out of a woman: milk her, ride her, train her to bring in the paper and fawn at your feet. . . ."

"Plenty of women own their own houses, investments, businesses. . . ."

"Not with bank managers like you, they don't. I've told you: that's what I want the money for, to invest in a business, to have some income of my own."

"I'm sorry," Peter said, standing up, "but your husband is the man to talk to first."

"This interview will be over when I decide it's over," Grace Hill said. "Sit down."

Peter stayed on his feet and waited.

"You know, I could make things fairly unpleasant for you around here."

Peter did not reply.

"Feller does listen to me about some things. He trusts my woman's intuition, and, if I tell him I think it's pretty odd for a man like you to have left the city to come out here to this cancerous carcass of a town, if I suggest that there must be something peculiar . . . He's a bright man, Mr. Fallidon, but he's very suggestible. He's trusted some people in the past and been disappointed."

"I can imagine he has," Peter said.

"Meaning?"

"Mrs. Hill, the bank has been closed for over an hour, and I have another appointment."

"With your little librarian? Or is she only a front?"

"Let me see you out."

"You'll regret this," Grace Hill said.

"I regret it now," Peter answered, in a tone so deeply ironic that it was almost neutral.

He had not had much appetite for dinner, but he fixed it for himself with the discipline of someone who has lived alone a long time and learned not to indulge his own negativity. There was nothing he could do to protect himself from Grace Hill. Neurotic malice could not be stopped. If she really did want money to go into business as a silent partner with Dina Pyros, why didn't she want to discuss it with her husband? Surely, something of that sort to occupy her would seem not only reasonable but a relief to Feller Hill. Probably then, she wanted the money for something else. Dina Pyros did not seem to Peter the sort of woman who would want or need a partner. As her bank manager, Peter knew how successful she had been without help from anyone. Might he speak to Feller himself? No. To intrude himself in any way into Feller's relationship with his wife was to sponsor the disaster Grace Hill promised him. Peter did not really believe Feller was the suggestible fool his wife made him out to be. Victim to her in some ways, yes, but surely not to her random malice.

He did not want to think about it any longer. He tried to distract himself with the notices pinned up in the lobby of the old movie theater which was used for these concerts. Incredible that a town of this size didn't have a concert hall or little theater.

"How are you this evening, Peter?"

"Fine," Peter said, taking Carl Hollinger's offered hand. "Miss Setworth, how are you?"

He liked both these old people. He did not know why he was mildly surprised to see them together. Probably they had been together before at one of these concerts, but tonight they had something of the look of a couple about them, not simply two old friends sharing a taste.

"Waiting for Harriet?" Ida Setworth asked.

"Yes," Peter said. "She seems to be a bit late."

"We probably ought to go in," Carl said.

Peter did not go in with them. He waited a moment longer. It wasn't like Harriet to be late. He tried to think if she had told him about a meeting or something she had to do for her mother. Anyway, she had her own ticket. There was no real problem. But Peter waited until the ushers were closing the doors before he hurried in to take his own seat.

He tried to listen, which was usually no more of an effort for him than seeing. But it was as if the volume had been turned down or he was too far away from the players, aware instead of the sharp, hateful voice of Grace Hill and the empty seat beside him, discordant anxieties which played against a music that seemed dull, thin, correct. Where was Harriet? If something had happened to her, no one would think to notify him, not at once anyway. It troubled him to realize that, if she had been in an accident, he would be more apt to hear it reported on the late news or to read about it in the morning paper than he would be to receive word from a friend or official. One of the virtues of Harriet was that he could be totally unaware of her while she sat beside him at a concert. He could absorb himself in the warm perversity of a dominant second violin, the deep extending support of a cello. Yet without her, he could not listen at all. Finally he gave up any attempt and simply waited for the performance to be over.

At intermission, he went to the phone and called her apartment, but there was no answer. Then he called the Larson house, but there was no one home there, either. Had something happened to Amelia Larson? He wanted to call Harriet's mother, but he hesitated. What if Harriet wasn't there? He would only worry the old lady.

Peter could not go back to hear the second half of the program. He waited in the lobby to make certain that Harriet didn't come in. When the doors were closed again, he went out onto the street. There was no sign of her. He drove by her mother's house to see if her car was there. It was not. But perhaps she'd gone home by now. He crossed town again and drove slowly by the old house, looking for her Volkswagen. It was not there. Not knowing where else to go, he parked his car and simply sat. Perhaps he should go home, but, even if she thought of calling him, she would not try to reach him before the concert was over. Where was she? What had happened to her?

This was just the kind of anxiety Peter did not want and could not bear in a relationship. Harriet Jameson, so dependable and independent and undemanding, had seemed to him a woman he could trust not to do this sort of thing to him. No Grace Hill, who must spend most of her neurotic energies concocting sexual and social anxieties for Feller. No Rosemary Hopwood, either, who, though she was a sensible enough woman obviously, would threaten a man by the attention she attracted without any effort, would seem to him a possession to live up to while she quite unconsciously refused to be a possession. So undeniably beautiful, the no less so as she aged, he would always have to think of what

64

could happen to her, what the loss of her would mean. Harriet: nothing could happen to someone like Harriet. But what had happened to her? It was ridiculous for him to sit here. Whether she'd call him or not, he should go home. Just as he was about to turn out into the street, he saw her Volkswagen pull in two cars behind him. His relief exploded in his chest like rage.

"Where in hell were you tonight?"

"Peter!" Harriet said, startled at seeing him there in the street and at his apparent anger.

"I was at the hospital with Miss A."

"What's happened to her?" he asked, baffled at his own lack of control.

"Nothing. It's that Kathy's having her baby. I just went down to keep Miss A company."

"You might have let me know."

"Why?" Only as she asked the question did she remember the concert. "Oh, Peter, I'm so terribly sorry. I completely forgot. Dina brought the chest over and told me about Kathy, and I . . ."

"I see," Peter said. "It was stupid of me to be concerned. Good night."

"Peter?" He had turned and was walking back toward his car. "Peter, I'm so really sorry. I don't know how . . . Couldn't you come in for a drink?"

"It's late. I've had a bad day," he said, not looking at her as he got into his car. "Good night."

He pulled away from the curb, leaving Harriet standing in the street.

"Oh Peter!" Her own regret turned suddenly into anger, and she wanted to shout after his car. "You don't really care whether I live or die anyway!" But she didn't. She just stood there, stupid with misery.

❋

"I wonder what did happen to Harriet tonight?" Ida said, as they drove back to her house after the concert.

"Don't know," Carl said. "He left after the intermission."

"Yes, I noticed."

"The something of true love ne'er runs smooth," Carl said.

"I thought you thought it didn't have anything to do with true love."

"I said I didn't think he'd marry her."

"Which is not the same thing?" Ida asked, sounding arch in a way she wasn't sure she liked.

"Some people can and some people can't," Carl said.

"Will you come in for a drink?"

"It's late," Carl said. "Thanks."

He showed her to the door and only touched her arm in saying good-night. Ida stood in her own front hall, feeling uncertainly guilty. The emotional debt most girls learn to accept in high school Ida had never experienced before. What, after all, should she owe Carl? He had said he loved her. But some compliments are too expensive to return without real consideration. Still, she felt ungenerous, and she did not like that.

"Well, I offered him a drink," she said. "He doesn't usually even wait to be asked."

It occurred to Ida then that Carl felt as burdened by what he had said as she did. Perhaps he even regretted it.

"How silly we are, past all that complication and then inventing it!"

❋

Once Harriet had left and the doctor suggested that Kathy try to sleep awhile, Amelia settled herself again in the chair she had claimed when she first arrived. Now there were two men also waiting, a young truck driver who wanted this second child to be a boy and a prematurely balding man who sat apparently absorbed in a book. It was a good time for Amelia to rest, but the amount of walking she had done had stirred the arthritic pain in her joints which sent sore messages along her skin so that even to rest her hands in her lap was awkward. Defense against that was concentration or distraction, not a nap. But she was very tired in a way that she had not anticipated, and it made her a little afraid. Beatrice had always been fearful in these last hours, as if disaster and death were her images of birth. There had been deaths. There had been deformities. But, in thirty years of vicarious labor, the habit was hard and perfect birth. What troubled Harriet—the pointlessness of it for Kathy—and the emptiness that Kathy herself anticipated had troubled Beatrice as well. Amelia couldn't accept or couldn't understand that. The child was born into the world and for it, whatever the circumstance. Then why was she fearful?

Had the energy of her faith come all those years from the need to reassure Beatrice? Or at least counteract her?

Too old, she was simply too old. "We're all too old to be doing what we're doing, but we go on doing it." A good man, Carl Hollinger, and it couldn't be easy for him to spend the time he did at the Veterans' Hospital with the collective stench and senile promise of what each death would be until his own. Pain: her own, Sister's, Kathy's, the fierce, outraged face of birth.

"Amelia?"

She opened her eyes to Rosemary Hopwood and was for a moment confused.

"What time is it?"

"A bit after midnight," Rosemary said.

"You shouldn't be down here at this hour," Amelia said.

"I was restless," Rosemary said. "I thought maybe you'd like company for a while."

"You've been worried about Kathy."

"Not seriously," Rosemary said, but her face was strained.

The young truck driver was dozing. The bald man was still intent upon his book. It was very quiet.

"I'm sorry I missed meeting Agate this afternoon," Amelia said. "I hope it wasn't hard on her."

"No," Rosemary said. "But I was interested in her reaction. She thought maybe she'd better stay right away since you'd have no one to look after you now."

"No one to look after me?" Amelia smiled, pleased and amused.

"Why don't I take you home now? You could come over early in the morning. Kathy's asleep. I've just looked in on her."

Someone cried out. Everyone in the waiting room looked up to the space in front of him. Then the balding man put down his book and left the room.

"That will have wakened her," Amelia said.

The cry came again, not so surprised this time. There was pity in it, not like self-pity, detached, as if the mind could express sympathy for the struggling body. There were several sets of hurrying footsteps, voices in the corridor. The young truck driver, looking casual enough, stood up, stretched, and left the room. Amelia started her own process of getting up.

"I'll go," Rosemary said.

"No," Amelia said, for she seemed refreshed from the nap she must have taken and wanted to move against her own pain. "Kathy doesn't call, but she'll want me."

"I love you, Amelia Larson," Rosemary said, kissing Amelia on the cheek.

"It's nice to know," Amelia said, though the declaration had fallen short in the wide space there was to her own need. "Go along home now. I'll phone you tomorrow."

Kathy would hear her coming down the long corridor and compose her face. "A good brave girl" she wanted to be, and maybe she'd be able to manage it for herself. Being good at pain, for most people, was a matter of practice rather than courage, or so it seemed to Amelia.

"How is it now?" she asked as she swung into Kathy's curtained bed and look at the whitely wakened face.

"I think maybe I've begun, too," Kathy said.

"Good."

"But maybe it's only her baby," Kathy added, an uncertain shake in her voice.

Amelia smiled at her.

"I mean, like wanting to throw up because somebody else is," Kathy tried to explain, then suddenly grunted and closed her eyes.

"That's you, all right," Amelia said. "And that's fine. Get the idea, get the rhythm. It's hard work, child, but you're good at that."

After a moment Kathy eased herself again and took her breath. Then she said, "They try to tell you, but it isn't like they say."

Amelia had trouble hearing her because of a sharp complaint from the woman in the next bed and the busyness of nurses around her.

"Time for you now," one of the nurses said.

"I wish it was for me," Kathy said.

"It will be; just go with it," Amelia said.

It was clear that her hard labor had begun, but, as the hours passed and each of the other two women went in to be delivered, Kathy stayed caught in the prerhythm of pain. There were nurses to talk with her, guide her. The doctor was there, his tired young face sometimes intent, sometimes impatient, knowing he had been called back too early. He and Amelia went into the hall occasionally, taking coffee together.

At six o'clock in the morning, Kathy whispered to Amelia, "Am I going to die?"

"No, child. You're going to have a baby."

"All right, Kathy," the doctor said. "Let's get this job done."

As they wheeled her into the operating room, Amelia went back to the waiting room, empty again, her own. She sat down in her chair and immediately slept, exhausted and peaceful, her part of it done.

"Miss Larson?" The doctor shook her gently. "Miss Larson?"

"Over?" she asked, opening her eyes.

"Over," he said. "A nine pound, four ounce girl."

"I'm not surprised," Amelia said.

"I've called you a cab, and don't argue with me," he said, as a nurse came into the room with a wheelchair.

"I can walk," Amelia said.

"You worked nearly as hard as she did."

"All right. Just wheel me down to see her before I leave."

"You're a good, brave girl, Kathy," Amelia said and saw the characteristic euphoric smile of accomplishment that comes of birth. "And that's what you've had. We'll all get some sleep now, and I'll see you tomorrow."

The nurse wheeled Amelia out into a sunny morning. What an old fool she must look, carried out in a wheelchair after having someone else's baby! Without Sister, she had no style. Sister had been her style, her right arm, the last bit of strength she did not have by herself. It didn't really matter, however, since Sister was not there to mind.

VII

AGATE, IN A YELLOW COTTON SHIFT and sandals, lounged in the early sun on the front steps of the Larson house. She had rung the bell when she first arrived just a little after seven, but either no one was home or everyone was still asleep. As she debated walking back to a small store several blocks away to buy something for her breakfast, a cab pulled into the drive. Agate stood up and walked down the steps to meet it.

"Good morning," she said to Amelia. "I'm the new maid."

"Agate?" Amelia asked.

"Yes. Are you Miss Larson?"

"Yes," Amelia said. "I'm just getting back from the hospital."

"You've been there all night?"

"Yes," Amelia said. She was paying the driver. "Don't get out, Freddy. Agate will get me out. Stand there, and give me one hand."

"Have you had breakfast?" Agate asked.

"I don't think I have," Amelia said. "Now stand up ahead of me, two steps. That's it. Thank you, Freddy," she called over her shoulder. "Isn't Cole home?"

"Nobody answered the bell."

"He's probably asleep."

"Shall I get you breakfast?" Agate asked.

"You haven't even seen the kitchen."

"Does it look different from other kitchens?" Agate asked.

"I expect not." Amelia unlocked the front door and went in.

"Then why don't you go right to bed and I'll bring you something. Do you need help now?"

"No. I'll tell you," Amelia said. "The kitchen's right down the . . ."

"I'll find my way. What will it be?"

"No coffee. I'd like juice, hot milk, perhaps an egg, whatever you want to do with it," Amelia said, turning herself into the chair lift.

Agate went off in the direction Amelia had indicated, the adventure of the morning modified by the concern she felt at the color of the old lady's face. Maybe she always looked like that, but Agate doubted it. She wondered if, once she'd made Miss Larson breakfast, she'd better call the doctor. Poached egg, probably, and there were the eggs, the orange juice, the milk. The girl who had been keeping this kitchen was tidy. After Agate had opened cupboards to find pans and china and a tray, she poured herself a large glass of milk.

"There you are," she said to her stomach. "You'll have to wait for more."

Within ten minutes she had the breakfast ready to take up and decided, at the bottom of the stairs, to give herself a ride. She pressed the button to recall the chair lift, then climbed aboard with the tray. It hummed steadily until it got to the landing where it strained and jerked a little, threatening the milk and juice. Agate, who had been reading the mottoes with amusement, had to turn her attention to the balance of the tray. Wouldn't do to have the first thing she served awash in itself.

"Did Rosemary Hopwood bring you over?" Amelia asked from her bed.

"No, I walked."

"Walked!"

"I like to walk," Agate said, putting the tray in Amelia's lap. "And I thought you had to have somebody to cook breakfast."

"It's very nice," Amelia said, "but your room isn't ready. . . ."

"Doesn't matter. I'll find my way around."

"Perhaps when Cole wakes up . . ."

"Do you want more butter?"

"No, thank you. It tastes very good."

"You must be hungry."

"I'll be down again in the early afternoon. Then we can have a real talk."

71

"Will you sleep?" Agate asked.

"Yes, easily."

"What will Cole want when he gets up?"

"Eggs and bacon, fruit, coffee, toast. He probably won't be up before ten."

"I don't know how to bake bread," Agate said. "I notice that's homemade."

"Thank fortune," Amelia said.

"Are you all right?"

"Yes, just very tired. Thank you, child. It's a very kind thing you've done, getting here this morning."

The old lady was falling asleep as Agate took the tray. Probably that was all she needed. Agate needed food. The sooner she had some breakfast, the better. Seated at the kitchen table with a plate of eggs and toast, Agate felt relaxed and content.

"Maybe what I've wanted all along was to be some old lady's maid," she said, and then she laughed.

A large, ugly cat appeared and made a single, commanding noise.

"Who are you, hideous?"

She got up to look for the cat food she had seen in one of the cupboards, but the phone was ringing.

"Larson residence," Agate said.

"Is that you, Agate?"

"Yes, Miss Hopwood," Agate answered in a tone she hoped would indicate pride in being a menial.

"How did you get there?"

"I walked."

"But Miss Larson wasn't even expecting you, and you have the whole staff here in a state."

"Somebody had to cook breakfast," Agate said.

"What do you want to do about your clothes?"

"I'll pick them up sometime," Agate said.

"Would you like me to bring them to you?"

"That's kind of you," Agate said, liking Miss Larson's word, given her own tone.

"I'll be by later this afternoon," Rosemary said.

"Oh, about the books," Agate said. "You might just donate them to the library there."

"Of course," Rosemary said with answering sarcasm.

The cat did not weave about Agate's legs as hungry cats are

supposed to. It stood in the middle of the kitchen and glared at her.

"All right," Agate said to it as she hung up the phone. "I agree. The customer on the spot should get the attention, but that's not how the world works."

She found the box of dry cat food and was shaking some into a plastic bowl when Cole came into the kitchen.

"Who are you?" he demanded.

"Everybody in this house is such an awful color," Agate said. "Hangover? Bad trip?"

"Who are you?"

"And as good-tempered as the cat."

"Look," Cole said. "I want to know who you are and what you're doing in this kitchen."

"I'm feeding the cat, and I'm about to feed you, since Miss Larson seems to want it done."

"Oh," Cole said. "I'm sorry. You're the new girl. Is Cousin A home then?"

"Cousin A?"

"Miss Larson."

"Yes, she's gone to bed. How do you want your eggs?"

"Actually," Cole said, "I'm not all that hungry. I think I'll just get some juice or something."

"Coffee?"

"Ah . . . no, thanks. Well . . ."

"I've made a pot."

"Okay, thanks."

"Don't mention it."

"Is your room fixed? Have you been shown around?"

"No, not yet. Doesn't matter."

"I don't think Kathy had time to pack or change her sheets or anything," Cole said, sitting down with juice and coffee at the kitchen table.

"You really do look awful," Agate said.

"I feel awful."

If you didn't know, Agate in her yellow shift did not look pregnant. But Cole did know. Her naturally ample figure would have intimidated his uncertain appetites anyway, but the thought that she was beginning to swell with the blood and milk and sea wash of birth sickened him newly with the pity and horror of it. He assumed that Kathy was dead. Now knowing he would have to

73

watch Agate ripen for the same fate, he couldn't drink his orange juice.

"Maybe I'll get some air," he said, and he fled.

"Christ!" Agate said to the cat. "He's like something out of an English novel."

At least he wouldn't be an important nuisance. With one old lady, nearly dead asleep, and one wilting tulip of a boy out in the air, Agate could begin exploring without fear of interruption or discovery. Her interests, for the moment, were relatively innocent. She did want to find her room and her way about the house. Its treasures, frailties, and secrets would be distractions and entertainments for other days, when she was bored with and powerless over her own.

✳

"Are you interested in these, Dina?" Rosemary asked.

Dina turned away from her Saturday beer and looked at the paperbacks Rosemary Hopwood was holding out to her.

"Where did you get a collection like that?" Dina asked, amusement strong enough to make its way through the murk of her hangover.

"From one of the girls at the hostel."

"Sure. Never can get enough of these," Dina said. "I'll even give you twenty cents a piece."

"Fine."

Dina got to her feet and went to the ancient cash register which rang with simple authority. She took out two dollar bills and handed them to Rosemary.

"Thanks."

"Who was the girl?" Dina asked, carefully not looking at Rosemary.

"Who had the books?"

"No," Dina said. "The one in your car yesterday."

"Oh," Rosemary said. "That was Agate, the girl who's going to Amelia. Why?"

"I just wondered," Dina said.

They stood, caught in each other's misunderstood and misplaced jealousy, with nothing clear to say to each other.

"I owe you a dinner," Rosemary said finally, not as she had planned to say it. What she had intended to be casual came out as a taunt.

"You don't owe me anything," Dina answered, and what she had meant to be truthful sounded simply surly.

"Would you come to dinner?"

"At your place?"

"Yes."

"When?"

"Whenever you say," Rosemary answered.

"I don't . . . you know . . . dress or anything," Dina said, looking down at herself.

"Tonight? Tomorrow night?"

"I was going down to Nick's," Dina said.

"I see. All right," Rosemary said, and this time the tone, unplanned, was neither angry nor embarrassed. The mistake she was making was beyond that.

"What time tonight?" Dina asked.

"Seven?"

"All right."

"I'll see you then," Rosemary said, and she turned and walked away past the idle curiosity of the boys by the stove, the books, the chairs on the wall, into the heat of the June afternoon.

It was three o'clock. She could deliver Agate's clothes, see Amelia, and still have time to get to the stores before they closed. The menu had been fixed since early this morning when Rosemary was driving up and down F Street after even Amelia had refused her distraction.

✳

Out of her shower, Dina wandered into the kitchen and poured herself an ouzo, then went back into her bedroom and looked at the clothes in her closet. There was the gray suit she had worn to Nick's wedding eight years ago, the black suit she kept for funerals, and the violet linen she had bought a year ago in April to wear when she first called on Peter Fallidon, the new bank manager. She had not worn it. Why should she wear it tonight to have dinner with Rosemary Hopwood? She had even eaten at Miss A's in her boots and trousers, but always she was there on the pretext of furniture of some sort. That was how she presented herself in any house in town, whether Harriet Jameson's or old Miss Setworth's. She wasn't invited to the Hills'. There were Dolly and Sal, of course, but they were different, apt to be in boots and trousers themselves after business hours. Rosemary hadn't said, "There's a bureau I'd like to sell," or "Could you advise me about what sort of piece I need in the dining room," or "Stop for a drink when you deliver that bookcase." She had simply said, "Would you come for dinner?" There wouldn't be anyone else there. Dina understood that. But they would sit at a dining room table. There would be wine in good glassware.

"I told her I didn't dress."

There was a clean pair of chinos she had intended to wear to Nick's tonight and the sweat shirt she never worked in, but that would be either an ignorant or a belligerent way to dress when someone had asked you—just asked you—to dinner, like a friend. Even if Harriet Jameson had ever said, "Come for a drink," just for that, Dina would have put on clothes. But nobody ever did say that, and she was out of the habit of dressing.

The girdle she found and pulled on held her as firmly as trousers did, and she liked the feel of stockings and the slip Sal had once given her, saying, "Just because you ought to own one." The dress was not so reassuring, for it left her strong, muscled arms exposed. She had a sweater around somewhere, a white one sent from Greece, from a sister she did not know. The shoes, though odd in balance, posed less problem than skates or skis, on both of which Dina was competent. They made her feel as if going out to dinner at Rosemary Hopwood's were a kind of sport.

Then she thought of the truck. She couldn't drive the truck, dressed like this. If it had not been Saturday night, if she had had more than half an hour, Dina Pyros might have gone out and bought herself a car for the occasion. She felt that whimsical.

"So they call you a peasant," Nick had said to her when she was still a kid. "Be a proud peasant.' '

Call a cab. That would mean, of course, that people in town would know where Dina had gone for dinner, dressed as if she had been invited. But Rosemary Hopwood had invited her. She called a cab.

"Hey, Dina!" Freddy said. "You look like a million bucks!" And he scrambled out of the cab to open the door for her.

"Make it fifty thousand," Dina said, liking to be modestly accurate without anyone's being the wiser.

"Where are you going?"

"To Miss Hopwood's."

Rosemary had sold the family house in the Larson's neighborhood and bought one that had been built ten years ago by an eccentric only son who then killed himself there. Designed for a single person with too much of a taste for privacy, and then marked by his death, it had not been salable until Rosemary offered half what it was worth and moved in.

"All houses survive people. It's not the sort of thing that troubles me," Rosemary had said. "He had excellent taste."

What for him had been finally an unendurable turning in on himself was for Rosemary a sustaining peace, imitating the nature if not the style of Ida Setworth's singularity.

This evening she had dressed no less carefully than Dina, discarding the bright tent, held at the throat by gold butterflies and then falling freely to the floor, she often wore when she had someone in for drinks. Instead she put on slacks and a long, tailored tunic. Would Dina like drinks in the patio? She sat often enough at the back door of her shop, taking the sun. Would Rosemary know what to say to her? If she actually turned up. Rosemary was not at all confident that she would.

At seven precisely, the doorbell rang.

"Hello," Dina said.

"Hello."

"Am I too early?"

"No, of course not," Rosemary said. "Come in."

"I've always wanted to see this house," Dina said. "But I was afraid I'd buy it."

"Well, come in," Rosemary said, and she took Dina's hand. "I'll show it to you. Then you can decide where we'll have drinks. I couldn't."

"Was this carpeting here when you bought it?" Dina asked as they stepped down into the living room.

"Yes—and a lot of the furniture, too. The family didn't want any of it, and I liked it."

"I can see why," Dina said.

"And I liked the fact that it had a dining room," Rosemary said.

"I knew there'd be a dining room."

"Did you?"

"Yes," Dina said.

"The kitchen's peculiar to work in. He was tall and left-handed," Rosemary explained. "Shall I get us a drink while we're here?"

The bottle of ouzo was on the counter with glasses and a pitcher of water.

"You're a little bit Greek," Dina said, taking the glass Rosemary offered. "I thought we'd drink gin."

"Would you rather? I have some."

"To me it's like perfume," Dina said smiling. "Something to wear, maybe."

"The best way to the other side is across the patio," Rosemary said, and she opened one of the glass doors and waited for Dina to go out before her.

"I like this," Dina said.

"Then let's stay awhile. I'll show you the rest later."

Gradually, as they walked through the house, Rosemary became accustomed to Dina in a dress, perhaps because she seemed so confident in the part she was playing in this costume, easier and surer than she had been in her ordinary clothes. Now, as she walked across the patio, precisely balanced, she was graceful in a way Rosemary could not have imagined of the Dina she had watched before, rooted in boots, strong, stolid.

"I care about fuchsias," Dina said, looking closely at the hanging baskets, and then she turned to Rosemary. "We're going to be friends, aren't we?"

Rosemary could not ask Dina what she meant by that. She felt the hope in Dina's voice but also the distance. "We are friends," she said.

Most people, waited on, flutter at or ignore small services. Dina received them with simple attention, a courtesy of compliments natural to her.

"Were you born in Greece?"

"Yes, but I don't remember it," Dina said. "I grew up with an aunt and uncle in Chicago. Then I came here to visit Nick. I liked the sea."

"Will you ever go back to visit Greece? Are you curious?"

"Afraid," Dina said. "I would not go until my mother died."

"I didn't come home until my mother died either," Rosemary said.

"Are you sorry?"

"No," Rosemary said. "We didn't understand each other. There was no point."

"I wouldn't understand my mother either," Dina said, and she smiled. "I don't speak Greek."

The silences that fell between them through the meal were nothing like the complete silence of their first meal together, nor were they awkward, attentive rather, to let in evening sounds, the wind coming up in the trees, the busy settling of birds. Rosemary looked at her guest, this foreigner, this friend at her table, amazed to see her there.

"Were you really tempted to buy this house?" she asked.

"Yes," Dina said. "It's different for me, though," and she hesitated before she decided to try to explain. "I have to think how to live. I have to decide. Am I a peasant or not? I don't know. And there's nobody to tell me exactly. I cracked myself up in a fine car. I'm better off in my truck. So I'm probably better off living over my shop."

"Why would you think that?"

"My mother and sisters are peasants," Dina said. "Why should I own a house? Unless it would be my dowry."

"Dowry?"

"Yes," Dina said. "Something to offer for a husband."

"You weren't joking?" Rosemary asked. "You want to marry?"

"Of course," Dina said. "It's different for you. You're a widow, yes?"

"No," Rosemary said.

"Yes," Dina insisted, "to some dead love."

"By that definition, there's nobody over fifteen in the world but widows and widowers."

"I am twice fifteen," Dina said.

Should Rosemary answer that she was three times fifteen? But Dina was serious. Since there had been no one to tell her how to live, she had invented this dowered virginity against all sense and appetite. It was ludicrous.

"That's too long to wait," Rosemary said.

Dina smiled to refuse the argument, nearly unaware of the desire she was about to resist, the assault on her mythology Rosemary intended, for Rosemary would not say again either "I love you" or "I want you like that" until she had made herself sexually clear. It might not be tonight. It might not be this week or this month, but she would finally be Dina's lover. Then she could say what she wanted. Now she said simply, "I don't really like your patience."

"Good," Dina said, believing she understood that. "I won't be patient for you."

VIII

CARL HOLLINGER WAS SUFFERING from nervous embarrassment. In the week since he had proposed to Ida, he had experienced an intensity of emotions he was too old to cope with. At times he deeply regretted having spoken to Ida at all and determined to tell her he now realized what a ridiculous suggestion it had been, but he knew perfectly well that he could say no such thing to her. Aside from its being both dishonorable and unkind, it was for most of each day untrue. What he really regretted was the hope he had made real, for now the discomfort of his loneliness seemed to him intolerable. He hated the pleasant house he and his wife had retired to five years ago. He couldn't work in the garden or in his study. He could not comfortably read the newspaper in his own living room. He went out for as many meals as he remembered, even for breakfast, and spent a great deal of his time at the public library with random rather than systematic reading so that he often could not remember what he had read or why he was reading what was in front of him. Once a week he visited the General Hospital. Twice a week he called on patients at the Veterans' Hospital, where he had been the chaplain before his retirement. But none of these tastes and duties which, until two years ago, had made his old age an interesting contentment gave him any satisfaction now. The sorrow he had known during the first year after his wife died gradually gave way to irritable self-criticism which he had known was destructive and had tried to control. But he could not live happily alone. It was not his nature. Why should he endure it when Ida might provide a return to the domestic center of life? His impatient need of her brought him as close to lust as he had been for years. His shame at his inability to deal with loneliness humbled him. Ida had no such need and no such weakness. Why should he hope that answering his would have any appeal for her? But he did hope, and to distract himself from that was even more difficult than finding an escape from grief.

On Monday morning, he was on the library steps before it opened, a declaration of impatience he had never allowed himself before so that he had never seen before the number of people who were willing to suffer the humiliation of their loneliness so publicly. Old people, more than a dozen of them, who were regulars like himself, stood about or sat on the steps in the sun. Several had learned to talk at each other, but most were silent, occupying small, isolated spaces of their own, staked out the months or years ago when they had resigned themselves to this way of passing the time between important deaths and their own. Probably the talkers went elsewhere, to the benches outside the courthouse, to the train and bus station waiting rooms if the weather was bad.

"Good morning, Mr. Hollinger," Harriet said as she came up the steps with her key. "You're early this morning."

"My watch was wrong," Carl said.

"It's a lovely day to be in the sun," she said. "I should think you'd be tempted into your garden."

"We missed you Friday night at the concert," Carl said, and was immediately sorry that he had when he saw the expression change on Harriet's face. "I hope nothing was the matter."

"I went to the hospital to see if I could do anything to help Miss A. Kathy was having her baby."

"Ah," Carl said. "I didn't know. I should stop in and see her."

"I simply forgot the concert," Harriet confessed.

"It was pleasant enough but nothing to be really sorry you missed."

Harriet unlocked the large front door, and Carl held it open for her. None of the others seemed in any hurry to come in out of the summer morning.

"I didn't mind missing the concert," Harriet said quickly. "But it was very rude to forget Peter."

"He'd understand," Carl said.

"I'm afraid he didn't," Harriet said, and to the confusion of both of them she began to cry. "I am sorry," she said, recovering. "It's not important at all. I think I just don't like being in the wrong like that and upsetting someone else. It's silly, really."

"Silly to be concerned about someone else's feelings?" Carl asked, gently teasing her, wanting to comfort her.

"Oh, Peter doesn't matter to me at all, Mr. Hollinger," Harriet said. "What I mean is . . ." and she hesitated, obviously near tears again.

"That you wouldn't want to worry anyone," Carl finished for her.

"May I tell you the truth?" Harriet asked with a sudden, angry earnestness.

"If you want to, of course."

"I would like to worry someone. I really would. But it would have to be someone who cared about me."

"I feel exactly the same way."

"You do?"

"It's something some people never outgrow," Carl said. "Maybe it's not such a bad thing. And, Harriet, people don't worry about people who don't matter to them, not much anyway."

The others had begun to come into the building now, and the telephone on Harriet's desk was ringing.

"Excuse me," she said.

Carl hesitated a moment and then went into the reading room. If Peter Fallidon had no intention of marrying Harriet Jameson, he should stop seeing her. Carl could not say why he felt Peter would not marry. He was not a cold man, but there was something rigidly self-sufficient about him, not at the social edges but at the center. Peter Fallidon would not find it difficult to go home at night to the task of preparing his own meal and eating it alone. He would never be driven out to escape solitude. Like Ida, he would have made for himself a cheerful discipline, even a pleasure, out of singleness. Still, for Ida it was a necessity which she found the courage to serve. For Peter it was a choice. And he should be free to make it only if he really could live without worrying much about other people or mattering much to them. It was quite wrong of him to teach Harriet the peripheral pleasures of companionship without taking responsibility for them.

The stern tone in Carl's head warned him. Wasn't he really lecturing at Ida? And certainly, if she decided she wouldn't marry him, he would not want her to decide, as well, that she should not see him any more. Would that occur to her? She had said that night, if he wanted a wife, he should stop "hiding" with her. But, at their age, that was ridiculous. Was it less ridiculous at Peter's and Harriet's? There certainly didn't seem to be anyone else who was being discouraged from courting Harriet because of Peter. At least, with Peter, she had the peripheral pleasures, and that was better than nothing. If that was all Peter could offer her, if that was all Ida could offer him, why judge them for it? Carl knew why. He couldn't stand the idea. He wanted to walk into Peter Fallidon's office and say not "If you don't intend to marry Harriet, leave her alone" but "Marry the girl!" Peter should come down here to the library. Maybe now, while he was occupied with business and energetic in his health, being alone had its virtues, but did he want to grow old like one of these rheumy, rheumatic old men who shuffled in out of the sun every day to the files of old newspapers? Carl sighed. He doubted that there was a bachelor among them. Peter, in his old age, would be no more baffled by loneliness than Ida was now. Harriet? Well, she would have lived her whole life in the library, anyway. But what a waste! Even now for him, at his age, it was a waste. Couldn't Ida see that? If they had no more than five years, no more than six months, why should they live even a moment not worrying much, not mattering much to each other, when from that center flowed the love one had for everyone? A profane view for a minister, but for years Carl had suspected that his love of God was supported by his love for his wife rather than the other way round. And he could not feel guilty about it; it was too good a thing to mistrust. Even now in his loneliness, when to love God was a requirement without comfort, he did not mistrust human love.

"Daily bread," he said and realized that he spoke aloud, but it was not an unusual thing here among books and old people used to talking to themselves.

Carl closed the book he had not been reading and went back out to Harriet's desk.

"Are you busy tonight?" he asked. "I'm going to be fairly late at the Veterans' Hospital, and I won't want to cook myself supper. Would you have some with me?"

"Why, thank you, Mr. Hollinger," Harriet said. "That would be very nice."

"I'll pick you up around six," he said.

If he and Harriet had to suffer, there was no real reason why they should suffer alone. He thought of Kathy. Given her shyness, it would be better to call on her with Amelia. Perhaps he would stop at the Larson house now. It was about time for Amelia's midmorning coffee, and she liked company.

"Cole's at work," a tawny-eyed, ample-bodied girl informed him at the door. "And Miss Larson's in bed, doctor's orders."

"I'm sorry," Carl said. "Is it serious?"

"She needs rest, the doctor said."

"How about callers?"

"I don't know," Agate said. "Do you want to see her?"

"Could you just tell her that Carl Hollinger is here?"

"All right."

"Thank you."

Carl was surprised at the alarm he felt, for at their age it was surely more surprising to find a friend well than sick, but Amelia, much more than Maud Montgomery, who bragged about her strength, or Ida, who simply did not inform people of her ailments, had a strong constitution which seemed hardly affected by emotional or physical strain.

"She says you're to come up," Agate announced as she came back down the stairs. "I'll bring you some coffee."

"Oh, don't bother. I'll stay only a few minutes."

"Miss Larson says you *expect* coffee," Agate answered with mock firmness.

The girl's tone, tilting toward rude familiarity so different from Kathy's shy politeness, reassured Carl, for she did make Amelia sound like herself.

"What's this all about?" he asked, standing in the door of her bedroom.

"Nothing but four months of biscuits and too long a night," Amelia said cheerfully, but her color wasn't good. "I'm to be starved and bored for a week. So much for modern medicine. Come in, Carl."

"I was just stopping by to see if I could arrange to take you down to Kathy," Carl said, taking a chair that had been moved near the bed.

"I was going to call you," Amelia said. "Rosemary's going down, and Harriet will, but, since I can't, I'd be awfully glad if you did as well."

"I'll go from here. Now what else can I do for you? If Cole's gone to work, you must need some errands run."

"That's no problem. I can send Agate by cab."

"Quite a change from Kathy," Carl said, smiling.

"Isn't she? She doesn't even know *how* to bake bread."

"Is she managing for you all right?"

"Perfectly," Amelia said. "She's simply taken over. I think she's going to be a bit bossy, and she hasn't a manner to her name, except as a way of being funny, but she is funny. I haven't laughed so much since Sister died. I'm sure Maud won't approve."

"She wouldn't in any case," Carl said.

They heard Agate coming up the stairs.

"Here's your coffee," Amelia said.

"I hear you're taking good care of Miss Larson," Carl said, taking a cup from the tray Agate offered. "Thank you."

"She just doesn't want me to tell people what a terrible patient she is; so we made an agreement not to complain about each other. You don't get coffee."

"I know. You needn't remind me," Amelia said.

"I found the Teflon frying pan in the bottom drawer of the stove. It was full of pork fat, but Kathy didn't use it before she'd scrubbed it clean. The only Teflon left is around the handle bolts where she couldn't get at it."

"So it won't do?"

"Not without butter, and you're not having butter."

"Order a new one then," Amelia said.

"Yes'm, Miss A," Agate said and did an Aunt Jemima strut out of the bedroom.

"Are they always critical of their predecessors?" Carl asked.

"Not always," Amelia said. "But it's not unusual. Kathy was too busy with her own mistakes to notice, or at least she never said."

"What are all these boxes?" Carl asked.

"Sister's diaries. I'm reading them before I burn them."

"Are they witty?"

"I suppose they are," Amelia said. "Is it always the unhappiest people who are?"

"Beatrice wasn't really unhappy, was she? Critical, yes, but not unhappy."

"She was never content with herself. I know that, but I find it peculiar to read her saying so. I was so content with her."

"Why do you read them?" Carl asked.

"I don't know. A way of passing through grief, is it?"

"I used to have answers for questions like that," Carl said, and he took Amelia's hand.

"We're bad at missing people, you and I," Amelia said.

"Is there anything I should take to Kathy?"

"Jawbreakers," Amelia confessed.

"Out of the penny machine?"

"That's right. And thank you, Carl."

"I'll come by again in a day or two."

✳

July 1, 1939: How can Sister really mean that it doesn't matter how Bill Hopwood died? Of course, if he committed suicide, it shouldn't be in the paper, but we should know. If he had a heart attack at the wheel, an autopsy would show it. Esther won't agree to an autopsy. Is she so afraid? Is she so sure? He wasn't ever stable, not even as a boy. Still, to live to nearly fifty makes suicide unreasonable without troubles over money or something of the sort. He would have been a happier man with troubles. Was it just two months ago he said, "When we die, it will be of boredom"? He never could make a decision, not even to marry. But he wasn't really unhappy with Esther. Except for losing the boy. But that must be ten years ago now. And Rosemary, even before that, was his favorite. A vain thing people do, loving the children who take after them. Rosemary would be better off with more of Esther's toughness and less of his temperament, particularly now. An odd thing to see beauty change sexes from father to daughter, mother to son. If I'm going to believe that Bill Hopwood is dead, I must know how and why. Was he having an affair? Was he ill? He could not have been too bored to go on living—that isn't possible.

July 2, 1939: Ida, come from the Hopwoods, said Rosemary wasn't speaking to her mother—at a time like this! But Ida knows no more about it than the rest of us. Esther says the funeral has to be tomorrow, whether all the family can get here or not. It can't be on the Fourth of July. Amelia is arranging to have casseroles sent over. That's what Esther did for us when Mama died. Should I speak to Rosemary? Sister won't discuss the idea. Who is close to the child? She can't behave this way now. If people think

Rosemary blames Esther, they'll also think Bill killed himself. I don't know what to think.

July 3, 1939: Of course, Esther wouldn't cry. She's like Sister in that. And Rosemary is hardly more than a child. It's hard for any of us to believe he's dead. Because it was a sudden accident? Because we don't understand it? Why do I feel frightened in a way I did when Father died? We've buried Mama and Aunt Setworth and now Bill Hopwood just in the last eight months. "We begin to bury ourselves," Ida said. I believed so little in Bill's life—no more than in my own. It's a hard walk for Sister to the grave, but she always goes. "Accept it," is all she will say. Aunt Setworth taught her that: "One of the hard poems, child." For Ida and me it has to be a joke. I can't accept it. Why won't Rosemary cry?

July 4, 1939: Sister and I sat in the turret tonight to watch the fireworks down at the docks. They are no comfort.

July 5, 1939: Rosemary has gone. Esther won't talk about it more than to say "She wanted to, and I thought it best to let her go." At sixteen? And she's moving into Rosemary's room, as if she expected Rosemary would never come home again. When Ida asked her what she was going to do, she said, "Just what I've always done . . . nothing." Are we simply born to bury each other? And help each other kill the time until the time.

❄

Carl, driving back into town from the Veterans' Hospital, had a sudden image of his wife, not as she was in those last sad months before she died but years younger, laughing at him. And somehow that laughter was related to Kathy this afternoon, sitting very solemnly in her bed, sucking one of the jawbreakers he had brought her. He wondered if on the next occasion of her having a baby, there would be an earnest young farmer to take his place who could sit in dumb adoration of that pregnant cheek. Then he heard his wife's voice, still uneven with laughter: "There must be a great deal of silliness in the day of any good man, Carl. Isn't that a lucky thing?" But it hadn't to do with anything he had done or told her about, had it? Wasn't it some foolishness between them? Some comic turn of love in the day? He couldn't remember. Did Ida know how to laugh like that? It was probably something you couldn't learn by yourself. It was certainly easy to forget by yourself. It was as if Kathy with her jawbreaker *was* his wife. To be reminded of someone by another's gesture or tone or attitude wasn't surprising, but to have his bright, articulate wife come to him in the face of Kathy was nearly perverse. Except

87

that to have loved the silliness of one person was to make loving anyone's silliness possible. The other faces of the day, with that gift, could be endured. If Carl felt a threatening connection between himself and the old men at the library, he was still healthy and independent enough to offer a detached sympathy for the men at the Veterans' Hospital. Amelia was a different matter. He must speak to Harriet. Amelia was very fond of Harriet.

IX

THERE WERE RESTAURANTS other than Nick's: half a dozen dairies
of varying dullness, a steak house, a seafood restaurant where the
food was very good and the service very bad, a few motel and
hotel coffee shops a step up from the greasy spoons and drive-ins,
but Nick's was the only place with a style that could make you
forget you were going out to dinner simply because you did not
want to eat at home. Nick's could have been successful anywhere
else as well, and that's what happened to restaurants that did
succeed: their owners left for the larger appetites and wallets of
the real cities. But Nick Pyros would not leave. He had a house,
a wife, a couple of children, and this was his sort of town. He'd
chosen it.

It was really two halves of one place, a dining room and a
café, mercifully separated by the kitchen so that the loud music
of the café threatened the nervous systems of the diners only
when both kitchen doors happened to open at the same time.
Though that occurred on an average of once every five or six minutes, no one enjoying the intervening quiet ever complained. For
those who talked, it provided a moment to eat. For those who
were silent, it was company. For those of uncertain social habits,
the jarring noise relieved them of any guilt of their own. But perhaps the acceptance was for the music as well. It was Greek. Like
the menu, the jukebox offered only two or three North American
choices, whatever was the musical hamburger of the moment.

And a kid could eat a hamburger if he really wanted to, either in the dining room or the café, but it wasn't the thing to do. Nick had trained his customers to tiropeta—a kind of cheese pie with many layers of thin pastry and a thick, savory filling—if they were snacking, to lamb dishes and eggplant if they were ordering a meal.

But more than the music or the food, it was the dancing that drew people of all ages to Nick's. Even on a weeknight there was always a nucleus of half a dozen men, either immigrants like Nick or first-generation Greeks, who kept a sense of that rhythm of manhood which would call them to their feet at any time. Singly at first, later often together, some simply assertively and some with real authority, they danced. Local boys, used to showing off to anything but music, watched during the early evening, but, as the hours passed, they too would get up, their first solos drunken and sheepishly imitative, even mocking, but the music allowed for that. Within it a number of them had learned to dance so that the crowd's response would change from cheerful jeering to stamping and table-beating approval. Weekends the place was always jammed, and after eight the dining room was opened to music and dancing as well. Any night there were Greek sailors in town, it was hard to find a place to stand. Women were not forbidden to dance either by rule or custom, but not many did except when the sailors were there, teaching them what would not have been allowed in Greece.

The sailors had been in town for a week because of a delay in loading lumber, caused by a series of the usual errors in planning. Deadlines here were rarely met, not because there were strikes but because owners of timber clipped trees like coupons, when they needed the cash, without regard to mill needs or foreign orders. The uncertain supply of logs made work at the mills uncertain, and whether there were logs or not, most mills shut down for the opening of the hunting and fishing seasons. Another thirty years and there would be nothing left of the already vastly depleted forests; so why not spin out the process a little longer? If a ship waited in the harbor, sailors danced in the town, and whoever was paying the bill probably knew nothing about it and did not care.

For Nick, it was good business: free meals and drinks for a dozen sailors who, by their presence, tripled his take. At five-thirty the first had arrived, and by six o'clock locals who usually didn't drop in until after eight were already coming to have dinner and claim their space for later in the evening.

Cole Westaway was already settled at a table by himself when Carl and Harriet came in.

"Hi, Cole," Harriet said. "Isn't the new girl a good cook?"

Cole tried to stand up and nearly tipped over the small table in front of him. "I just thought while Cousin A was in bed it would be easier for Agate not to have to bother with me."

"How is she?" Harriet asked.

"Better, I think."

"Is it a good idea for her to have company?"

"She'd love to see you," Cole said. "She always does. And I think she gets a little depressed, just staying in bed and reading Cousin B's diaries."

Carl wondered if he should ask Cole to join them, but the boy was obviously embarrassed to be found eating out in the first place. Better let him alone. Carl and Harriet had just settled at a table of their own when Dina Pyros came in. She stopped at Cole's table, and for a moment it looked as if she might join him. Then she went to sit by herself at a table for four, where almost at once she was joined by the two women who ran the corset shop.

"Do you know what Dina said to me the other day?" Harriet asked, her voice pitched so carefully low that Carl had to strain to hear her. "She said that a woman should marry, any woman."

"Do you think she's wrong?"

"I don't know. It just surprised me, when *she* said it."

"Knowing what should be isn't hard," Carl said with some dryness. "Accepting what can be seems to me the problem."

"I owe you an apology about this morning. It's hard to explain. . . ."

"There's no need to. . . ."

"It's just that Peter was so angry the other night, and I was upset by it. I've thought of phoning him, but somehow I can't. I don't phone Peter. That's one of the things I think he wouldn't like. So I sent him a note. He must have had it this morning. He often does call me at the library or at home right after work. He didn't call. There's not much else I can do, is there?"

"Are you in love with Peter, Harriet?" Carl asked.

"I didn't think so," Harriet said, bleakly honest. "Months ago, we had a talk, and we agreed we weren't really interested in each other, but, as Peter put it, we could be convenient for each other —friends."

"Maybe that wasn't a very good agreement."

"I couldn't really think of any reason to refuse," Harriet said. "But maybe now there is one."

"For Peter, you mean?"

The kitchen door swung open, and six fast bars of Greek song canceled Carl's reply.

"I beg your pardon?" Harriet said.

"For either of you," Carl repeated.

"I guess, when I forgot, I stopped being a convenience," Harriet said. "Once when I was just a girl, my mother asked me to take my little brother and sister shopping with me. I did it, cheerfully enough, but then I forgot them. I mean, I simply left them in the store and got all the way home before I remembered. They were tiny—about three and five at the time."

At that moment, the street door opened, and Peter Fallidon walked in.

"Oh dear," Harriet said.

Peter caught sight of Cole just before he noticed, with acute embarrassment, Harriet and Carl. He spoke to Cole, and then he deliberately moved to greet the others.

"Won't you join us?" Carl suggested.

"I'd like to," Peter said. "But I've just told Cole I'd keep him company. I got your note, Harriet. Thank you."

"I just wanted you to know how sorry I was. . . ."

"Have you heard about Miss Larson?"

"Yes," Harriet said.

"The new girl called to tell me there won't be dinner on Wednesday."

"No, I thought there wouldn't."

"Doesn't even seem to be dinner for Cole," Peter said, glancing back at the boy. Then he caught sight of Dina, nodded and smiled. "Everybody seems to be here tonight. Well . . . enjoy your dinner."

"That's good advice, you know," Carl said gently to Harriet. "Why not enjoy it?"

"I don't know why I involve you in all this nonsense," Harriet said. "I don't see how you can enjoy yours."

"The older you get, Harriet, the gladder you are of lively problems, and you're very charming not to realize how flattering it is for me to be confided in."

Peter had stopped at Dina's table, his smile a little strained at the bad jokes Dolly and Sal were sharing with him. He waited for a pause and then said, "If you're in the bank any time this week, Dina, I wish you'd stop in to see me."

"All right," Dina said, her clear gray eyes alert with questions she would not ask.

"Just some business that might interest you."

Then Peter returned to Cole, who had nearly finished his meal.

"Are you planning to stay awhile?" Peter asked. "I don't want to hold you up."

"I was planning to stay."

"You look tired."

"First day at the mill, I guess," Cole said. "Takes a while to get used to it."

"Hard not to be able to go home for dinner."

"Oh, I could have gone home. It's just that . . . I didn't really know where I should eat."

"How do you mean?"

"Well, with Cousin A having her dinner in bed, I didn't know whether I should sit in the dining room or suggest that I eat in the kitchen."

Peter grinned at him. "You'd better solve that problem or you may have to eat out every night for a week."

"I know, and I wouldn't mind that, but I guess Cousin A would think it was funny."

"What's Agate like?"

"Oh, I don't know," Cole said.

"Bad cook?"

"Oh no. She cooks all right." Cole waited for Peter to order. "She's different from Kathy. Kathy would have just gone ahead and set my place. But I don't think Agate's used to being a . . . a servant. She doesn't act like it anyway."

"How does she act?"

"Sort of like a . . . well, just like a girl. She jokes a lot. Tonight when I got in, she was sitting in Cousin A's chair in the study reading the paper. There's no reason why she shouldn't. Cousin A's in bed, after all. She said something like, 'The master's home from touring the cotton, is he?' in a cornball southern accent. So I told her I'd be going out for supper, and she just shrugged, but maybe I hurt her feelings."

"Well, she was bugging you. Just tell her what you want."

"Sure," Cole said, with a wry grin. "All I have to do is figure out what that is. There have to be more choices than master or slave."

"She's paid."

"So am I. I still don't like taking orders, but I'd rather take them than give them. Ever meet a sadder combination? An army mentality in a conscientious objector."

"Are you going to take that route?"

"Can't," Cole said, "not legally anyway; so it's jail or Canada."

"I was in the navy. It wasn't all that bad."

"So was my dad. Maybe he was a bastard before, just a one-armed bastard after. But I still think maybe he wouldn't have slugged so hard with two arms."

"What happened to him?"

"Don't know. He took off."

What should Peter say: that he was sorry? that he hadn't even had the benefit of a bad father himself? That letting women run you and the world was no solution? Nobody had shown Peter that alternative of domestic kindness and unworldly idealism which Cole was trying to struggle into. Could Peter say it wouldn't work?

"You don't approve," Cole said.

"Of what?"

"Me."

"Why shouldn't I?"

"Because you think the army would make a man of me."

"Don't hang that cliché on me, Cole. I don't know what I'd do now in your shoes. It was a different scene for me, for all of us."

"You'd go."

"All right. I'd go. Maybe you will, too, when the time comes, for the same reasons."

"What reasons?"

"Bad alternatives. Not being enough of a romantic to be that kind of rebel. Inertia."

"No good reasons at all?"

"Sure, but I thought you were asking about the real ones."

"I wasn't," Cole said. "I don't want to know things like that."

"Well, Mr. Fallidon!"

At the sight of Grace Hill, both Peter and Cole got to their feet, Peter quickly bracing the table between them.

"Hello, Mrs. Hill," Cole said against Peter's silent nod.

"I didn't know you were interested in this sort of thing," Grace

Hill said to Peter, the malice in her eyes amused. "And Miss Jameson at another table . . . with a minister. Pre-wedding plans? Or is this . . . ah . . . a new arrangement?"

Peter looked beyond her and asked, "Isn't Feller with you tonight?"

"He doesn't come to places like this. He thinks it's slumming. I didn't know you were old enough to drink, Cole. Is Mr. Fallidon trying to persuade you to open an account?"

"He . . . I . . ." Cole began.

"Ah, there's Dina." Grace Hill waved.

Dina stood up and came to Grace. "Why don't you let them sit down?"

"Do," Grace said to the men.

"There's an extra chair at our table. There isn't at this one."

"Nobody suggested that I was welcome," Grace said, "but that's why people sit at tables for two, isn't it?"

"Often," Dina said. "Come on."

Cole sat down and said, without looking at Peter, "I suppose you have to be polite to her."

"Marginally," Peter said.

"I'm not old enough to drink . . . not for another five months," Cole said, staring at his beer in moral gloom.

Peter was not free to get up and walk out before he had finished his dinner. The price of the resulting embarrassment and gossip was higher than he could afford. Since it was futile to regret his ever having come to Nick's tonight—as futile as to regret he had ever taken the job of bank manager in this town eighteen months ago—he defended himself against such temptations by concentrating on the astringent clarity of the wine, the sudden assaults of music, withdrawing into his senses.

Cole, aware that he had been temporarily deserted, looked around the room over the heads of the other diners with the casual indifference of someone ignoring an epileptic fit. Harriet, seeing him so stranded, wished she could send him some comfort. How often she had found herself without the ease of actually being alone, isolated in Peter's presence. Sometimes he had turned his attention to something else, but more often he simply withdrew without warning or explanation.

"Do you understand people, Mr. Hollinger?" she asked. "I suppose you do."

And she saw, as she spoke, that she had brought Carl Hollinger back from some retreat of his own. Maybe Peter wasn't peculiar. Maybe all men went into themselves like that from time to time. A nervous defense, as women were likely to chatter. Grace Hill chattering now. If Dina had been a man, the listening light in her face would have gone out by now. But Harriet didn't talk a great deal. She didn't make demands. She forgot.

"I was thinking about Ida Setworth," Carl said, realizing that Harriet was uncertain of his attention. "And loneliness."

"Does she seem to you lonely?"

"No, but I don't really understand why she isn't."

"I don't think loneliness has to do with whether you're with people or not," Harriet said. "Look: Dina's lonely right now, and so is Cole, do you see?"

"Are you?"

"No, but I can talk with you," Harriet said, an easy frankness she regretted at once for the shadow it cast across the old man's face, because, of course, he was lonely, and what attention had she paid to that, involved in her own more interesting pain?

Suddenly the lights went up; the speakers on the kitchen wall crackled into the wild center of a fast dance; and through the kitchen door came a line of sailors with several trapped girls, feet stuttering in uncertain effort, saved from falling by strong hands on their hips, from real humiliation by encouraging laughter. They swung round the long, narrow center of the room, the leaders disappearing back into the kitchen just as the music stopped. People clapped for those left behind, who grinned as they untangled themselves from the dance. One sailor leaned on Cole's shoulder, picked up his beer, and drank to Peter. Two stood by Dina, asking her why she was sitting down in here, why not in there with them, with the dancing. Well, they would dance for her here. The music began again, slowly this time. With the sharp snap of a handkerchief, which invited a partnership, with the formal stamping reply, the two boys danced, the handkerchief held high between them, while across the room the sailor who had drunk Cole's beer did a solo, insolent and sexual, for Peter. Cole, who had practiced this dance for nights in his own room, felt a sharp envy for the strutting confidence before him, and he could see by Peter's face that he was both impressed and entertained.

Others of the dancers were finding extra chairs and drawing up to tables which they had been encouraged to join. Waiters hurried to clear away the last of the dinner dishes so that there would be room for the beer and wine being ordered.

"Do you want to stay?" Carl asked, for, at the sight of the insolent sailor, he had felt an alarm for Peter or for Harriet, as if one or the other should be protected.

"I love the dancing, but if it's late . . ."

"Not at all," Carl said.

And why should he be alarmed? If the boy's dance was the social equivalent of a long, bragging, dirty story, it was no aesthetic equivalent, and Carl admired Peter's candid appreciation of it. Carl needn't feel a shocked missionary at a native feast when even dear, prim Harriet took innocent pleasure in it.

"They always dance for Peter," Harriet said. "Someone told me they want the praise of the handsomest man in the room."

"In order to impress the ladies?"

"I guess so, but I don't think we have much to do with it really. It's more like sport, like the Olympic Games. Greece must be a wonderful country."

And, as if to prove Harriet's point, the most accomplished of the dancers leaped high, doubling his knees to clear an invisible barrier, and the table-pounding and shouts of approval began.

Peter was ordering more beer. Dina was firmly refusing to join the men on the dance floor. Grace Hill was silent, watching Dina, the sailors, Peter, and Cole with intense interest that shifted only occasionally to Harriet and Carl, those refugees from a Sunday school picnic, unless she had been very much mistaken, which was comically possible. Grace Hill liked the sailors, their sycophantic sexuality such a contrast to her own heavy-muscled, sluggish sons, who would breed, she supposed, like beached fish on waterlogged girls.

"Dance, Dina," she called over the music. "Go ahead and dance."

"She doesn't want to," Sal explained, already slurred, blurred by beer and sound, her hand on Dolly's immovable thigh.

"Go ahead and dance, Cole," Peter was saying as the sailor who had chosen them snapped his handkerchief in mocking invitation.

"I don't really know how," Cole said.

"Go on. Do what you want to do."

The sailor, laughing, put away the handkerchief and pulled Cole to his feet. Then, facing into the center of the room, arms on each other's shoulders, they did the fine, nearly military folk dance, the basic steps of which almost everyone who came to Nick's had learned. Cole, shy and too light on his feet, was nevertheless confident. As he kept pace, the sailor shouted amused approval and called for more difficult variations. Cole knew them all. And as the watchers cheered and pounded, he gave in to his ambitions, challenging the speed of the music. At the frantic end of the dance, he and the arrogant Greek stamped and posed in front of Harriet and Carl's table.

"Marvelous, Cole," Harriet said, clapping and laughing. "You're just marvelous!"

The sailor, younger than Cole by a couple of years, held out his hands to Harriet, but she shook her head firmly. He shrugged and turned away to Peter, who offered him a drink.

Now Grace Hill's chant had been picked up by other people who had crowded around their table. "Dance, Dina, dance, Dina, dance."

But tonight she would not. There was no one here to please. She would please herself and sit. Or she would get up and leave, go back to the shop and work and wait. She could not; Grace Hill would go with her. But she could ignore the chanting. Across the room, she watched young Panayotis taunting Peter with the same invitation. Dance. Dance. Dance. He sat, in the same refusal. Panayotis, Peter: the same name. So Cole and Panayotis were dancing again, a competitive dance for the attention of their father, who had refused to father anyone. Still, he was chosen. Panayotis, growing proud of the grace of this tall, fair, foreign boy, became teasingly, lewdly seductive. As Cole turned free into a step of his own, Panayotis leapt suddenly and caught himself with knees clenched around Cole's rib cage, the shouts of the crowd covering Cole's own cry of surprise, but he held his balance until Panayotis dropped back. Peter was laughing at them both, proud, indulgent of them. As he looked round to signal the waiter for more beer, the easy love aroused in his eyes turned on Harriet. Caught by it, she couldn't look away quickly. Nor could he.

"I think maybe I'd better go," Harriet said to Carl. "I've got some work to do at home before tomorrow."

As they found their way carefully around the dancers, Peter stood up.

"Perhaps," he said, "since we're not going to Miss Larson's on Wednesday, we could go out for dinner."

"Oh, I . . ."

"Could I pick you up at around seven?"

"Well . . . thank you."

"Good night, Peter," Carl said. "I think they're going to have you on the dance floor if you stay much longer."

"A good reason for me to leave soon myself. Good night."

"Those youngsters get pretty wild, don't they?" Carl said as they walked to his car. "I thought Cole was going to be knocked down."

"He's steadier on his feet than he looks, or than he knows."

Cole, carefully feeling his rib cage with his elbows, was not sure he was not in some way broken. He did not want to dance again, either alone or with Panayotis, who, discouraged, drifted over to Dina's table.

"Knock the wind out of you a bit?" Peter asked.

"Yeah," Cole said. "I didn't expect it. I've seen them do it lots of times, but I didn't expect it."

"It looked all right," Peter said. "You didn't look surprised."

Which is the point, son, the difference. Was that all? You simply learned to express no surprise at bodies hurling themselves at you in fury or lust, stood your ground until they dropped or fell away? An ugly image. Still, it suited people like Grace Hill, studying him now from across the room. Not Harriet. But he felt as if he had been trapped tonight by Harriet just the same. By the circumstances, honestly. But if she hadn't been at Nick's, he would have seen her some place else. You couldn't live in a town like this and simply ignore or forget anyone for long. She had apologized. But he still smarted from the fear he had felt. Dependence. If you walked away from that, the dependence on the family you were born to, did you always choose its equivalents wherever you found yourself? Grace Hill could be Peter Fallidon's blood kin easily enough. As Harriet Jameson was the girl who had never been "good" enough for him, another way of putting that she was too "nice" for him, too far above the vicious, empty restlessness of his inheritance, her simple kindness called "prissy" and "old maidish"; so the Harriet Jamesons could always be made to feel grateful for whatever attentions he offered, resigned to his basic rejection of them. All right, and the punishment he took came not from Harriet but from Grace Hill, who was not really dangerous, because she would never accuse him of anything he felt guilty about. People like her, like his sisters and

99

mother, were more inventive than imaginative and nearly ignorant of real guilts because they had no knowledge of real
virtues. And that was probably why Feller Hill could stand his
wife. But why would he choose to?

"Dina's going to dance after all," Cole was saying.

"I must go," Peter said.

He was glad that he had been sitting near the door because,
now that Dina was on her feet, the crowd would move in, taking
everyone with it into the dance. He stood and put a hand on
Cole's shoulder to keep him from standing, too.

"Tell Agate what you want," he said.

X

AMELIA LARSON COULD NOT GET UP at the end of the week. She had phlebitis.

"I must get a nurse then," she said to the doctor.

Agate wouldn't hear of it. And because she argued that it was easier for her to wait on Amelia than to cook for another person, Amelia agreed to getting along without a nurse for a while.

"But this isn't the job you were hired to do," Amelia said. "I must pay you at least another hundred and fifty dollars a month."

"That works out to five dollars a bed bath."

"You don't get any time off."

"Sure I do," Agate said. "Cole and I have great evenings of gin rummy, and since I'm already winning most of his mill money, you'd better save the extra hundred and fifty for his fees this fall."

"You're not gambling."

"Nobody'd play gin rummy just for fun."

Amelia was not used to being physically tended. Though she worried about the extra burden it put on Agate, she was frankly grateful not to have a brisk and professionally cheerful woman constantly about. Agate, random and inventive about her duties, kept the days from turning into boring routine. Amelia got her breakfast within an hour of the usual time—never late, almost always early because Agate liked the morning. Lunch and dinner were less predictable. Sometimes Agate brought the evening meal before Cole got home from the mill. Sometimes she not only waited for him but enlisted his help. He would arrive in Amelia's room with a card table, then rescue precariously balanced trays sent up on their own by chair lift, Agate bawling out comic instructions from the bottom of the stairs like a short-order cook or a cockney kitchen maid. Finally she herself would arrive, usually with beer she was drinking from the bottle, and they would all eat together. Amelia supposed, once she was up again, Agate would always eat with them. She knew that Cole helped Agate now with the cleaning up. Nice of him. And why not have an extra and helpful youngster about the house rather than a servant? Fine, but Amelia was aware that, while she lay helpless, Agate was reversing the pattern of authority, which made it difficult for Amelia to correct Agate ever.

"Does she always wear shorts?" Maud Montgomery asked after she had sent Agate from the room with sweet peas she'd brought to Amelia.

"No," Amelia said. "She usually changes into blue jeans for dinner."

"And you don't say anything to her?"

"No," Amelia said. "I'm afraid I don't. It seems such a happy accident that she turns out to be a natural and willing nurse, as well as a good cook, I decided not to object to her dressing like one of the family."

"One of the family! She's five and a half months pregnant, A. It's disgusting."

"How's Arthur?"

Maud did not want the subject changed, but she could not refuse to answer that question in detail whenever it was asked. Over the years Amelia had learned not to be disgusted by the intimate knowledge she had of Arthur Montgomery's bowels, blood, and glands. If Maud could not return such charity for pregnant girls, she could be distracted. And Agate, who took to Maud no more than Maud took to her, had the sense not to be blatantly rude to her—only about her. Maud Montgomery was Agate's most successful imitation. Amelia nearly regretted that she couldn't encourage Agate to perform for others of her friends.

"Now tell me about *your* pain," Maud said.

It was not a subject Amelia discussed, even with herself. The perversity of most aging bodies was that in aid of one ailment you alarmed another. Amelia preferred to be preoccupied with Agate's body, or Cole's. Agate probably was drinking too much beer. She bought it herself, however, and it seemed enough of a gesture for her. Amelia hadn't smelled marijuana since Agate moved into the house. Cole wasn't getting enough sleep. Still, he looked well, sun-caught. She only hoped Agate was joking about the gambling, but Cole was so conservative about money that Amelia couldn't really imagine him losing his fall fees.

"Agate's getting *fat!*" Rosemary Hopwood said with firm humor, as she took eleven o'clock coffee with Amelia, who was resigning herself to Sanka.

"I'm afraid she is," Amelia said. "Somehow, under the circumstances, I don't find it easy to scold her."

"I can see that."

"Of course, I know this business about watching weight is sensible, but sometimes I think it's overdone. A bit of plumpness isn't unattractive."

"No," Rosemary said.

"I wonder if it has to do with just lying here: everyone seems to me lovely to look at these days. Not that you aren't always. But is it the color you have on?"

"Probably the medicine you're taking. Or Agate's putting LSD in your Sanka. Incidentally, any problems there, do you think?"

"A lot can go on that I don't know anything about, but I don't think so."

"Ida seems to think she's doing a fairly good job."

"Dear Ida. She probably had a good look around the kitchen before she left yesterday. You know, *she* doesn't look well. I don't know what it is. Her hair maybe? What is it?"

"She's bought some new clothes," Rosemary said cautiously.

"The heat never has suited her."

"How's Cole?"

"Just fine. Agate seems real company for him. Kathy never was. Didn't she look well before she left?"

"Yes. Is there anything you'd like me to say to Agate? Do you want me to tell her to stop wearing those dreadful shorts?"

"No," Amelia said. "There are things Agate needs to do."

"Are you still reading those diaries?"

"Not much in the last week or so. I've had a happy amount of company. But I must get back to them, I suppose."

"Is there anything about my father?"

"In Sister's diaries?"

"Yes. He always liked her, I remember," Rosemary said. "He

used to say they shared the same unsatisfied tastes."

"Did he?"

"Beatrice thought he killed himself, didn't she?"

"She may have wondered about it," Amelia said.

"Mother wanted people to think he had. I've never known why, really. I know it looked as if she was trying to cover it up at the time, but she wasn't. She was trying to create doubt. I just wondered if Beatrice . . ."

"She didn't see why he would, given who he was," Amelia said, then hesitated.

"What?"

"She didn't think anyone could be too bored to live."

"Is that what she said about him?"

"It was what he said about himself and about all of us. He and Sister shared a dislike for the town, for the life here."

"Beatrice could have left, surely?"

"She did leave," Amelia said. "She wasn't much older than you were. She was away for nearly three years. Then Papa died . . ."

"And she felt she should come home?"

"In a way," Amelia said. "She wasn't really happy away from home."

"Neither was I."

"For nearly twenty years?"

"That's an exaggeration, I know," Rosemary said. "I suppose I enjoyed myself in a way."

"Why did you come back?"

"I don't really know. I didn't know what else to do, I guess. There wasn't any reason to stay away any longer."

"Are you sorry?"

"No," Rosemary said. "I'm very glad I came home."

"I believe Sister was, too. But she expected more."

"More of what?"

"Herself, the people around her. Some more than ordinary love."

"But she had that . . . from you."

"Sisters," Amelia said, in vague dismissal.

"Did you ever want to get away, Amelia?"

"I? No. I would have enjoyed traveling more. We could have, really. My hip was the excuse, Sister's nerves the reason. But I like what's familiar. I always have. It's enough for me."

Talking with Rosemary tired Amelia. It was not simply the shape of Rosemary's head. Amelia sensed the same kinds of tension in Rosemary that had been in Beatrice, and she felt required without knowing what she could do or say. It was Rosemary's desire to understand things no longer useful, like her father's death. It was as fruitless for Amelia to be trying to understand her sister's life. She did not want to, not in the way of assigning blame or value, not even for simple insight. What was the good of that, now that Sister was dead? Yet Amelia did turn to the diaries again when Rosemary had left. Hers a more than ordinary love? Precisely not. Vestigial? Not exactly.

"You're not going to read that now," Agate said, coming in for the cups.

"Why not?"

"Because it plays hell with your blood pressure, for one thing."

"Don't be silly!" Amelia replied, a rare impatience in her voice.

"Anyway, it's time for your bath."

"At noon?"

"Anything written in the Good Book that says you can't have a bath at noon?"

"Harriet was explaining to me the other day about divergent thinkers," Amelia said, setting the 1945 diary aside and leaning back on her pillows.

"That's what we both are," Agate said. "That's why we get along so well."

"I'm a divergent thinker?" Amelia asked, surprised.

Agate stood with a tray in her hands and gave Amelia a long, serious look. "Yeah."

"I've come to the conclusion that I don't much like thinking . . . of any kind," Amelia said. "It's age, probably."

"No, it's not," Agate said. "I don't like to think either, except to rock somebody else's boat. Now, don't pick that up again while I'm gone. I'll be right back."

Obedient, Amelia dozed instead, and when Agate came back, she found the old lady asleep. She had had too much company, and she had too much on her mind. Agate picked up the diary to put it back in one of the boxes out of Amelia's reach. She had already glanced at one or two of them. Nothing she'd seen so far made her understand why they upset Miss A as much as they obviously did. There seemed to be more weather reports and card games than anything else. Oh, and funerals. It was pretty clear that Beatrice Larson wasn't what you'd call a cheerful woman.

✻

November 5, 1945: Cousin Hetty is to marry Sam Westaway, come home without an arm. Would he have wanted her otherwise? A pretty thing, but dim-witted. Still, some of us can be grateful there are cripples who need us.

✻

"Christ!" Agate said softly.

Amelia stirred but did not wake. Agate put the diary into the box and went quietly out of the room. The thing to do with those diaries was to burn them as quickly as possible. Surely, she and Cole together could either persuade Miss A or, if necessary, just go ahead and burn them. No, not Cole. He needed permission to breathe.

"She's got to stop reading those damned things," Agate said to Cole as they ate supper at the kitchen table.

"It's not exactly something you can tell her," Cole said.

"Why not? I mean, my God, there's this creep of a sister saying things about 'cripples who need us.'"

"Have you been *reading* them?" Cole asked.

"Only a page or two here and there," Agate said, as if that were not the point.

"But they're Cousin B's private diaries!"

"Cousin B, baby, is dead. Cousin A, like in the alphabet, comes first. I bet Beatrice even resented that."

"Look, Agate, I don't really think things like that are any of your . . . our business. I mean, what you're doing is . . . dishonest, prying like that, disrespectful. It's . . ."

"*Is* your mother dim-witted? Is that where you get it?"

"What do you mean?"

"Well, that's what Cousin B thought."

"Agate, I can't sit here and let you talk about members of my family like that," Cole said, whitening in his effort to sound dignified. "You behave as if you had some right . . ."

"Oh, okay, okay. Skip it."

"I can't skip it. Now that you've brought the subject up."

"Forget I brought it up."

"Is that true, what Cousin B said about my mother?"

106

"She said she was pretty," Agate said.

"And dim-witted?"

"Yeah."

"I wish I'd burned those diaries the day we were cleaning out the attic," Cole said.

"Right. You're beginning to get the point."

"The point is, *you* shouldn't be reading them."

"All right," Agate said. "Why don't you tell her I'm reading them? Then maybe she'll let you burn them."

"You want me to say that?"

"Why not? It's a quick way to get rid of them."

"But Cousin A trusts you. If she found out you'd done a thing like that . . ."

"You make it sound like a major, bloody crime," Agate said.

"When somebody trusts somebody else, right in their home . . . I mean, you could snoop into anything. . . ."

"Snoop!"

"Well, you could!"

"I already have," Agate said, her eyes wide and yellow, her voice pitched spookily low. "I know where you keep your jockstrap, poor son of a one-armed father!"

"I suppose you found out that in the diaries, too!"

"Where you keep your jockstrap? Nope. That was all on my own. I'd just been ironing some shirts for you and . . ."

"That my father lost his arm in the war."

"Actually I overheard you talking about it on the phone."

"Oh, Agate!"

"Why be so up tight about everything anyway?"

"You and I just don't think the same way about anything," Cole said. "We might as well come from different planets. You just haven't got any . . ."

"Morals?"

"All right, no. You haven't got any morals."

"Listen, you repressed little faggot, just because . . ."

"That's enough!" Cole shouted, and he got up and left the room.

"Ball kicking isn't really such a good sport," Agate said to the ugly cat. "But he hasn't been exactly forward in suggesting anything else. Gin rummy, for God's sake!"

Now she was sorry she had suggested that Cole tell Miss A about her reading the diaries. If Cole was right, if Miss A found such behavior really offensive, then she might decide that getting rid of Agate was the easier solution. There were half a dozen docile, dutiful girls waiting to take her place, and Rosemary Hopwood was right: Agate certainly had no place with them. She couldn't go back to the home. And now that she could feel and see the baggage of life she was carrying around inside her, she knew she couldn't strike out on her own as she had at other times. Miss A wouldn't throw her out, surely. But Agate didn't even want to be put in the position of having to plead to stay. She liked the fond tyranny she had set up over that strong old lady. Easier to pacify Cole. She had been rude to him. Probably his feelings really were hurt.

"Cole?" she said quietly outside his shut door. "Cole?"

He opened the door no more than six inches and said, "What do you want?"

"Look, I'm sorry. Could I talk with you for a minute?"

"Now?"

Agate censored impatient obscenities and said, "Just for a minute."

Cole opened the door wide enough to let her in. She saw that he had been sitting at his desk; so she went across the room and sat on his bed. He stayed at the door, his back to it, as far from her as the room would allow.

"It was a bad idea," Agate said. "In the first place, I haven't really been reading the diaries. I saw what I told you when I was putting one away, that's all. The point is, they upset her. That's all I want to stop. If telling her that I'm reading them would upset her more, then that's stupid."

"How can I believe you're not reading them?"

"I'm just trying to figure out how to keep her quiet and get her well."

"Why do you think I'm a faggot?" Cole suddenly burst out.

"Oh, hell, Cole, I don't think so. It's just a playground game: you say I have no morals; so I call you a faggot."

"I shouldn't have said that," Cole said. "I'm sorry."

"So we're sorry, but I'm serious about those diaries."

"Agate, I just wouldn't dream of telling Cousin A what to do about something like that. I mean, she's like my grandmother. Maybe it's different for you. You take care of her; you can say different sorts of things to her. You don't seem to worry about what you say."

"Maybe sometimes I should. Diplomacy isn't my strong suit.

It's not a matter of telling her what to do but giving her the idea that she ought to get rid of them somehow."

"Maybe Harriet could," Cole said. "Maybe you should talk to Harriet."

"Wouldn't you talk to her? You know her. I don't really, and I'm supposed to be just the maid around here."

"But you see her," Cole said. "I haven't seen her since I started work."

"Okay, I'll try."

Cole hadn't moved from the door, though he was more relaxed, leaning with his hands behind his back, braced on the doorknob.

"Oh, another thing," Agate said. "I thought I ought to get some clothes, something to fit the two of us."

Cole blushed as he said, "There are some uniforms in your closet that . . ."

"I'm not really the uniform type. I wondered if you'd be around Saturday afternoon so that I could go into town."

"Sure."

"What are you so bloody nervous about?"

"I . . . I don't think you should be in my room. I . . ."

"Oh."

"I don't mean anything. I just mean it probably doesn't look . . ."

"Who's looking?"

"Just because I care, just because I want to do the right thing . . ."

"You're a refreshing change," Agate said in a virtuous tone totally unlike her own, "for a poor girl like me so used to being taken advantage of."

"Don't make fun of me!"

"Why not? You're funny. I'm not going to rape you, I promise, though I'd be doing you a favor."

As Agate got up off the bed, Cole opened the door. Then, as she was going through it, he said, "I just don't know how to joke. I don't know how to kid around."

"Don't worry about it. The straight man always gets the laughs anyway."

Agate went back down to the kitchen to clear away the supper dishes. Cole didn't have the guts to be a faggot, just to worry about it. Why shouldn't she bait him? Bastard! Prick the size of a jelly bean!

109

"Often men with smaller than normal sexual organs, because of a sense of inadequacy, turn to members of their own sex . . ." Cole had read in a secluded corner of the library, and he remembered it now as he looked down at his own erection, unable to judge, since he had always been shy in public toilets and gym showers, since he had not been in the army, whether he was smaller than normal or not. Nowhere had he ever found simple statistics. So what good had it done to take Cousin A's measuring tape from her sewing basket? None. "Faggot." Cole could still feel the pressure of Panayotis' cock in the cavity between his ribs. And it was to that memory he masturbated, canceling out Agate's widespread thighs which had so recently threatened his bed.

Agate, similarly rejected, hadn't the energy or imaginative patience for such relief. Even her anger could not sustain itself for long. She never had attracted "nice" boys who, when their appetites finally moved them past their courage, chose less ample mountings than her own. The men who wanted Agate were those who had already made the mistake of marrying those tight, compact little cunts, more designed for jackhammers than human flesh. And showing them what they had missed and would continue to miss had its pleasures. Agate never took a man more than three or four times, just long enough for it to be really good. On the form she could be honest when she said she did not know who the father was. She could only be sure that he had fathered before, that no green seed grew in her now. Some comfort? Some. But she felt heavy, slovenly, sad, as she climbed the front stairs to Miss A's room.

"Tired tonight, Agate?" Amelia asked, looking up from the evening paper.

"Full of life," Agate answered.

"Sit down a minute. Sit here." Amelia indicated a chair that was right beside the bed.

"I thought maybe you'd like something to drink."

"Not just now."

When Agate sat, Amelia reached over and took her hand. Agate looked down at the old hand over hers, joints swollen, liver spots stretched on the tight, sore skin. Where did the comfort come from out of all that unspoken pain? Awkward to sit there, her jeans straining like an outgrown skin of her own, her breasts straining against the inadequate hammocks of her bra, her elbow straining back to leave her hand where it had been taken.

"You're a comfort to me, Agate, a real comfort."

She was not going to bawl like a kid. She simply was not.

"I've got to be some comfort to myself pretty soon," Agate said. "I'm going to go downtown and buy me some tents. Not uniforms. Tents. Bright ones."

"Go to Harden's and charge them to me."

"Nope. I've got to spend all this money I'm making on something."

"Why not save it?"

"I don't need it. I never have."

XI

"FELLER WISHES I wouldn't be seen by myself at Nick's. By myself means not with him. Feller wishes I'd find something constructive to do. Other women get themselves involved in church groups or charitable organizations. Rosemary Hopwood won't let a pregnant girl in the same block with me. Is she jealous? I could at least be a den mother. Cubs! As if my own three didn't gnaw at my bones enough now. At least, Feller says, I could stay home more often in the evening. To watch him get a hard on over his court cases or dividends and then want to take it out on me? I hate men."

Grace stamped out a cigarette and looked at Dina, sitting away from her in the armchair.

"Do I have to get myself a drink?"

"No," Dina said, and she got up and took the glass from Grace. Grace followed her out into the kitchen.

"You don't care whether I live or die. That's what I like about you. I don't think you even care whether I keep my clothes on and go home, do you?"

"No," Dina said.

"I don't either. That's a fact."

"You're getting drunk." Dina handed Grace a fresh drink.

"That's right."

"Why don't you get something to do?"

"Pardon me?"

"I said . . ."

"Pardon me? Pardon me?"

Dina shrugged and went back into the living room.

"I *have* got something to do," Grace announced to Dina's back. "Something very interesting."

Dina didn't respond.

"But I have to plan it carefully. Take my time about it. I don't want it just to be uncomfortable for that faggoty bastard. I'm going to see him run out of town."

"Your own husband?" Dina asked.

"No, sweetheart—that cock sucker, Fallidon."

"What have you against him?"

"His money-colored eyes."

"He's a better man than we'd get again in a long time."

"*Man?*"

"Man," Dina said.

"He's probably being blackmailed by every sailor off that ship."

"Why did you tell him you wanted money to invest in my business?"

"Pardon me?"

"I said . . ."

"Pardon me? Pardon me?"

"Don't do anything stupid," Dina said. "There are so many people who could do so much to you."

"What do you mean?"

"Just that."

"Look, nobody tells Mrs. Feller Hill to bugger off and gets away with it."

"Anybody can. I can."

"Baby? You aren't mad at me?"

"I'm tired of you," Dina said.

"But you're not mad at me?"

"I could be."

"Please don't be mad at me. Please."

"Then don't be stupid. Don't hurt yourself any more."

"If I could just have some money. If I could just have a little bit of money . . ."

"What you need is a little sense."

"I'm nothing but a bloody slave. Just because Feller knows, just because he can hold it over my head . . ."

Dina closed her eyes for a moment.

"You don't have to worry," Grace said. "You don't care anyway, do you?"

"No."

"I could go home right now. . . ."

"This is the last time," Dina said.

"That's what *I* say."

"And now it's true."

"Doesn't matter to me."

"I know," Dina said.

"Or you."

"No."

✳

Harriet had imagined that, on the night they went out to dinner, she and Peter would talk about it. Then, out of understanding, she would say it was best for them not to see each other. She had worried mainly about how that could be arranged. They would have to telephone each other more often to assure not meeting than they ever had to be together. But they mustn't go on seeing each other simply because it was easier. What had never occurred to Harriet was that the subject would not come up. At dinner they chatted about everyone else. Then they sat in customary side-by-side absence from each other through a movie. Harriet wasn't troubled. Over Miss A's recipe for hot chocolate or something stronger back at her apartment, they would talk. Peter didn't come in. She could not even tell that he was evading anything. He seemed simply tired.

"Would you like to take a drive on Sunday, maybe out to the beach? I haven't been yet this summer," he'd offered instead.

"Shall I bring a picnic?"

So here she was chopping celery, slathering mayonnaise across bread, still dutifully keeping her side of what was no bargain at all.

"I like your tuna fish sandwiches," Peter would say.

"Thank you," she would answer and then look for something as innocuous to compliment him with. "What a nice place you've found for a picnic."

He would smile, with his teeth, his potentially grief-stricken eyes uninvolved.

"Actually they're seasoned with arsenic, you . . . heel!"

114

If she ever did dare to get angry with him, that would be exactly the trite sort of thing she'd come out with, sitting scrawny-thighed and sharp-elbowed in as apologetic a bathing suit as she could find at Harden's, which carried nearly nothing but bikinis in her size. "The figure of a girl still," her mother said, in a tone of dubious surprise. Picturing herself on the beach with Peter, she had an inverted image of the Charles Atlas cartoons: a spindly, nearly breastless woman having sand kicked in her face by 40-26-39, Peter dashing off on muscular, hairy legs after breasts and beach ball.

But she was a person, not a cartoon. And so was he. If she could only talk to him. Well, she did talk to him. She had told him a lot about her family, her growing up, the books she read. In some ways she talked more easily with Peter than she did with anyone else. And he talked with her, too, told her things about the bank he wouldn't have told anyone else. He had even spoken several times with a mild, distant bitterness about his mother and sisters. She knew he still sent money home but did not, in other ways, have anything to do with his family. They simply didn't talk about themselves, having established from the first that there was nothing to say.

"There is something to say, Peter."

"What is that?"

All the things to be said were, of course, for him to say, and if he wouldn't, couldn't, didn't know, then what could she do?

"Why don't you love me?"

"Because you're a prissy, bony, dull, no longer young woman . . ."

"Those aren't the real answers, are they? Are they? Am I really stuck with those?"

All the badly invented conversation. She should be grateful it never did take place.

Peter was knocking at the door.

"That's a pretty dress. Is it new?"

"You always notice."

She wasn't going to be able to bear it. Not for a whole afternoon, the terrible nourishment to her starved vanity that simply being with him was. Why did he have to be so cruelly good-looking, so markedly polite, so indifferent? But there he was picking up the picnic basket. Then there she was sitting in his car, a rare treat which was being offered for the second time within a week. Crumbs. Birds lived and sang on them. And enjoyed the air.

"It's lovely air," Harriet said.

"I wish I could remember to enjoy it the way you do."

From F Street they turned onto Main and drove along the sea-wall. There on the walkway was the awkward line of pregnant girls, setting out into the Sunday sky.

"I wonder how Cole's getting along with Agate," Peter said.

"I think they're making friends. He helps her a good deal now that she's nurse as well as cook."

"He's such a self-conscious kid. He reminds me of me at his age."

"Were you like that?"

"Sure. When you don't have a father to watch or teach you, or when your father doesn't know even as much about the world as you do, when there isn't anyone to ask all the stupid questions . . . Do you know what Cole wanted to know? Where he should eat because Miss Larson was sick in bed."

"Poor Cole."

"And it is a matter of life and death," Peter said. "If you don't learn, you harden into a different sort of hysteria."

"How do you mean?"

"You . . . close out."

For fear of making a gross mistake, Harriet did not reply. Was he trying to explain himself? He couldn't be. He did know where to eat. He had found the answers to all the stupid questions. Was he trying to say something to her then? For certainly she hadn't learned. And she did close out. She was closing out now. But she didn't know what else to do.

"Does this look like a good place?"

"You always find good places."

Now what would she say when he spoke about the sandwiches? She and Cole.

"Did you bring a suit?" Peter asked, seeing only her towel on the back seat.

"I have it on underneath."

"Oh."

"The material they make them of now dries right away."

"I guess it does. When I was nine, I had a good case of sitting in wet wool, and I'll never trust a suit again, no matter what the label says, even if it's true."

Harriet laughed. "I did that, too."

"What kids are missing nowadays!"

Then they were walking along the beach, looking for agates, and Harriet, absorbed in the search for the light-struck clarity of those small stones, forgot that there was anything to be nervous about.

"There. There's one," and she picked it up, brown filtering to amber. "She does have odd eyes, doesn't she?"

"Who?" Peter asked.

"Agate."

"I hadn't noticed."

"She's beautiful in a way I'm not used to," Harriet said. "I've never seen anyone like her before."

"Vulgar."

"Is she?"

"I think so," Peter said.

"But I'd think she came from a good family."

"That doesn't prevent vulgarity, even encourages certain sorts."

It was that sort of confidence in him Harriet envied. Nobody from good families here was vulgar, nobody born into them anyway. She saw another agate.

"There. That's the color of Dina's eyes."

"Yes," Peter said, looking.

Harriet was about to say the only interesting thing she had to say about Dina, but she remembered, in time, why she shouldn't.

"I wish there were more people in this town like Dina," Peter said.

"Oh?"

"She has real business sense. I wouldn't be surprised if, before she's through, she could buy and sell some of the people who treat her as if she were just one step up from the junkman."

"Does anyone treat Dina like that?"

"Sometimes I think all of us do, but she's too proud to care."

A hard judgment, unless you agreed that everyone treated everyone else with some indifference.

"Is this a good place to stop?" Peter asked.

"Yes, lovely."

She helped him spread the towels and anchor them with rocks. Then she opened the picnic basket and set out sandwiches and fruit, poured the iced tea from the thermos. They sat. Peter picked up the plastic bag from his place and opened it. Harriet watched him look at the sandwich and then bite into it. He chewed carefully and then swallowed.

"I like your tuna fish sandwiches," he said.

"Why don't you love me, Peter?"

For once the expression of his mouth and eyes coincided, tense with surprise. Then he said, "You don't love me, do you?"

That she should, whether he did or not, had never occurred to her.

"I don't know," she said. "You've never let me try. I mean, you haven't wanted me to. I've tried not to. I don't know. I want to, but not if . . ."

"Not if what?"

"No," Harriet said. "That would be as bad a bargain as the one we've already made. Isn't it funny? I never heard that before."

"What would be as bad a bargain?"

"Loving you only if you loved me."

"I don't see why. Loving someone who can't love you is simply painful."

"It's not a bargain."

"Harriet, I do care about you . . . more than I've let you know, perhaps, more than I realized myself until the night you didn't turn up at the concert. I was terribly worried about you. I found it very painful. That's all."

"What do you mean, that's all?"

"I wasn't relieved when you were all right. I was angry."

"Why?"

"I don't want to worry, not about anyone."

"Well, no, of course not."

"I can't stand it," Peter said.

"I think what I want to say," Harriet continued carefully, feeling oddly calm, "is a warning. I know you don't want to love me. I do want to love you, and I'm going to try. I don't mean I'm going to try to seduce you. I'd be too embarrassingly bad at it. I'm simply going to go ahead and worry about you when I feel like it. If you can't stand that . . ."

"I can't stand worrying about you."

"I'll try not to worry you then."

"You are worrying me right now."

"I'm surprising myself," Harriet said. "I love your face when it goes together like that, even in a frown."

"Harriet . . ."

"I might even kiss you before this day is out. I won't compete with the tuna fish. I won't chase you down the beach. I'm a prim, shy woman. But even prim, shy women sometimes kiss people."

"You're a very pretty, appealing woman, but I . . ."

She put a hand over his mouth. "Stop there. That's all I want to hear. Just go ahead and eat your sandwich."

He held her hand and kissed her palm gently. Then he gave her the first smile she had ever seen in his eyes also, rueful, guarded. And he gave it to the sandwich as well, as if it might easily be poison, whether he liked it or not.

❈

"Is something the matter, Dina?" Rosemary asked, pulling a footstool nearer the chair Dina was sitting in.

"I couldn't say."

"Why not?"

"If you have a real friend," Dina said, "you begin to see that all the things you just don't say to other people you can't say anyway. You don't know how."

"Try."

Dina shook her head.

"Are you afraid I wouldn't understand?"

"You have degrees in understanding," Dina said, smiling.

"What is it?"

"Do you ever try to help someone and make it worse instead? Because you find out you really can't like, don't care, are even a little afraid?"

"Yes," Rosemary said.

"What do you do?"

"Call in someone else, usually."

Dina gave a short laugh. Then she looked at Rosemary seriously. "If you got a little afraid of me, who would you call?"

"I don't think I could be afraid of you like that. I was talking about my job."

"Who would I call then?" Dina asked.

"If you felt like that, you wouldn't have to call anyone. You'd just go away, wouldn't you?"

"I'm talking about Grace Hill," Dina said flatly. "To begin with, it was like the kids: better at my place than on the streets. I don't have to like every one of them. I don't even have to pay much attention. Furniture's my job. So a woman needs sometimes, occa-

119

sionally . . . a place. She comes occasionally."

Dina gave Rosemary a clear, uncommitted look.

"And you . . . don't even necessarily have to like every one of them," Rosemary said quietly.

"They come in. They . . ."

"The way I did," Rosemary said.

"Yes . . . like that."

"And you say, 'up to you.' "

"Mostly."

One of many. Like the kids. Well, what else could be true?

"What does Grace want now?" Rosemary asked.

"What she's always wanted and got: some repairs and refinishing," Dina said. "One day her husband's going to get impatient. One day . . ."

"Can't you stop her? Can't you tell her you don't want . . ."

"She knows that. Nobody wants Grace Hill. There are people like that."

"You feel sorry for her," Rosemary said.

"I don't really care."

"I don't think I know what you mean."

"I'm only sorry she's the way she is. She's a mistake."

"Will she come whether you tell her she can or not?"

"I never tell her she can."

Rosemary had been kneading Dina's palm with her thumb, and now she felt Dina shift slightly in the chair. Rosemary moved her hand so that it rested lightly on Dina's arm. She did not want Dina to move away.

"Sal and Dolly are always saying to me, 'You'll get more than you bargained for with that one.' "

"Have they said that about me?" Rosemary asked.

"Yes."

"What did you say?"

"Nothing."

"What did you think?"

"I thought 'less.' "

"Who was right?"

"No one," Dina said. "Do you understand me? Do you understand what I say?"

"Partly," Rosemary said. "It's always harder to understand something important when it has to do with me, too, with how I feel and what I want."

"Yes, I know that."

"I wish you wouldn't see her at all. I wish you'd stay here to avoid her."

Dina shook her head. "I can stop her. I feel guilty about it. And worried. She doesn't like Peter Fallidon. He wouldn't lend her money. Now she wants to start some kind of scandal. I can't stop her at more than one thing at a time."

"What kind of scandal could she start about Peter?"

"He likes boys," Dina said. "It's ridiculous. Men do like boys."

"You don't mean he's homosexual."

"She would put it that way."

"But Harriet Jameson . . ."

"Do you think he's interested in Harriet?" Dina asked.

"Well, they're together a lot," Rosemary said. "No one would pay any attention to a rumor like that, Dina. They'd be crazy to." As she said it, she knew it wasn't true. "And, anyway, you can't ruin your own life to protect someone else from a rumor."

"It's not a matter of ruining my life really. I just don't like her much."

"Would she try to hurt you?"

"Me? How? There's nothing to hurt. I don't owe anyone any money. I'm my own boss."

"You think Feller might . . ."

"He might hurt her. He might throw her out finally. She wouldn't know what to do."

"He's got the children to think of."

"Yes," Dina said. "She's not as bad a mother to them as she claims, but she's not good."

"Peter could simply say he'd refused to lend her money."

"Well . . ." Dina said, and then she reached out and took Rosemary's chin in her hand. "If you ever don't much like me, you'll tell me. Yes? Then I'll go."

"That's not my problem, darling, and I can't imagine that it ever would be. Am I supposed to say the same thing to you?"

"You're my friend."

Rosemary understood now what Dina meant by that. She was singular for Dina that way, not simply another of the women, another of the kids, who left themselves like pieces of furniture to be repaired and renewed at George's. Rosemary was, at the same time, reassured and inhibited by that knowledge, for what set her apart from the others for Dina also seemed to require that

121

she accept Dina's sexual isolation. That was impossible, for the more familiar Dina became with Rosemary's needs and desires, the more obsessed Rosemary was with Dina's aloof body.

"Why don't you spend the night?" Rosemary asked.

"I don't sleep in front of anyone," Dina said.

Rosemary laughed. "You have such a funny, exact way of saying things sometimes."

"Because English is my second language and I don't have a first."

"That's the way you think about women, too, isn't it?"

"I don't think about women much," Dina said, turning an amused look at Rosemary.

"It's dangerous to be so arrogant, Dina Pyros."

It was such a clear, clearly defined face, like a landscape in the high, bright light of day. Rosemary took Dina's head in her hands with desires she was not allowed.

"It's dangerous to be anything else," Dina said.

✳

"There is something faintly ridiculous about any relationship that's a matter of choice," Ida said.

She and Carl were sitting out on Ida's front terrace, watching the late sun on the sea.

"Essentially ridiculous," Carl said. "And what relationship isn't a matter of choice?"

"Blood relationships."

"Do you think so? Amelia and Beatrice didn't have to live together."

"No, but they didn't have to decide to in any public sort of way either. Why *essentially* ridiculous?"

"Because what we need of each other is, I suppose," Carl said.

"What I need is to look proud rather than foolish."

"And surely that's ridiculous."

"I suppose so, but there it is."

"Do you mean that you'd marry me if it didn't make you look foolish?"

"I mean I can't get past that difficulty to consider any of the real and serious problems. There may be a good many."

"Getting married is really a very temporary embarrassment. We could do it somewhere else."

"Yes, there's that."

"Ida?"

"Yes?" She turned to him.

"I would make you proud."

"I know you would. That's what makes me feel so foolish. What would that make of the pride I've pretended all these years? I'm sorry to behave like a schoolgirl. Give me a month, Carl. I will think, and then we'll discuss it seriously."

"All right."

"Essentially ridiculous," Ida repeated, as she might have a line of poetry for the pleasure of hearing it again.

XII

AGATE, IN AN ANKLE-LENGTH orange shift and barefooted, opened the door to Harriet Jameson in day-old seersucker with an armload of books.

"What a glorious color!"

"The house needs cheering up," Agate said. "Could you talk to me for a couple of minutes before you go up?"

"Certainly."

Harriet put the books on the stairs and then followed Agate down the corridor, expecting to be led into the kitchen. Did Peter think Agate's refusal to wear uniforms vulgar? Harriet wasn't easy with the term, applied to Agate. Flamboyant, certainly, and native to some other climate, but Agate wasn't ample in the way of *National Geographic* islanders or peasants. Her frame was large, as were her gestures, as if she might be used to living on the stage, an opera singer, and the material that fell from her shoulders was expensively bright. Even her bare feet, long and high-arched, had style.

"Let's sit in here," Agate said, turning into the library.

Harriet was surprised at the ease with which Agate took Miss A's chair. The jars of cream, nail scissors, and book on the table by it obviously belonged to Agate.

"It's about the diaries," Agate said. "We've got stop her reading them."

"Why?"

"They're making her sick."

"She has phlebitis," Harriet said.

"She has an enlarged and heavy heart."

"Why do you think it's the diaries?"

"They make her relive a lot of things no one should have to go through more than once. They make her think about things she can't do anything about."

"How do you know that, Agate? Does she talk about them?"

"Some," Agate said. "She doesn't have to. I just have to look at her after she's spent a couple of hours with them."

"Surely, if she wanted to stop reading them, she could."

"She's hung up about them. She thinks she's got to. I want to burn them."

"They may be very important records," Harriet said.

"For some timid gossip two generations from now who wants to be known as a local historian? Who cares? They're killing the old lady."

"Surely that's an exaggeration. It's . . ."

"She loved that bitch of a woman, Harriet."

Harriet started at the use of her Christian name. "Who?"

"Beatrice. God knows why. But she did."

"Beatrice Larson was a witty, handsome, great lady," Harriet said.

"She was a bitch."

"Why are you saying that, Agate, when you didn't even know her? Of course Miss A loved her. She's still grieving. Miss B hasn't been dead for more than seven or eight months."

"All right. Let her grieve—without visual aids."

"Why would you get that impression of Miss B? Whoever has talked about her like that? I can't imagine."

"No one. Couldn't you take a look at one of the diaries? Maybe if you saw one, you'd see what I mean."

"You haven't been reading them, have you?" Harriet asked, amazed.

"You and Cole! What difference does it make?"

"A great deal."

"All right. I've read a page or two while I've been putting them away. That's all it takes. Do you want to know the kinds of things I think make Miss A unhappy? Beatrice says things like, 'Sister is so simply grotesque,' and 'Some of us have to be grateful there are cripples who need us,' and . . ."

"Not really," Harriet said quietly.

"They aren't things she probably didn't know anyway, but . . ."

"Not really."

Harriet stared at the chair, now moved back from the comfortable circle, in which Miss B had always sat, and she tried to recall the presence of the elder Miss Larson, the tones in her voice. Sometimes what she said to her sister, repeated, could have sounded cutting or cruel, but the tone of her voice tempered everything with love, until last year when her speech began to go, of course.

"The way she wrote it down," Harriet said, "it might seem to have a different tone from the one she intended."

"So why not get rid of them?" Agate said. "Cole thought you might be able to persuade her. . . ."

"I don't know."

"Will you try?"

"I'll do what I can," Harriet said, getting up.

She walked slowly back down the hall, picked up the books, and started up the long stairs, pausing to look out at the rose garden, the paler blooms bright in the summer evening. Why hadn't she encouraged Miss A to burn them in the first place? "Some shy gossip two generations from now" or right now. Harriet had been curious. If all inner thoughts were not irritated or bitter, self-defeating or self-righteous, certainly enough of them would be to make the few good revelations small compensation. Miss B had been a bitter woman. The pride, the wit, the handsomeness made you think of her differently, that was all.

"Is that you, Harriet?"

"Yes," Harriet called, hurrying then.

"I thought I heard you come in earlier," Amelia said, as Harriet crossed the room to greet her.

"Yes. I stopped a minute to talk with Agate. I hadn't really got to know her well enough to know what kinds of books she might like to read."

"I'm afraid she doesn't get much time to read. I have too much."

"Are you still reading the diaries?" Harriet asked to that easy opening.

"Off and on," Amelia said.

"They trouble you."

"Yes, they do."

"Then why go on? She wanted you to burn them."

"I couldn't catch her tone," Amelia said. "There isn't any point in thinking now about what else one might have done twenty, thirty, forty years ago."

"No point at all."

"She was my right arm. I was her lame leg. She always claimed she needed one, that I could have got along quite well without it. I never knew how to imagine such alternatives. I knew what she meant about herself, of course. Well . . ."

"What did she mean?" Harriet asked.

"That being whole and handsome can be harder. I see that. It's probably easier to learn not to use the excuse you've got than to be born without one."

"Excuse?"

"For lack of courage. For self-indulgence. I could think, from the time I was a child, every time I climbed a flight of stairs, 'There, I haven't indulged myself.' My father even thought I was developing a kind of smugness. Pride for Sister was harder. She tried to be proud of loving me, but that got tangled with a failure of nerve, need. Perhaps all relationships have something of that in them."

Harriet watched the mindless activity of Amelia's hands as she talked. They moved lightly up and down her arms, following the routes of otherwise ignored pain.

"Do stop reading them," Harriet said.

"No," Amelia said simply. "By now I'll finish them."

There was no more Harriet could say. She could only distract Amelia with other topics for the hour of her visit.

"Did you persuade her?" Agate asked, as she let Harriet out the door.

"No," Harriet said. "And I'm sorry. It's something she has to do."

Agate made no comment.

❋

Though Agate liked the library in the evening, she had discovered the attic as a daytime retreat when Miss A was resting and there was nothing urgent to do in the kitchen. Occasionally she wandered among the furniture and boxes on the dance floor. One morning she found a trunk full of hats that must have gone back to Mrs. Larson's youth, and she entertained herself with trying them on. She looked at old photographs, too, and from those in

Miss A's room Agate could identify some of the faces. She could also identify a man who must have been Rosemary Hopwood's father. And there were a number of pictures of Ida Setworth as a girl and young woman, a bump of a nose and an amount of embarrassing hair, often arm-linked with Beatrice, who had been beautiful, even in those comic styles and slightly out of focus. But sometimes Agate did not explore. She sat on the turret bench, high in the morning light, and watched the society of birds. One morning, as she shifted her unaccustomed weight awkwardly to stand up, the seat gave slightly. Examining it, she saw that it opened, not up on hinges, but across on notched slides. It did not move easily, but she got it open far enough to be able to put a hand down into the storage space underneath, and there, one by one, she retrieved the six missing diaries. Here, anyway, were six years Miss A didn't have to live through again. And the thought of being able to burn them somewhat eased the frustration of not being able to get the others away from Miss A. Agate took them down to her own room, intending to dispose of them when she next used the incinerator in the basement, but, as Miss A had done before her, Agate glanced at a few pages before she put them away in a drawer.

＊

May 16, 1913: I have told Papa today that I want to go to the Seminary. He is pleased, though the decision comes two years late by his calendar. I don't know how I can leave. I know I must.

October 12, 1913: There is no pleasure in this martyrdom of self-exile. There is no good reason for it, either. I paint flowers on paper, on canvas, on china. I have no gifts, except social malice, which is more useful to me here than at home. This morning, walking under the medicinal eucalyptus, I saw a girl with a withered arm and further along, by the bridge, I wept.

December 2, 1913: I will go home for Christmas. Papa has sent the boat ticket. It is easy to lie in letters. Perhaps I will not find it difficult even when I see them all. I am learning a kind of indifference in any particular moment. There is, among these unimportant strangers, at least an absence of guilt and shame.

December 24, 1913: Ida and I walked along the seawall today, the first time I have been away from Sister for more than a few minutes. A cruel choice, I think. Ida admires my independence, knowing nothing about it. Why have I all the opportunities other people envy and might use? When we got back, Bill Hopwood had come to call. He's in a restless depression. Like me, who enjoys pain, he invents it to endure it.

✳

"Sick," Agate said, pushing aside some underwear and dropping the books into the drawer.

But, as she was fixing lunch, she thought about Beatrice Larson and wondered why she was so archly self-pitying and self-lacerating. The entries, specifically silly, confessional only in generalities, would never reveal what she felt shamed and guilty about. Probably there was nothing. Did Miss A know, or did she wonder? Was she reading to find clues? There was nothing. Born that way. It was hard to imagine a masochistic baby. A bad subject.

"You know, you've got two fortunes in hats up there in the attic," Agate said as she gave Miss A her lunch tray.

"You've found the attic, have you?"

"What are you going to do with them?"

"One day soon all that has to be cleared out," Amelia said.

"Have you looked at them recently?"

"No," Amelia said.

"Wait a minute."

Agate left the room. When she returned, she was wearing a huge hat, crowned with large bunches of violets, the color of the shift she had on, but she carried herself with such dignified theatricality that she might have been about to christen a ship or welcome royalty.

"That's my mother's," Amelia said, smiling; however, Mrs. Larson had never worn it that way, being, though not unnaturally balanced, as dependent on solid ground as Amelia was.

"But there's a really wild one," Agate said, and she stepped back into the hall out of Amelia's sight for a moment. "How do you like this?"

Her head was alive with parrot feathers.

"Good heavens!" Amelia said, laughing.

"Oh, you chicken reel," Agate sang, "how you make me feel. Say, it's really so entrancin', who could ever keep from dancin'." And she certainly couldn't, inventing between Charleston and cakewalk. "Put all the other fine selections right away. That am the only tune I want to hear you play. Keep on playin' chicken reel all day!"

Amelia was wiping the tears from her eyes.

129

"But you haven't seen anything yet," Agate promised.

The show of hats continued, Agate pacing carefully so that her performance would not really tire Miss A.

"I could swear that was Aunt Setworth's," Amelia said. "But what would it be doing in our attic?"

"Did Aunt Setworth have a real nose?"

"No more than Ida."

"Then it can't be her hat."

"There, now that's Sister's. How can it be so funny now? She was beautiful in it."

"*She,*" Agate said, with great haughtiness, "was beautiful in anything," dropped out of sight and turned up again in crushed tulle and smashed velvet, tying a shredded bow under her chin, "even bottom-of-the-trunk."

"Oh dear," Amelia said, struggling to catch her breath. "You really should be on stage, Agate."

"I am," Agate said, taking the hat off. "Most of the time."

"Yes, I know."

"I like it. It's where everybody ought to stay. This one really ought to be burned."

"Yes," Amelia agreed.

"And while I'm at it, why don't I start getting rid of Miss B's life work here."

"I haven't finished with those," Amelia said.

"Some of them you have."

"You know, they aren't all here. You haven't, looking around up there, found any more?" Amelia asked.

"If I had, I wouldn't tell you," Agate said, taking the lunch tray.

"Why not?"

"Just an excuse to stay in bed another week. I'm getting you up on Friday."

"I hope so," Amelia said, doubtful.

"By the way, who was so hung up on Dickens?"

"My mother," Amelia said.

"All the pages are cut. I couldn't believe it. The only thing any-one read in my grandmother's library was *Godey's Lady's Book.*"

"And where did you learn 'Chicken Reel,' for heaven's sake?"

"On a crank-up Victrola in our attic. His Master's Voice."

A funny mixture of things, that child. If Sister had still been alive, Agate would have killed her, up there in the attic among all the old hats and private papers, down in the study, leafing through Mama's Dickens. If she found the diaries, she might very well not tell Amelia. Would she read them? She'd discover nothing but the terrible, ordinary pain of a homesick girl or the uncertain bitter sanity of a middle-aged spinster in menopause. Which Amelia already knew.

"Agate?" Amelia called after the girl.

"Yes'm?"

"It's a good idea. Why don't you and Cole start burning them?"

"Tonight," Agate called back, and then Amelia heard her singing, "I got life! life! life!"

✳

"How did you get her to agree?" Cole asked, as they had supper in the kitchen.

"I gave her a hat show," Agate said.

"A hat show?"

"That's right."

"The ones she hasn't read as well?" Cole asked, giving up, as he so often did with Agate, any attempt to understand her explanations.

"Well, some of them. We haven't negotiated the whole lot, but I don't think there will be any problem once we get going. We're going to burn up old Sister Bitch, what do you think of that?"

"I wish you wouldn't keep calling her that," Cole said, but resignedly.

"Admit it. You didn't like her, did you?"

"I really did. She was funny . . . in a dry sort of way."

"I'll bet."

"Well, sarcastic, the way you are."

"And I don't crack you up all that often. Why should she?"

"Oh, I don't know," Cole said. "Do you know that Greek ship went out last night? One of the sailors wasn't on it."

"Jumped ship?" Agate asked, interested.

" I guess so."

"Did you know him?'

"Not really. He was down at Nick's a lot, is all."

"Would Nick help him?" Agate asked. Cole had told her enough about Nick's to make her curious and also determined to go there once Miss A was well enough to be left alone for an evening.

131

"I don't think so. Nick's a pretty tough guy. And he wouldn't want to get mixed up with the law."

"So where would he go?"

"I don't know. He's just a kid. I mean, he's a couple of years younger than we are. He doesn't even really speak English."

"That makes it kind of rough."

"Yeah," Cole said. "I wondered if he'd go to Dina."

"She's the one who has the furniture place?"

"Yeah. She's Nick's cousin, but she doesn't speak Greek either. Still, there's always a bunch of kids around her place, and she's not all that particular about things ... grass and that sort of thing; so maybe she'd help him. But I don't see what he thought he could do."

"Can't even score very well without English," Agate said.

"I suppose he'll get picked up in a couple of days."

"Poor kid."

"Yeah," Cole said.

Increasingly, they had moments of this kind of simple agreement, basic loyalties they shared, no matter how at war their styles. They went upstairs when they had finished cleaning up in a harmony of purpose to begin the task of burning the diaries.

"Not those," Amelia said, on Cole's second trip. "Those are the later ones I haven't read, aren't they?"

"This one," Cole said, fishing a diary out of the box, "is 1926."

"Oh. Then you must have taken the other box down already."

"Shall I get it?" Cole asked. "Agate's just starting the fire." Amelia smiled, shaking her head. "She shifted the boxes. She will have her way, won't she?"

"I can stop her," Cole said, turning quickly.

"Don't. She's right."

Down in the basement, Agate was working fast to make a fire of those last years. By the time Cole arrived with the final box, she had got rid of most of them.

"You weren't supposed to burn those," Cole said.

"Has she noticed?"

"That you switched the boxes? Yes."

"What did she say?"

" 'She will have her way,' " Cole said. "You really do get away with murder."

"Exactly the opposite," Agate said. "Now you tend this. I have one more small batch to get."

Cole had begun more slowly to burn the pain of years Amelia had already endured when Agate came back with the six diaries she had found.

"What are those?"

"I found them this morning. Nobody's going to read them."

"Does she know?"

"No," Agate said. "And now, Sister Bitch, whether there's blackmail money in these or not, whether there's excuse in them or not for your lame brain, nobody's ever going to know."

"What could be blackmail money?" Cole asked, disdainful.

"I think she had incestuous tendencies," Agate said with deep melodrama.

"For whom?"

"Miss A."

"Oh, Agate, for God's sake!"

"Never mind. Whatever might not be fit for a young boy's innocent eyes is now condemned to flame."

"How can you even make up such ideas?"

"Talent. Raw talent."

Cole found himself, for a second, tempted to snatch one of those books from Agate's hands, and he was immediately ashamed of himself. He knew perfectly well he'd find no such lurid confessions in anything written by Cousin B. And why should he want to know anyway?

Upstairs Amelia did not quite doze, remembering Beatrice young in a hat. Then Bill Hopwood under the tree she had so often climbed as a child. He was crying. It had never been a real choice for Amelia, not after Sister came home to stay. People had always assumed it was Beatrice who gave up a life of her own for Amelia. Beatrice thought so herself, needing to. It didn't matter. It never had. Then that fragment Agate had been singing repeated itself in Amelia's head: "I've got life! life! life!" Amelia accepted that sentence and was smiling as she fell asleep.

XIII

It was saturday, and Dina was sitting at the back door of the shop with a bottle of beer, out of habit rather than need. She had taken off her sweat shirt and rolled back her shirt sleeves. Instead of boots, she was wearing a pair of new sneakers and thinking of taking them off. She should get some sandals, why not? She didn't always have to be dressed for moving furniture, even here in the shop. One of the cats, sniffing and then rubbing itself against her toe, took hold of a lace and pulled. Dina reached down and rubbed the base of its tail. Then she pulled off the shoe and looked at her bare foot. "The sun makes a Greek dirty," her aunt had said. Nick didn't take the sun either. But Rosemary had laughed at that. "Your face is a gorgeous color. Why not the rest of you?" Was she lying in the sun now? Dina shifted slightly against that thought, but the image of Rosemary's naked back, softly rounded buttocks, and long, slightly parted legs, was easier to call up than dismiss. Dina took off her other shoe and then stretched until she could feel the edge of the step sharp against her back. She was going to buy a car, but not a sports car again. A Volvo perhaps. Charles Ries next door had one. Ann Ries liked to put the passenger seat right back and take a nap on the way home from work. If Rosemary wanted to go up into the mountains for the day, she could just put the seat back on the way home and sleep, there beside Dina while she drove. "Why don't you spend the night?" Rosemary had suggested it as a quite ordinary idea. Perhaps, between friends, it was. Dina remembered in school that girls asked each other over for the night. Dina knew so little about being a friend, having a friend. How often, for instance, did friends meet? If you were at school, if you worked together, even if you just drank at the same place, there was no question. You saw each other, as Dina understood was the custom in Greece, every day or nearly every day. But Rosemary didn't go to Nick's. "How do I see you next time?" Dina had asked. "Return my invitation," Rosemary answered simply. While Grace was still apt to drop in, it was not easy for Dina to ask Rosemary to her apartment. Getting rid of Grace was taking time, but soon, perhaps, Rosemary would come over without difficulty. Still, the apartment wasn't right for her. Maybe, after all, Dina should buy a house, but the only house she had ever really wanted to own was Rosemary's. One could be built. Extravagant to build a house just to entertain a friend? Not if that was what one did. Dina liked the sun on her undefended skin. One afternoon she would lie in the sun at Rosemary's. They would have cold, fresh drinks with ice. And they would talk. Perhaps Rosemary would tell Dina about the way she had lived before she came home, the low octave of her voice easy to listen to.

"Dina?"

"Hi, Cole, You haven't been around in a while."

"No," Cole said. "Working at the mill and Cousin A being so sick . . ."

"How is she?"

"Really better. She gets a bit tired still, but that's all."

"Rosemary says Agate's working out all right."

"Oh yes," Cole said, sitting down on the step next to Dina. "But she hasn't had any time off since she came. I offered to stay home so she could go to a movie or something, but I guess going out on her own wouldn't be much fun."

"No," Dina said.

"Kathy never did, but Agate's different. She's used to having fun."

"Mmm," Dina said. "She looks it."

"Well, you know what I mean."

"You want a beer?"

"No thanks," Cole said. "Thing is, Agate would like to go to Nick's."

"Well, no harm in that, is there?"

"If I took her?"

"Oh."

"It would look funny, wouldn't it?"

"I don't know," Dina said.

"It's kind of a problem. Agate's been really wonderful to Cousin A all these weeks she's been sick. She's more like a . . . I don't know. She doesn't seem like a maid. She asked me if I would take her to Nick's."

"Well, take her."

"Somebody like Mrs. Montgomery might . . ."

"I haven't seen Mrs. Montgomery drinking at Nick's lately," Dina grinned.

"And Mrs. Hill," Cole added.

"You afraid of Grace Hill?"

"Not afraid, exactly."

"Have you asked Miss A about it?"

"Not yet," Cole said. "I was going to ask Peter. Then I thought maybe you . . ."

"It's not exactly my field," Dina said. "Why not ask Peter?"

"I guess I wanted to ask somebody who would say it was all right," Cole said, smiling.

"Ask Miss A then."

"You don't think she'd mind or worry about it?"

"I don't know," Dina said, "but I don't think she'd say no."

"Probably not," Cole said. "You been playing tennis?"

"No" Dina said. "I don't even know how to play tennis."

"Oh."

"These are cooler," Dina said. "When you have them on."

"They would be," Cole said.

They heard the shop door open, but neither of them turned around. There were already half a dozen kids by the cold stove, and there would be more as the afternoon went on. Then the hard, high-heeled steps told them it wasn't just another kid, but Cole and Dina kept their backs to the sound.

"Wait until you hear this!" Grace Hill announced.

Dina looked up, clear-eyed and bland. Cole looked at his feet.

"Mr. Fallidon is in jail."

"Don't make bad jokes," Dina said sharply.

"He's not," Cole said, getting to his feet.

"Oh yes he is," Grace said triumphantly. "With a smorgasbord

136

of charges to choose from. Everything from aiding and abetting to indecent assault of a minor."

"What happened?" Dina demanded.

"The police found Panayotis at Mr. Fallidon's apartment in an ever so slightly compromising circumstance."

"I don't believe it!" Cole said. "I don't believe a word of it!"

"Jealous?" Grace asked. "I wouldn't be. You could be in jail yourself."

Before Cole knew what he had done, he had slapped Grace Hill in the face. She stood, stunned for a moment, and then she said, "And now we can arrange that for you on an assault charge. Call the police, Dina."

"Get out of here," Dina said quietly.

"Call the police! I have a witness."

"You've got witnesses all right, for all kinds of things. Now get out."

"Do you mean to tell me that you're going to side with this little . . ."

"I'll break your teeth myself. Now get out, and don't come back."

The kids by the stove were standing now, watching and listening. A couple moved over toward the back door.

"I have witnesses," Grace Hill shouted, gesturing to them.

"You heard her," one of the kids said. "Get out."

"My husband's a lawyer! My husband is Feller Hill!"

"Poor bastard," the kid said.

"And don't think I can't wipe the floor with you, you little pot-smoking punk. I'll have you all in jail," Grace shouted, but she was moving toward the door. "You're going to regret this, Dina."

Dina had turned away from her and simply stood, waiting to hear the door slam, which it did.

"Well, that's fair warning, kids," Dina said then. "Better clear out now and spread the word that George's is hot, for a couple of weeks anyway."

"What happened, Dina?" one of the kids asked.

"None of your crapping business, buddy," another said. "Come on. Dina says out."

Cole had not moved from where he stood when he hit Grace Hill, his hand still smarting. Dina put an arm round his shoulder and shook him gently.

137

"Come on. Come to," she said.

"I hit her."

"I should have done it myself . . . months ago."

"She wasn't lying, was she?"

"I don't know," Dina said. "I think we'd better find out. The trouble is, Feller Hill is Peter's lawyer."

"Oh, God!"

"I'm going to go over to Nick," Dina said. "If they have that kid in jail, he can't even speak English. Nick can find out what's happened faster than anyone."

"What shall I do?"

Dina paused. Who could help Peter? Harriet Jameson? Not on a thing like this. Miss A? Not yet. "I think you'd better not do anything or say anything to anyone. Will you be at home later on?"

"Yes, I guess so."

"I'll phone you there."

Cole helped Dina lock up the shop without further conversation. They left together and stood for a moment on the sidewalk.

"Do you want me to take you over to Nick's?" Cole suggested.

"It might be faster," Dina said, looking at her truck. "I've got to buy myself a car."

Cole drove with his ordinary nervous care, but he felt criminal in a way he didn't understand, as if they might be apprehended at any moment and charged with complicity of some sort.

"Don't talk to anyone," Dina said as she got out of the car. "I'll call you later."

"All right."

"And, look, if Grace does lay a charge against you, if the police turn up, don't say anything. Just get Miss A to call her lawyer."

Cole nodded, trying to call up an image of himself in a cell with Peter and Panayotis, a prospect which paralyzed him momentarily. He still couldn't believe that he had hit Grace Hill. It had not ever occurred to him as an idea, not even after he had done it. So to do something unthinkable was as simple as that. Peter and Panayotis. Cole forced his imagination to falter. He was driving out toward the beach. He musn't see anyone. He musn't speak with anyone. The criminal weight in his chest forced him forward over the steering wheel.

"Go on. Do what you want to do," Peter had told him.

Peter in jail. Indecent assault. Had Panayotis been with him all these days and nights?

Cole turned off the road and parked in the tall, dry grass that grew in the sandy soil. Sand dunes blocked his view of the sea. "Peter."

He put his head down on the steering wheel and wept, whether in jealousy or horror or fear or grief he could not have said. An unthinkable pain, the mind lost to it.

✱

Peter Fallidon did not have a cleaning woman. "What do you want me to do?" one of his sisters had been in the habit of shouting at him. "Go out and clean people's toilets?" That indignity had been invented by their mother, who apparently once for a week or two when they were small had taken some sort of honest job, something neither of his sisters ever intended to suffer. Though the attitude infuriated Peter, he had never been able to hire anyone to clean for him. It disturbed his privacy, he explained. Actually he didn't mind the job, and this Saturday morning he was grateful to have something to occupy him. By noon, in that small apartment, there was nothing left to do. Without any interest in eating, he fixed himself lunch, ate it, and tidied the kitchen after himself. Then he went into the living room and sat down with a book. It would be better if he could go out, drive to the beach or up into the mountains, but he had to wait for a phone call or a pounding on the door which might come in an hour or a day or . . . No, Feller would almost certainly call before evening, once Nick Pyros had talked with the boy and Feller had talked with Nick.

"I can't represent you both," Feller had said at the police station last night. "I'll have to get the boy another lawyer. It may take a couple of days to get all this untangled. But we will get it untangled, Peter. So just go home and try not to worry about it."

"Right. And, Feller, thanks."

A manly handshake, self-conscious with all that had been discussed. Without Feller's help, the police might very well have laid charges. They could still, of course. They had only his word that he hadn't been harboring the boy all this time, that Panayotis had been with him no more than half an hour before the police arrived. If only the boy could speak English in any useful way, but he couldn't explain to the police any more than he could to Peter where he had been and why he had chosen to turn up at that hour at Peter's. Oh, his hopes were crudely clear enough; he had the street language for that. He had been more genuinely baffled than Peter could understand when he was refused. All right, Peter had bought him a few beers one night. Even a kid would not assume from that that Peter might take him in, hide him from the police, keep him as a bed servant. Panayotis had been very angry when the police arrived, sure apparently that Peter had called them, arranged this trap.

If no charges were laid, if the details of Panayotis' arrest were kept out of the paper, if Nick Pyros kept the episode to himself . . . too many of them. Whatever happened, Peter was through in this town. It was too good a story to be left untold: the bank manager and a Greek boy. Even if it didn't get out, Feller Hill would never look at Peter Fallidon in quite the same light again, whether he believed the story Peter had told or not. For something, obviously, had put the idea in the boy's mind, however erroneous it was. Feller Hill didn't go to places like Nick's. Well, Carl Hollinger did . . . and saw Peter buying beer for the kids. Why had he done it? He had been feeling sorry for Cole . . . and for himself. Then, when Grace Hill came in, he had wanted to show her how invulnerable to her insinuations he was, how freely innocent. Would Feller tell his wife? Peter tasted the bile of rage in his mouth. He was through, whatever happened. All the years of patient, negative decency to become the kind of man people could respect, whether they liked him or not, a man with authority and influence, a man with some vision . . . a New Yorker ad for the trust department. Peter Fallidon, from bitter little bastard angry enough to be awarded the Navy Cross, to bank manager and Rotarian in a place nearly the size of a city, back to bitter little bastard in a night. Because of a bitter little bastard who thought he saw a short cut to such salvation. There wasn't any.

"I'll pay his lawyer."

Like buying the beer. The gesture of a free and innocent man. How could Feller Hill ever understand such acts, such people, as himself . . . or even his own wife? To be born in this town, to inherit it as a right, even without money, was to be given decency as a place to begin and to fall back on. Feller Hill could not know every time he got up on his hind legs that it was an awesome view from a dizzying height. And he had taught his sons to walk long before they would find out that their mother was a bitch, if they ever did. Two-legged creatures, all of them, Cole, too, for all his uncertainties.

Harriet. He could not bear to think of her, as he had begun to think of her. What an irony it was that the only person in town who might understand his innocence was Grace Hill, because she could understand Panayotis' need, like her own. And, perhaps, Dina, who put up with Grace in much the same way Peter felt indulgent of Panayotis, for knowing how hard it was to choose decency instead. But Harriet? For Harriet, a ship-jumping, cock-selling kid was not even a legal problem, except that she happened to have been associated for some months with a local bank manager who . . .

The phone rang.

"Hello?"

"Peter?"

"Yes, Harriet."

"I bought a roast this morning, and I wondered if you'd like to come over tonight and help me eat it."

"Thank you," Peter said, "but I can't tonight. I . . . there's . . . it's . . ."

"That's all right. It was just a thought."

"How are you?" Peter asked, automatically.

"Just fine. How are you?"

"Oh, fine."

"Well," Harriet said with forced cheerfulness, "perhaps some other time."

"Yes," Peter said.

"Good-bye then."

"Good-bye."

It was the only phone call that came. Through the afternoon and early evening Peter waited, trying to spend the time with some thought of what he would do, how he would hand in his resignation if he was allowed to, where he would go, but, until he knew that he would be free to make such decisions, it was impossible to formulate them clearly. At ten thirty, when he was considering taking a drink and trying to get some sleep, there was a knock on his door. The police again, he supposed, come to lay charges this time. He walked to the door and opened it.

"Feller! You shouldn't have come over. You could have phoned."

"I needed to see you," Feller said, and he added quickly, "I think it's safe to say that there's going to be no problem for you."

He was Peter's age, but he looked ten years older, deep bays of skin defeating his hairline, his crop of hair sparse and graying, his mouth deeply bracketed with lines, his skin stained with customary tiredness. And tonight there was more than the usual strain in the fast-blinking eyelids, the burdened shoulders.

"Let me get you a drink," Peter said.

"Thank you."

Feller stood, looking at the books on Peter's shelves, at the orderliness of all the objects in the room, until Peter came in with a drink for each of them.

"I can't tell you how grateful I am . . ." Peter began.

Feller shook his head. "Pyros' version of the boy's story, though it's pretty garbled still, makes it clear that he had a mistaken idea that you'd help him. The police are going to want to talk to you again tomorrow. Under the circumstances, I have to advise you that you must have another lawyer."

"Besides you?" Peter asked.

"Instead of me. I can't deal with the case any further."

"I don't quite understand," Peter said carefully.

"It's difficult," Feller said.

"Of course, if you don't want to . . . for personal reasons, then . . ."

"My wife told me tonight that you'd refused to lend her money."

"That's right."

"She's behind all this, Peter," Feller said, and then he put his face in his hands in a shame or grief that was silent.

Peter could not say or do anything. He simply waited.

"I haven't really sorted out the legal problems," Feller said finally. "I don't know whether you'll be asked . . . In any case, you've got to have another lawyer."

"You mean, she put Panayotis up to this?" Peter asked.

"Yes," Feller said, and he looked at Peter. "My wife's a very sick woman. I've got to do what I can to protect her, for her own sake, of course, but for mine, too, and the boys'. It may be, with psychiatric evidence . . ."

"Look, surely somehow together we can sort this out," Peter said. "It's not as if we were in a big city where nobody gives a damn. Nobody's going to lay any charges that don't have to be laid. You persuaded them not to charge me, after all."

"I didn't think you'd done anything," Feller said. "Neither did they. It's not the first time a kid's jumped ship here."

"But has"—Peter forced himself to that first name—"Grace done anything that has to be charged?"

"You've got to talk to another lawyer. I can't advise you on this. I simply can't."

"If I'm asked to lay charges, I simply won't do it," Peter said flatly. "I don't need a lawyer to advise me about that."

"You do," Feller insisted. "If there are simply rumors, if you don't have a chance to clear yourself . . ."

"Do there have to be that many rumors?" Peter asked, who had been ready to leave town on the evidence of much less threat only hours before.

"When I got home tonight," Feller said, "Grace was hysterical. She'd been assaulted, she said, by Cole Westaway."

"Cole!"

"She went to Dina's this afternoon. Cole Westaway was there. She thought you'd be in jail and told him you were—for indecent assault of a minor. He slapped her. It was only then that I realized she was the woman Panayotis was talking about; otherwise she wouldn't have known anything about it. So I confronted her with it. She began to talk about the loan . . ."

"I probably should have spoken to you about that," Peter said. "But she didn't want you to know, and, since I couldn't anyway, I . . ."

"You've got to think of yourself. Whatever you have to do . . ."

"I'm not going to do anything."

"You must see another lawyer. I insist."

"Feller, this is a human thing . . . between friends, in a human place."

"It's a human place all right," Feller said bitterly. "What do you think people like the Larsons are going to do with the tales Cole's bringing home?"

"I can handle that."

"Can you?" Feller asked. "Not one of those people has had anything to do with me since I came home with Grace seventeen years ago. It's a smug, cruel, narrow-minded little sewer."

"Miss Larson?" Peter asked, baffled.

"The elder Miss Larson."

"Well, she died before I had much sense of her."

"I keep forgetting," Feller said.

"I'm not going to do anything, Feller. Not even resign."

"We'll talk about it again when we've both had some sleep."

"All right, but I won't have changed my mind."

They stood. Peter took Feller by the shoulders. "I'm sorry as hell."

"Yes, thanks. So am I."

*

Dina tried to get Cole at home in the late afternoon and again after dinner.

"I don't know where he is," Agate said irritably. "He was supposed to be home for dinner, and then we were going to Nick's. Maybe he decided he'd rather drink alone."

Dina phoned Nick's, but Cole wasn't there. She had invited herself to Rosemary's for the evening and was already half an hour late. She thought of phoning Agate again and asking her to get Cole to telephone Rosemary's when he got in, but she didn't want to sound urgent.

"I'm worried about him," she confessed to Rosemary, having recounted the details of the long afternoon.

"Could he have gone to Peter's?"

"He thinks Peter's in jail."

"What a sick, sick bitch she is," Rosemary said.

"Cole needs to know that, specifically."

"Do you want to go out looking for him?"

"Maybe if we just swung by Nick's . . ."

"Come on."

"It's probably silly," Dina said.

"Well, doing something silly is better than sitting around worrying about him."

"I should have paid more attention to him this afternoon."

"You can't give absolute attention to everybody, Dina."

"No."

*

"I'm getting worried about Cole, Agate," Amelia said at ten o'clock, when it was time for her to go upstairs to bed. "He doesn't usually go off like this without saying anything. Are you sure he didn't say anything?"

"Don't worry about it," Agate said. "I bullied him into saying that he'd take me to Nick's tonight. He didn't think you'd approve. Anyway, he didn't want to. He's probably waiting it out

144

in a movie somewhere until we've both gone to bed."

"You wanted to go to Nick's?"

"It sounded entertaining."

"You need some fun. I'll speak to Cole."

"You wouldn't mind?"

"Why should I?"

"What would Mrs. Montgomery say?" Agate asked, putting on a Maud Montgomery face.

Amelia smiled. "She's a good soul, all the same."

"But don't say anything to Cole," Agate said. "I'll just hit him over the head a couple of times with a rolling pin when he gets in. That will take care of it. Now, it's time for you to turn in."

"I hope he's not late."

✳

Cole had no idea what time it was when he came in through the kitchen door. Nor could he have accounted for the hours that had passed. The empty ache in his stomach reminded him that he had not eaten. He stood by the refrigerator, wondering if he would attempt food, a gesture toward stopping that simple pain, anyway. He was pouring himself a glass of milk when Agate, in a light summer robe, came into the kitchen. He didn't so much drop the bottle as simply let it go, tipping over the glass as it fell. He watched the pool of milk form around his feet over bits of broken glass.

"Why not try a beer?" Agate suggested without moving. "Or is that the trouble?"

Cole didn't answer her.

"What's the matter?" she asked then, going over to look at him more closely.

"I dropped the milk," he said.

"Why?"

"Don't know."

"Where have you been?"

"Nowhere," he said, not evasive, simply factual.

"Have you eaten?"

"No."

"Well, wade out of that stuff and go sit down. I'll get you something."

"You don't have to."

It was Agate's turn not to answer. It wasn't alcohol, and he didn't use anything else. But something was wrong, really wrong. He sank down in the chair, put his chin in his hands and stared ahead of him, taking no notice of Agate as she cleaned up the milk and then went about making him a sandwich.

"Dina was trying to get you earlier," Agate said finally, as she put the sandwich and a new glass of milk in front of him.

"Oh."

"She phoned a couple of times."

"I wasn't home," Cole said.

"No," Agate said without much energy in her sarcasm, "you weren't."

"What time is it?"

"About three."

"It wasn't in the paper," Cole said.

"What wasn't?"

"Thanks," Cole said, nodding to the sandwich.

"What wasn't in the paper?"

"What did I say?" Cole asked.

"What's the matter with you?"

"Tired," Cole said. "I'm awfully tired." He picked up the sandwich and took a bite of it. Then, as if he'd just remembered, he said, "I'm sorry about Nick's tonight. I just couldn't make it."

"We all have our busy days," Agate said.

"Yeah."

She watched him eat. It was the only entertainment he provided, having nothing more to say. He was the awful color he had been when she first met him. Any blond got such easy mileage with suffering. She could be into the last aria, TB, gout, and voice strain overcoming the final high notes, and she'd still look an ad for a good laxative. Why had Dina been trying to reach him?

"Is it something about that kid?" Agate asked.

"What kid?"

"The one who jumped ship."

"That cock-sucking bastard," Cole said, nearly under his breath.

"Who've you been playing with to learn such bad language?"

"You."

"Me?" Agate answered in surprise. "That wouldn't have been my first guess."

"All of you!"

146

Agate looked around her. "How many of me do you think there are?"

"Stop talking to me like that!" Cole said angrily, getting to his feet.

"What in hell's eating you?"

"I hit a woman today," Cole said.

"I'm supposed to be impressed? Run from the room screaming? What?"

"Don't talk to me like I'm the village idiot. . . ."

"King Cole, from now on . . ."

He had taken her by the shoulders, as if to shake her, needs scattering in his eyes like broken glass, not knowing what he was doing, what he wanted done to him. Agate stepped toward rather than away from him, hands on his rib cage, not hard and breaking, simply holding him there to give him balance.

"Agate . . ."

She lifted her mouth to his, taking her name from his tongue, as if they—mouth, tongue, name—all belonged to her. Against him, separating them, was the object of her belly. But her hands moving now, one to the small of his back under his shirt, the other to his cock, distracted him from that horror of life, growing there, his need growing, being made known to him.

"We can't . . ." he said, turning his mouth from hers. "I can't . . ."

"You don't even know," Agate said, touching him carefully and surely. "Come on. Come upstairs . . . to my room."

He let her lead him, so tired he stumbled on the stairs, let her kiss him again, let her hands move against his skin, his hairless nipples, his lean, tight buttocks, his cock rising to whatever judgment, helpless finally, glad to be, even as he felt her go down on him, as a boy might, as a man might, as anyone might but never had, to suck the need out of him. He came and slept.

"You're all bastards," Agate said quietly. "Well, we all are really," the sweetness of green seed in her mouth.

Where was the anger, the sense of revenge? She had never had a boy before, lying naked and asleep on her bed, his hands and genitals in the same rhythm of collapse, comic, vulnerable. Mythical. How would he be in the morning? Horrified. In a moral sweat to get rid of her or marry her. She was going to have to be fairly careful with him for some hours, until he felt well enough to remember the simple pleasures of rape. She covered him,

147

wrapped her robe about her and went to Cole's room to sleep, but the child in her was restless in desires of its own. She lay, her hands on her belly, unwilling jailor to this punishing life, refusing to think, unable to stop.

XIV

THOUGH AMELIA HAD BEEN UP every day for two weeks, this was
the first morning she had come downstairs for breakfast. Peter
and Harriet were coming for dinner that night, her first dinner
guests since she'd been ill, and she wanted to help Agate as much
as she could. She realized, by the uncertainty of the routine, that
Cole and Agate must be accustomed to having breakfast in the
kitchen. There was an embarrassment between them about who
would clear away the fruit dishes and who would feed the toaster.
Cole was, in nearly any circumstance, even more nervous than
usual these days. He had been since the night he had stayed out
so late, apparently to avoid taking Agate to Nick's. But whatever
disagreement there was between them, they'd work it out better
without interference.

What concerned her more was a conversation she'd had with
Rosemary several days ago, during which Amelia learned that
Agate hadn't made up her mind what she was going to do with
the baby when it was born. Amelia herself had no convictions, but
experience had shown her the importance of a firm decision well
before the birth of the child. Agate had only two months now,
and it was time for her to face the problem. Perhaps today wasn't
the day to bring it up, but Amelia could always find a reason
these days for postponing anything difficult. She had not completely recovered, she told herself, but she knew that, at her age,
she wouldn't. This growing tiredness of spirit was irreversible,

and, therefore, like the pain she had learned to ignore, she must learn to ignore reluctance.

Cole had hurried through his meal and excused himself to take his dishes to the kitchen.

"I'm going to arrange flowers when I won't be in your way in the kitchen," Amelia said to Agate.

"Any time," Agate said. "There's not much to do."

Cole came back into the dining room and stood.

"On your way, then?" Amelia said, smiling at him.

"Yes," Cole said." About tonight . . ."

"They'll be here about six thirty; so you'll have plenty of time for a shower and a look at the paper."

"The trouble is, I might have to work late. I wouldn't want to bother anyone. I thought maybe I'd get something downtown."

"And miss Peter and Harriet?" Amelia asked.

"Well, it's just that I might be late."

"That doesn't matter. They'd be really disappointed not to see you."

"And I told some of the guys I might go to a movie. . . ."

"You do what you want, of course."

"I'll get here if I possibly can," Cole said quickly. "Well, I guess I better . . ." If he finished his sentence, he did so as he went through the kitchen on his way out.

"Does he not want to be here tonight?" Amelia asked. "He's usually very pleased to see Peter and Harriet."

"Oh, you know Cole," Agate said.

"In ways."

"More coffee? Or do we behave as if feeding a couple of people takes all day at a dead run?"

"If it really were coffee . . ." Amelia said wistfully.

"Think coffee," Agate said.

"All right."

Agate took the cup and went out into the kitchen, moving with a slowness not entirely accounted for by her increasing size. It was a lethargy that expressed restlessness. The novelty and real need in the house had vanished together, and Amelia saw that Agate was bored, therefore more vulnerable to worry.

"All the talking we've done," Amelia said, as Agate returned with her Sanka, "and I haven't any idea what you're interested in."

"I'm not."

"Truly?"

"No, not truly. I used to like acting and singing. I was going to major in drama until I realized that, the way I major in drama, I might as well be on a street corner as on a stage. I mean, I do major in drama. I don't need a degree in it."

"And now?"

"It's too early in the morning to make you laugh."

"It's never too early," Amelia said.

"Comparative religions. The mythology's fun. I always liked a a good story. But what really gets to me is comparative morality. So I'm probably an anthropologist, except they keep away from the moral issues, really. As a career, I'd like to write articles for ladies' magazines, sort of like Margaret Mead but more practical and preachy, like 'What Really Should Be Done with the After-birth' or 'Taboos, Uses, and Abuses of Menstrual Blood.'"

"What would you say?" Amelia asked, her own practical interests aroused.

"I'm not serious," Agate confessed.

"What are you then?"

"Oh, I don't know, I don't know," Agate said, rubbing her face as if it ached. "A bit fed up, I guess."

"What are you going to do with the baby?"

"Bake it? Stew it? Can't decide till I see it. I don't even know what color it's going to be."

"You can't wait until then. Or at least you shouldn't. . . ."

"Why not?"

"Because it's a matter of your life as well as the baby's."

"Well, I didn't make up my mind to have it, and I didn't make up my mind not to have it. If I don't make up my mind to keep it, if I don't make up my mind not to keep it, it will work itself out, as they say."

"Work itself out, yes, with some help from you, but then there it is, still needing help from you or someone. Either way, you have to plan."

"I've never been good at that," Agate said.

"Do you want a baby?"

"Any baby?"

"Yours."

"Mine," Agate said. "I don't know. If we turned out to like each other . . ."

"Could you support yourself?"

"I guess so," Agate said.

"What about your family?"

"They aren't fond of kids. They wouldn't just collect them any way."

"Do they know?"

Agate shook her head. "They think I'm in Europe. We're none of us letter writers, so . . ."

"If you had to work, if there was no one to look after a baby. . ."

"How would you like to have it?" Agate asked brightly. "I mean, along with me . . . if we turned out to like it, that is. If not, we could always find somebody who wasn't so particular, who . . ."

"Child," Amelia said gently.

"I wish you wouldn't call me that," Agate said, her eyes green with tears it was too late to stop.

"Child's a good name for you," Amelia said, hoisting herself out of her chair and moving around the table to Agate, taking the weight of her head from her hands and transferring it to her own old bosom. "Child."

Agate cried for a long time without any dramatic flare at all, noisily and soggily, and Amelia stood beside her, rocking her, rubbing her back, crooning at her as if she were a colicky baby. It was a kind of moral colic, very painful, nothing to worry about seriously, however. Finally Agate was quiet, but Amelia did not let her go. She held her quiet and waited.

"All right," Agate said, her cheek still pressed against that ancient warmth, "I'll tell her. I'll tell her I'm giving it up."

❋

Peter had to hurry, because this morning, remembering that he had not called Harriet since she'd invited him to dinner, he had phoned to say he'd pick her up to take her to the Larsons'. Though he had not really thought of her in days, Harriet was, in a way, very much a part of all that had been happening and changing in him. Now that he did think of her, he wished that they were going to have time to talk, for what he had thought would simply and properly shock Harriet he now hoped she might understand. For the first time in years, Peter wanted to explain himself. Why? He smiled. He approved of himself and he enjoyed it. He wanted to extend that pleasure.

The drive across town to Harriet's, then halfway back to the Larson house, which had once seemed an exercise in empty courtesy, was a pleasure to Peter this evening. It had been a gray, cool day, as so many were here even in the deep summer, the sea fogs protecting the town from the intense heat that lay just the other side of the coastal mountains. The lawns stayed green, the flowers intense in color—things Harriet saw and took delight in.

"Begonias," Peter said, testing his very recently acquired knowledge. "Marigolds."

Would he some day own a house and be a gardener? He'd never had a domestic image for himself.

Harriet was waiting for him outside the house. When he saw her, he glanced at his watch. He was only a couple of minutes late, and he knew her being there was not a reprimand but a simple thoughtfulness.

"How pretty you look," he said as he got out of the car to open the door for her. "And my favorite dress."

"Thank you," Harriet said.

"No books tonight?"

"I didn't think I'd bother. I'll be going over again in a few days."

"I'm awfully sorry I couldn't come over and help with that roast the other night," Peter said. "It was a bad weekend for me, and I couldn't really explain. . . ."

"It doesn't matter."

"Actually, it does," Peter said. "Sometime soon I'd like to tell you about it. How's your week been?"

"When you couldn't come, I decided to phone Mr. Hollinger and ask him. We had a lovely evening. He's so easy to talk to. I don't ever really forget he's old enough to be my father, but it's like being with a father you could only invent. It's a shame he didn't have children. He wouldn't be as lonely as he is now."

"How long has he been a widower?" Peter asked.

"Only two years, and his wife was a dear person . . . no, not 'dear', much more than that. She was very lively and funny and intelligent. They must have had a marvelous life together."

"Does he talk about her a lot?"

"Do you mean is he a bit of an old bore?"

Peter laughed. "I guess so."

"Actually . . ." Harriet hesitated.

Peter glanced over at her.

"He wants to marry Miss Setworth."

"Good for him."

"But she can't make up her mind. I think she wants to, but she says the whole idea is ridiculous."

"Why?"

"Well, I suppose, when you're that old—she's a lot older than he is—and you've never been married . . . I can remember my mother laughing about a woman only in her fifties."

"I don't see why," Peter said.

"No, I guess men don't," Harriet said. "I tried to explain to him how she might feel. Do you know, I was helping him to plan strategies for persuading her."

"Oh, Harriet, I love you," Peter said, embarrassed at that only after it was out.

"Aren't the begonias beautiful?" she said, turning away from him.

"I thought so on the way over."

"You won't say anything to anyone, though," Harriet said. "I think Miss Setworth's really horrified at the idea that anyone would know, particularly people like Mrs. Montgomery. And Miss A, too, I guess."

"Miss Larson wouldn't make fun of her."

"No, but Miss B would have. You know, I sometimes think she kept all three of them single."

"How?"

"Oh, I don't know. She always saw the ridiculous, but she never accepted it. She laughed *at* things and people."

"I don't think I would have liked that woman."

"Well, you would have, though. Respected her anyway. And she was very entertaining before she had her strokes. . . ."

"What were you going on to say?" Peter asked, hearing the uncertainty in her pause.

"A lot of people are remembered better than they were. In a curious way, Miss B gets worse, as if nobody ever dealt with the problems she posed at the time and wants to now that she's gone. Even Mr. Hollinger seems to resent her in retrospect. It's the diaries, I guess. They weren't pleasant reading apparently. Agate finally persuaded Miss A to burn them before she'd finished them. She started feeling better right away."

"Good for Agate."

"You know, you're wrong about Agate," Harriet said. "You should like her."

"Should I? All right, I will."

It was Amelia rather than Cole who greeted them at the door. Though Peter was delighted to see her, he noticed how much thinner she was, how uncertain her physical energy. But the welcome was reassuring. She was as glad to see them as she always was.

"I'm sorry Cole's not home yet," she said, as they went to the library. "He said he might have to work late, but I imagine he'll come in later."

But the half hour passed and Agate announced dinner.

"I guess we'd better not wait for him," Amelia said. "He said he might catch a bite downtown if he was very late."

"That's too bad," Harriet said. "It's ages since I've seen Cole."

Amelia led the way into the dining room and looked at the table. "What's this, Agate?"

"I've already had mine, and I haven't dropped dead; so you'll be all right," Agate said, to explain the two places she'd removed from the table.

Amelia was somehow troubled by being waited on in a way she had been accustomed to for thirty years. She had come to enjoy the company of both Agate and Cole at the table, their joint efforts to provide her with food and entertainment. Now, though Harriet and Peter sat down with her, she felt alone at the table without Beatrice, confronted, therefore, with the whole weight of responsibility again. She hadn't the energy. She had spent it on Agate this morning. Learn to live without it then, but under that sternness she was heavy with a sorrow only the children could relieve her of. Harriet was chatting about Carl. Amelia didn't want to think about Carl, struggling in his own loneliness.

"That's good soup," Agate said, as she took Harriet's and Peter's empty dishes. "You finish it."

Obediently Amelia picked up her spoon again while Peter raised surprised brows at Harriet.

"She bullies me," Amelia said in a happy tone.

Peter and Harriet, sensing Amelia's abstraction, found themselves talking often to each other as if she were not even in the room. Agate watched her with guilty concern. "Child" she certainly had been, to dump like that on a frail old woman who'd had enough dumped on her in a lifetime to deserve a permanent vacation. And why in hell did Cole have to be so spooked about the green-eyed bank manager? Agate hadn't taken to his arrogant formality the couple of times he'd come to the door with papers for Miss A to sign, but he was being pleasant enough tonight. At least Cole could have been there to help keep things going.

"This is delicious food, Agate," Harriet said.

"It certainly is," Peter agreed.

"Kathy must have been a lousy cook," Agate said.

"She made good biscuits," all three replied.

In that amusement, Amelia seemed to recover, but Peter and Harriet stayed for only a cup of coffee after dinner.

"For your first party, this is long enough," Harriet said.

"Well, soon again," Amelia said, without protesting. "And I hope Cole will be here, too. Agate?"

Agate was there at once, as if she'd been waiting in the hall.

"Will you show Miss Jameson and Mr. Fallidon to the door?"

"I'll get my map," Agate said.

"We really can find our way," Peter said, leaning down to kiss Amelia.

"Agate likes to ruin all her own acts," Amelia said, smiling. "She says it's where her greatest talent lies."

At the front door, they complimented Agate again. Then Harriet said, "She isn't really herself yet, is she?"

"It's the self you'd better get used to," Agate said. "When you've been dropped on your heart from the height of seventy-two years, you don't exactly bounce back."

"No, I guess you don't."

Harriet and Peter didn't speak until they were settled in the car.

"It's worrying," Harriet said then.

"Yes."

"I wonder why Cole didn't come home. He couldn't have worked this late, could he?"

"No."

Miss Larson's failing health and attention had depressed him, but Cole's absence had modified the story he thought he was going to tell Harriet, the self-approval in it.

"It's early," Harriet said. "Let's go back to my apartment and cheer ourselves up a little."

"All right."

Peter was used to sitting across from Harriet where he could see her, but now the Larson chest had taken the place of that chair. The only comfortable place to sit was on the couch with her. Instead of talking, Peter brooded on his own self-absorption, which had excluded Cole from his imagination, excluded everyone, really, except Feller Hill, in whose admiration and gratitude Peter had become extravagantly generous, understanding, full of kindly platitudes about decency and human concern. He had even gone so far as to explain Feller to himself, his good fortune to be born into this kind of world, where his wife could be sent to a psychiatrist instead of to jail, where a boy could be returned to his ship with protective explanations rather than deportation orders.

"Where do you go when you go away like that?" Harriet asked.

"Go?" Peter asked, startled.

"You haven't said a word for ten minutes. You often do that."

"I was thinking," Peter said, with that new rueful smile of his, "how self-absorbed I really am . . . and obviously demonstrating it at the same time."

"You're worried about something."

"I wanted to tell you a very pleasant sort of story for the sake of showing you what a decent, kind man I am, how well I acquit myself. In fact, I haven't spent a moment thinking about anybody but myself."

"That's probably not true. Why don't you tell me?"

He did, but instead of the superior moral tone he had enjoyed anticipating, he used the whole range of emotions he had actually experienced from the surprise of finding Panayotis at his door to the worry he had begun to feel about Cole.

"I am proud of you," Harriet said.

"Yes, well, that's what I intended you to say."

"Do you think out conversations with me ahead of time?" she asked.

"Sometimes."

"And then they happen?"

"Yes."

"And you're bored to death."

"Not at all," Peter said. "I'm reassured. I'm still in control. I don't have to deal with surprises."

"Not even pleasant ones," Harriet said. "Making up conversations with you does bore me. I've given it up. You should, too. You don't need to be that safe. I'm not that surprising. But Grace Hill . . ."

"She didn't really surprise me," Peter said. "I knew she'd do something."

157

"Why did Cole hit her? And why wasn't he at home tonight? Do you think he could imagine that you really were . . . attracted to Panayotis?"

"Why would he?"

"Well, it occurred to me," Harriet said. "And I would have hit Grace Hill, and I wouldn't have known how to see you after that, and I don't even feel guilty about loving you."

"Of course, any shy boy . . . " Peter began, and then he fell silent.

"Now, don't do that. Talk what you're thinking."

"Have I been . . . stupid about Cole?"

"I don't know. Do you want another drink?"

"I shouldn't," Peter said, looking at his watch. "I wish there were some way I could simply see Cole without having to set it up."

"Did you at all . . . want him?"

"Who? Cole?"

"No . . ."

"Panayotis? No," Peter said.

"I'm going to get you another drink."

They talked then at some length about Cole, about shyness in people, about Ida Setworth and Carl Hollinger. Finally Peter got up to leave. Standing, he kissed Harriet on the mouth, a nineteen-forties' movie kiss that embarrassed seven-year-olds and left the adults in the audience unmoved. Still, it was a beginning. Peter wasn't at all sure it could ever be more than that if he hadn't more help from Harriet than this, but perhaps in time he would.

XV

THE DOCTOR HAD GIVEN AGATE his now standard lecture on overweight, and, though she'd joked with him good-humoredly enough about developing a convincing figure for having spent the summer in England eating potatoes and jam tarts, she was irritable by the time Rosemary was driving her back to the Larsons.

"Anything you'd like to pick up in town?" Rosemary asked pleasantly. "I've plenty of time this morning."

"I get everything delivered," Agate said. "Except me."

"That, too, in time."

"How long have you been getting your kicks with unwed mothers?"

"Around six years," Rosemary answered evenly.

"I somehow thought it was longer than that. You didn't have yours and then just not graduate, stay on at the old school, so to speak?"

"No," Rosemary said. "I was in the psychiatric side before I came back here."

"Is that where you learned to keep your cool?"

"I suppose so."

"Or I just don't know over which tit the chink in the armor is."

Rosemary answered that with no more than a wry glance, and Agate turned away from her, resentful not so much of the person of Rosemary as of her lettuce-leaf trimness, her refined good looks, and her assigned authority. Rosemary knew that. Youngsters like Agate never threatened her temper. Quite the contrary. Agate's transparent moods, her vulgarity and impudence, were a relief from the sullen fright of so many of the others. If anything, Rosemary envied Agate her random assaults on other people's privacy or prudery. Why shouldn't she be irritable about the attempts to cut her down to size, in flesh, in uniform, in convention? Thank God for Amelia, who could not take such terms seriously either.

"I amuse you," Agate said.

"Sometimes, yes."

"I find you mildly entertaining, too," Agate said, in tonalities almost accurately Rosemary's.

"One thing I don't understand, and that's why you're having this baby."

"Oh yes," Agate said. "That's a thing I've been meaning to tell you."

"Good."

"I've decided to give it away or sell it or whatever it is you arrange. . . ."

"All right. You need to sign papers."

"But there have to be some riders," Agate said.

"Riders?"

"Yes. If it has more of anything or less of anything than expected, if it turns out to be an off-color joke of any sort, then I think we'll entertain each other."

"Are you afraid of things like that?"

"Not at all," Agate said brightly. "Some of us prefer to be freaks."

"I'm sure your baby will be fine."

"Are you? I thought you'd already lined up a circus agent who specialized in crossed-up chromosomes."

"I was only trying to warn you about drugs. I didn't mean to suggest . . ." Rosemary began, genuinely concerned.

"What do agencies do with the Amelia Larsons of this world if they happen to be dropped by accident-prone kids like me?"

"Lots of people are willing to adopt babies who, for one reason or another, have problems.'

"Like, some people prefer two heads?"

"Amelia's a pretty good example of what it means to be crippled," Rosemary said.

"Okay. If I have a baby like her, I keep her."

"People who take such children are usually pretty special themselves. They often have children of their own. They have the money that's necessary for doctor's bills. They're usually a bit older, more experienced. And, Agate, if there's anything seriously wrong with a baby, it's better, whether the mother can take care of it or not, to put it in an institution. It would be silly for you . . ."

"I'm a silly person," Agate said firmly. "It's that deal or no deal. If you're not interested, that's fine. If it comes out dull and whole, I'll sell it myself."

"Why do you feel so guilty?"

"I don't, and I'm not going to, ever."

"If that were true, you wouldn't be inventing punishments."

"This isn't my invention," Agate said, patting herself.

"It shouldn't be your punishment either."

"Don't try to sell me painless morality until you've been kicked in the belly and the ribs for a couple of months yourself. I haven't been playing with candles."

"Why weren't you taking the Pill?"

"I was, in an absentminded sort of way, and then, you know, it's like smoking for some people. You decide to give up men for a while, but then you're out drinking one night and you just absentmindedly reach for one, light him up, and there you are."

"Think about Amelia," Rosemary said. By now they were parked in front of the house. "She had a good life partly because of all this, the security, the love . . . "

"This is a paid commercial," Agate said.

"I suppose so," Rosemary admitted.

"Were you adopted?"

"No."

"What's your investment?" Agate asked. "I don't read it."

"I haven't one really. I just think you'd be much better off to give the child up, whatever happens."

"No investment," Agate said.

That got through to pain, but Rosemary didn't give any indication of it. Agate wasn't really interested in inflicting it; she'd take no real pleasure in being on target.

"Think about it a little more."

"While the old ones have a wild game of bridge."

"Are they coming tonight?"

"Yep, and for dinner, because I'm good for the gall bladder."

"You're good for Amelia."

Agate shrugged, then hoisted herself out of the car and labored up the steps. Knowing that Rosemary was watching her, she thought of imitating Miss A's gait, but that might strain her own heart. Rosemary Hopwood, taking graduate courses against pain and guilt and grief, hadn't quite made it, surely. Or had she? Nobody with teeth like that could be quite dead, unless she avoided people who liked to be bitten.

＊

Ida Setworth had made up her mind.

"Yes," she said to herself in the mirror, as unlikely a Molly Bloom as she could imagine, in a new dress her friends would not like any better than they had the others she had bought recently. "Yes."

The foolishness of it made her a little giddy but she had no fickle temptations. Her decision had been set by very simple reasoning: at seventy-eight she was unlikely to live long enough to regret marrying Carl Hollinger. The novelty of it would only have time to wear off in the grave. But, if she refused him, she would certainly begin to regret that at once.

The mechanics of change, which had troubled her at first, now seemed unimportant past telling Carl this evening on the way to Amelia's and then, if he agreed, telling Amelia and Maud at once. Having faced that embarrassment, she could certainly deal with whatever ceremony Carl suggested and then simply move into town.

She would miss the quiet of the country night, her view, the deep familiarity of her house, but those seemed small sacrifices for what Carl was offering her, a joyful companionship she had never admitted lacking. She hadn't lacked it really until he offered and she had an opportunity to refuse.

"Ida Hollinger," she said. "Mrs. Carl Hollinger." And thought to write out that name as any schoolgirl might.

＊

Carl had spent the day in his garden, something he had not done with pleasure since his wife died, but he had begun to feel that Ida soon would make up her mind to accept him, and he wanted to be ready for her. He had already repainted the guest room. He would not go as far as getting new slipcovers for the living room until Ida was prepared to choose the material.

Harriet had said, when the month was up, he should ask Ida again, and tonight he intended to, not when he picked her up but when he took her home. He could be that patient. Then, if she agreed, they would go out of town directly, marry, and grow accustomed to each other's company away from the amusement and curiosity of their friends. Ida was not going to refuse him. He somehow knew that.

The town, as he drove through it, was gentle with evening light. It was not really a chore ever to go to get Ida, but he would be very glad of a day when he did not have to travel farther than a room or two to find her.

The last stop light was red. He braked and looked at his watch. Six o'clock. He waited for the change. Green. A fist of pain, the weight of a falling planet, hit him in the chest. No instant of knowledge came with it. He was dead.

✳

Ida, who had cried so bitterly at the irony of being loved by Carl, did not weep when she finally located the fact of Carl's death two hours later by phone. In his car, at a stop light, dead.

She had already told Amelia to go ahead with dinner. She did not like to phone again now, though she knew Amelia and Maud would be worrying. But probably they had finished what meal they felt inclined to eat. That hard thing, "Carl and I are going to be married," did not have to be said now. She picked up the phone and dialed.

Cole answered.

"Could you put Amelia on?" Ida asked.

"Yes, Miss Setworth, right away."

"Yes, Ida," Amelia said into the phone, almost at once.

"Carl's dead," Ida said. "A heart attack, in his car, at the last stop light."

"Cole's coming out to get you," Amelia said.

"I don't really think . . ." Ida began. Then she said simply, "All right."

"He'll be there in just a few minutes."

"All right."

Ida went out onto the terrace and sat down to wait. Dying was

163

the only proper surprise any of them had to offer each other, one they were in some measure prepared for. She would not be the center of grief for this one. No one but Rosemary knew that Ida had been thinking of marrying Carl, and now she would not have to say so. Cole would take her to the Larson house to be one of the several mourning friends, as she had been for Beatrice. At the warm edge where she had always been. The only step for her to take, when the time came, was into the grave. Her brief holiday from that idea had not made her unfamiliar with it. But he had already taken it. Dead. Carl was dead.

"Miss Setworth?"

"Hello, Cole. I'll be right there."

But he got out of the car and came to her, offering her his arm. She took it, simply glad of the boy, to whose support she had no more right than she had to special grief. Gifts.

"You're a good boy, Cole, to take care of so many old women."

"It's hard to believe," Cole said.

"Is it?" she asked vaguely. "Yes, for you, young."

"He was . . . such a nice man."

"Yes . . . a good man. Did you have a chance to eat dinner?"

"Yes," Cole said. "Agate's kept some for you."

"That's kind of her."

And Ida imagined that she could eat, there with Amelia and Maud, while they watched and said the ordinary things that people say.

"A younger man than Arthur," Maud recalled, for no purpose.

"At least his loneliness is over," Amelia said.

"I really thought he might marry again," Maud said.

"At his age?" Amelia asked. "Dying is probably an easier solution."

"You sound like your sister," Ida said, cutting into a piece of ham.

"We blur," Amelia said, "as we age. And die."

"No," Ida said.

"Don't be perverse, Ida," Maud said. "It's not a time to disagree."

"No," Ida said, to agree. Safe. Safe next to the grave. Innocent. "Still it was unkind of him."

Agate came in to clear away the others' coffee cups. Cole got up quickly to help her, in the look they exchanged something irritable, needful, outside the circle of mourning.

If you, that have grown old, were the first dead,
Neither catalpa tree nor scented lime
Should hear my living feet. . . .

Let new faces play what tricks they will
In the old rooms; night can outbalance day,
Our shadows rove the garden gravel still,
The living seem more shadowy than they.

Beatrice would quote, "Cast a cold eye on life, on death."
Nothing of that freezing comfort in Amelia's honesty. Dull, direct,
loving Amelia, who had hurt them more with her goodness, her
contentment, than they could hurt her with their witty discon-
tent. Carl, unkind, dead. He had sent roses to Beatrice's funeral.
Ida had forgotten that.

But never asked for love; should I ask that,
I shall be old indeed. . . .

Ida wanted to go home, wanted to read her Yeats, play an ancient unreal Maud Gonne against her as unreal grief, who had
never had a moment of beauty, had only taken comfort from the
pointlessness of it in her best and beautiful friend, but she must
sit and eat a while longer among the living ruins of Amelia and
Maud, their faces bloated with customary sorrow, bored with
death only a little less than with life.

"Dessert, Miss Setworth?" Agate asked.

"Yes, thank you." It would pass the time.

"He never could learn to count," Maud said.

"Did you speak about arrangements?" Amelia asked Ida.

"He has a brother who'll come to bury him."

"It should be a nice funeral," Maud said.

"I hope so," Amelia said. "He always did such a nice one."

Like Aunt Setworth's wine cake or old Mrs. Larson's quilts.
And Amelia would walk to the grave, even at the risk of toppling
into it, not with any sense of drama, simply of what was fitting.
Ida, too, only making whatever gesture was required with some
moment of sharp whimsy. For Maud, every funeral since she had
been a young woman was a rehearsal of Arthur's. Perhaps Carl
was wrong. It might be unkind to rob her of that.

✻

Rosemary, without stopping to telephone, drove directly from
her office to Ida Setworth's, and she found Ida, as she expected

to, sitting on her terrace reading Yeats.

"I didn't hear until this afternoon," Rosemary said.

"Rosemary!" Ida said, looking up surprised.

"It's horrible for you. It's . . ."

"Don't ever say anything to anyone, will you?" Ida asked with some urgency.

"I . . ." Rosemary, seeing the distress in Ida's face, could not admit that she had blurted out to Amelia, "But Ida was thinking of marrying him."

"It was never anything serious," Ida said. "A silly notion . . . silly, old fools . . ."

"That's not the truth," Rosemary said, surprised at her own rudeness.

"It will do," Ida said sharply. "Anything else is an embarrassment to people . . . to me."

"Oh, Ida, Ida . . ." Rosemary said, putting a tight arm around this old lady, her friend.

It was criminal, this denying of Carl Hollinger, this leaving of him now as a lonely old man instead of the lively, loving person he had been. To save face. Rosemary felt the stiff, brittle shoulders, the unbending head, and knew Ida was looking out through the orchard to the graves of almost everyone she had known and loved, where day after tomorrow Carl would be buried beside his wife. Criminal, this living need of dignity against the defenseless dead. Her father, a possible suicide for some perversity of her mother's pride. But Rosemary, in an angry pride of her own, had not buried her mother. Did it, after all, make any difference? Rosemary had thought so, but she had not loved her mother. In angry concern, she held to Ida, her sense of all these things blurred in protesting tears.

"It's nothing to cry about," Ida said, taking Rosemary's free hand. "We're all too old to cry about. Don't. Don't, Rosemary."

"I'm sorry," Rosemary said.

"You can't have had supper."

"I came right out."

"There must be something in the kitchen," Ida said. "Come along. We'll look and see."

As Rosemary took lettuce and celery from the refrigerator, opened a can for Ida, and then went to set the table, Ida didn't really seem distressed. She might even be in some way relieved of the burden of choice. No investment. Not like Rosemary's mother, whose had been a passionately bad investment, but important, all-important after Jimmy died. If it had been her father instead, who had had no investments either except perhaps in her, would he have been, like Ida, relieved? Or forced to suffer no more than embarrassment? Something ugly in it all, perhaps in everyone. No. Carl had grieved. Amelia, too. Why hadn't Rosemary the decency to? She had even refused to weep for her father. If Dina cracked herself up tomorrow in that new Volvo of hers, would Rosemary be glad that no one knew about their relationship? Would she? Probably. She hadn't even risked lively confessions. What was independence after all but a denial?

Rosemary sat at the dinner table with Ida, appalled at them both, unable to think of the most ordinary things to say.

"You have to learn not to bury all the dead again," Ida said, "each time."

That firmness startled Rosemary. "What do you mean?"

"Just that," Ida said. "Just that."

"You mean, Aunt Setworth . . ."

"And your brother and your father and your mother, my mother, my father . . ."

"Beatrice," Rosemary said.

Ida nodded, "Her, too."

Rosemary wanted to shout at Ida, wanted to make her confess, for surely she had loved Beatrice, been in love with her but had never said, never done anything. . . .

"Ida, I'm in love with Dina Pyros."

Ida sighed. "Yes, I supposed you were."

"Is it ridiculous? Is it so ridiculous?"

"Yes," Ida said. "It can't ever be anything else."

"I don't really care."

"No, neither did Carl. Even, in some way, he found it a comfort, like his religion, I suppose. I didn't, don't, but I did think I just might manage it . . . with him."

"But you really loved . . ."

"Nobody," Ida said. "Or I wouldn't have minded so much . . . even now."

"Did Beatrice ever . . .?"

"Leave our graves alone," Ida said, but gently. "Ride by."

XVI

PETER FALLIDON went to Harriet Jameson, aware that she would need comfort and shaken in his own sense of mortality, for, since he had known that Carl Hollinger was courting Ida Setworth, Peter no longer thought of him as one of those marked and waiting, his life already accomplished or not. He had become for Peter a man with a lively problem, in some comic measure similar to Peter's own, full of silly, hopeful needs that might be answered. A couple of embarrassed bachelors, out of the habit of amorous persuasion, focused upon women whose graces had nothing to do with being courted. That Carl could be so intent upon a future and then simply not have one put Peter's own in jeopardy. Allotted time: thirty years? five minutes? Any stop light.

"It's hard to think about it," Harriet said. "Not like the others. They let you see them dying . . . even Miss A now. I'll hate it when she dies, but she begins to behave in a way to make it clear, like someone gathering up gloves and saying 'thank you' with a mind already in some other place. With Mr. Hollinger, it's as shocking as if one . . . of us . . . ."

"Yes," Peter said.

"And Miss Setworth there where she's always been, all her life, among the dead. Why didn't she just go ahead and marry him? But maybe that would have been worse."

"How could it have been worse?" Peter asked, almost irritably.

"To be a widow, to have someone else's name. Oh, I don't know. Embarrassing?"

Peter rubbed his face.

"Would you like something? Coffee?"

"Do you really think Miss Larson is dying?"

"Really? Yes, I do. It may take a long time, like Miss B, but she's begun."

"There's so much she might still do," Peter said.

"I think she's tired of that idea."

"Tired?"

"People do just get tired."

"I suppose," Peter said.

"But not Mr. Hollinger. It seems like an accident. I hate that. To suffer some lower form of fate."

"It wasn't an accident. It was a heart attack."

"I know that."

"Harriet?"

She turned to him from her sense of insult at this death.

"Let's not wait," Peter said.

"For what?"

"Let's marry. There couldn't be more harm in it than not."

Harriet looked at him and shook her head. "Harm."

"I'm sorry. I didn't mean it to sound like that. I meant that, whatever happens, I'd rather have married . . . you."

"In retrospect," Harriet said quietly, trying out the idea.

"Now, too," Peter said earnestly. "I'd rather. I'd so much rather . . ."

"Than what?"

"Than not."

Harriet sat without answering, her thin arms prim against her body, her eyes focusing through glasses onto her own hands.

"Wouldn't you?" Peter asked.

"I don't know. I think we should . . . do other things first."

"Other things?"

"What other people do . . . go to bed."

"You're not serious!"

"What if you couldn't bear me? What if I turned out to be one of those people who . . ."

"Don't be silly," Peter said. "We aren't adolescent. That sort of thing doesn't matter. It . . ."

"Doesn't matter?"

"Harriet, one of the reasons I love you is that you're not the sort of woman who makes something cheap of . . ."

"Nobody is a sort of anything," Harriet said, flushing. "I don't think you want to make love to me. I don't think I'm attractive to you."

"That's not true."

"You never touch me. In books men touch women." Harriet's tone was not accusing. She was earnestly trying to explain.

"Harriet," Peter said, taking both her hands, "we're both of us shy people. It doesn't do any good to behave as if we're not. Or to behave as if we didn't care about the things we do care about. I couldn't try anything out. Not like that. There are lots of things that people do, in books and out of them, that aren't for people like us."

"People like us?"

"Born decent like you, or trying to be decent like me."

"I don't think I'm that old-fashioned."

"Of course you are," Peter said.

"Maybe what I'm afraid of is that you're a prude," Harriet said, an uncertain amusement in her eyes.

"I am."

"And want to marry me just now because . . . because you feel threatened . . . old. . . ."

"There's that," Peter agreed, in an honest amusement of his own.

"And forget how little you want to worry about anyone."

"Or see that there are worse things than worrying."

"What?"

"Not."

"Would you want . . . a church? That sort of thing?"

"That's up to you."

"An old-fashioned prude would," Harriet said. "Why does Mr. Hollinger have to be dead? Why?"

Peter could put an arm around her then, lined up as they were together on the couch.

"And tomorrow, at the funeral, we'll have to pretend we don't know about Miss Setworth, her secret kept by probably half the people in town so that she won't know that we know. Love: the terrible secret people are suspected of unless they're married.

Then one always suspects they don't. People must talk about us now. Are we guilty or not? Are we? If I died today, if you died today . . ."

"Don't, darling," Peter said.

"I'm worrying you."

"We can stop being secretive. We can marry."

"Yes, all right."

The kiss she offered him tasted of salt.

✳

"The only decent thing for us to do is get married," Cole said, loading up the garbage to take out while Agate washed the dishes. "I've thought about it."

Agate yawned.

"Agate?"

"The thing about kid's books and songs that's always bored me rigid is the repetition."

"I'm prepared to marry you."

"Circumcised, anointed, and the lot?"

"Can't you ever be serious, not even for a minute?"

"Sure. I can hold my breath that long, too, if you like."

"Great!"

"Or my nose."

"Why don't you want to marry me?" Cole demanded.

"Why should I want to?"

"Well, you can't just keep . . ." Cole began, but trailed off.

"Whoring around? Why not?"

"What if you keep the baby?"

"Who said I was going to keep it?"

"You did, sort of. I mean, that night, you said you might if . . ."

"Well, that's none of your business," Agate said, and turned her energy to a pan.

Cole stood by the kitchen door and watched her, seeing the full, closed beauty of her face.

"Sometimes," he said, "it feels to me as if the baby were mine."

Agate plunged the pan to the bottom of the sink and threw her head back, opening golden eyes to a sympathetic, cynical audience on the ceiling. "The only thing of yours I might give birth to is an Adam's apple, and it wouldn't come out of my navel, either."

171

"That isn't what I mean. I mean, when I lie beside you some-times, when I feel it move, it's as if . . ." but he didn't finish.

"Go dump *all* the garbage."

"It's wrong to give it away," Cole said fiercely. "Even an animal doesn't do that. Even an animal . . ."

"You don't want to live in an animal world," Agate said, tight but aloof from his challenge. "It makes you sick to your stomach."

"It is an animal world," Cole said bitterly. "This house is like a human farm, bloody with birth or slaughter, nothing in between."

"Say, that's not bad, only human husbandry and human hus-bands aren't exactly the same thing."

"You think I'm not man enough. You think . . ."

"You still want me to make up a sad story about Agate and the skinny faggot? You still want to be hung up about that? Saved by a bad woman from a fate worse than death. Stow it."

"That isn't what I meant."

"You don't know what you mean."

"Neither do you," Cole said, "You're always pretending. You're no better than I am. You don't know any more than I do."

"You're a backward pupil," Agate said, grinning.

"You're a cow!"

They heard Amelia's heavy footfall beyond the kitchen door and froze.

"Enough bad temper here for me to think there's going to be a thunder storm," Amelia said. "Are we going to have a game of hearts tonight or not?"

"Hearts," Cole said, "yes. I'm just dumping the garbage."

"Is he ever!" Agate agreed.

"We're all tired," Amelia said, swinging herself over to a kit-chen chair.

"Cole said you went to the grave."

"Yes," Amelia said. "It's what one does."

"Like walking to your own. It's no wonder you're tired."

"I wanted to say something to Ida. I couldn't think of anything. Sister would have sensed it. She would have told me or anyway stopped me from saying such awful things in the first place."

"What awful things?" Agate asked, drying her hands now.

"I said on the night he died it was an easier solution to his loneliness than marrying again. I hadn't any idea he and Ida were thinking of it. It never crossed my mind until Rosemary told me the next day."

"So? You're right."

"No, child, I'm not. I'm wrong."

"You might have married him. You might have gotten away with it. But Miss Setworth? Not in a million years."

"I?" Amelia asked. "What an extraordinary idea!"

"Why?"

"You don't have the sense of what it is to be as old as I am."

"It's only that you don't think in formalities, and you never did, did you? You just go ahead and love people."

"Ida's loved people," Amelia said. "She loved Sister."

"I wish I could have met your sister, just once."

"I always could walk to the grave," Amelia said. "Walking away from it is what I can't do. I haven't got anything to say except 'accept it.'"

"What's wrong with that?"

"It's no comfort to anyone, and it's not good advice since no one can accept it."

"Don't you?"

"No," Amelia said. "I haven't accepted anyone's death ever. I think I should, that's all."

Cole came back in with the empty garbage cans.

"Maybe you'd rather go to a movie," Amelia said.

"No, cards is fine," Cole said.

"Or down to Nick's."

"I've had enough of Nick's," Cole said.

"Peter told me the other day that you were an excellent dancer," Amelia said.

"Not really. I learned a couple of the steps is all."

"He said he was hoping he and Harriet would see you next week."

"I hope so. I might . . ."

"That's what I told him," Amelia said. "I told him you were working overtime quite a bit lately."

"It's not . . ."

"Oh, for Christ's sake, Cole!" Agate burst out. "What's so polite about all the lies? You don't want to see him, so you don't want to see him. Why not say so?"

"It isn't that I don't want to see him. I . . ."

"Let's play cards," Amelia said, hoisting herself up. "There will be rain before morning, and we'll all feel better."

Rosemary lay listening to it on the flat roof above her head, wondering if across town it had wakened Dina. Or had it wakened Ida? She would listen to it falling on the new grave, and probably there would be poems in her head. Rosemary caught a line for herself, "Though you should lean above me brokenhearted, I shall not care," fished out of her adolescence somewhere. She never had read the hard poems willingly, only the romantic nonsense that nourished the crushes she couldn't expose in any other way. Less good-looking, she would have been said to moon. As it was, her mother would complain that she was brooding again. Brooding. But hatching nothing. It had always been easier to be loved, to let someone else play the fool. Like her father. Like Beatrice. Like Ida. The loved ones, who never made the promises, who never admitted the needs, who could always say, when it was over, "It was never anything but nonsense anyway." After a week, after three months, after five years, it didn't matter how long. But finally when you could see the pattern repeating and repeating itself, the defense wore thin. If it really was never anything but nonsense from the beginning, then you couldn't just assign humiliation at the end without taking some share in it. Not time and again. Saying to Jane's back, "I'm sorry. I just can't be melodramatic about it. If you need to get away, you need to get away." And to the lack of reply. "I don't take emotional tests. There isn't any point." And finally Jane had said, as tired of her own anger as Rosemary was, "I know, love: you didn't ask to be born, you didn't ask to be beautiful, and you certainly didn't ask to be loved. It's only the rest of us who are fools like that. We never quite believe what a bad joke it is, on you, too." Beatrice's bad joke. Not having to ask. But with Dina, Rosemary had. She had said, like the fool, "I love you. I want *you* like that." What good had it done? None.

"I want to be melodramatic about this," Rosemary said at the tempoed roof. "I want to pass the test."

A fool, in such a circumstance, would then go ahead and be melodramtic, invent the test—and fail it, for what would Dina say but "A Greek, to marry well, must be a virgin" or "I don't sleep in front of people" or not reply at all, except with the skilled sexual answers she had used from the beginning against which Rosemary wanted no defense. Why couldn't she say to Dina, "I'm no more tired of being loved than breathing in. It's just that I

174

want to breathe out. Reach out, before it happens again, before I stand there uncommitted at the crisis, and let you walk away, or walk away myself. Dina, I do love you. I do want you like that."

Why not? Rosemary got out of bed and turned on a light. Two in the morning. She put on slacks and a shirt, combed her hair, but left her face alone. Then she looked for shoes. Why bother? Barefooted, bareheaded, barefaced fool. In the rain.

There was a light above the shop. Dina was awake. Rosemary got out of her car and let herself in quietly with the key Dina had given her. She moved easily past the shapes of furniture into the workroom and up the dark stairs. At the door she hesitated, about to knock, but that was not the stance she had chosen. She opened the door instead and stepped into the room. There, in the bright red dressing gown sitting on the couch was a woman Rosemary had never seen before.

"Who are you?" Rosemary asked, baffled.

"What is it?" Dina called from the kitchen.

"Somebody's here," the woman said, without moving. "Somebody's just walked in."

"Rosemary!"

She could have retreated with an ironic apology. It was in her to be able to. But she didn't.

"I couldn't sleep," she said easily. "I saw your light on. I thought maybe I'd have a drink. . . ."

"Of course," Dina said. "Come in."

"Thank you."

"Well, in that case . . ." said the woman on the couch getting up.

"Don't rush off without getting dressed just on my account," Rosemary said.

The woman nearly lost her balance in her drunken attempt at dignified withdrawal into the bedroom.

"Do you want your clothes?" Rosemary asked, lifting up the neat pile on the chair.

The woman snatched them from Rosemary and slammed the door. Rosemary turned to the kitchen where Dina was fixing her drink.

"I don't need half the bottle, darling," she said. "Are you drunk?"

"Yes," Dina said.

"Who is she?"

175

Dina shrugged.

"You don't even know her name?"

"Alice."

"Alice," Rosemary repeated.

"I didn't know you'd be coming over, or I . . ."

"A customer, is she? Interested in a rocking chair?"

"She's a friend of Sal's and Dolly's. We were all drinking."

"Oh."

"She's had a row with her husband and didn't want to go home right away."

"Oh."

They stood in the kitchen and waited until they heard the bedroom door slam again and the main door open.

"Aren't you going to see her out?" Rosemary asked. "It's pretty dark down there unless she's been here often and knows her way."

"She'll be all right," Dina said.

"Will she?"

Dina moved out into the living room and through her bedroom to the bathroom. When she came back, she had washed her face and combed her hair. Rosemary sat on the couch still warm from Dina's recent visitor.

"You're angry," Dina said.

"Wouldn't you be?"

"I?"

"Yes, if you came to my house and found someone else there."

"Like that? I would be . . . embarrassed."

"I was lying in bed," Rosemary said. "I was listening to the rain. I wondered if it had wakened you. I wondered if I came here how I would find you, awake or asleep. It was a silly idea. But then it was all nonsense, wasn't it, from the beginning?"

"Nonsense?"

"Yes," Rosemary said, hating her coolness, her irony, but choosing it. "A pleasant sort of nonsense."

"Not for me," Dina said. "You're my friend."

"I'm another one of your pieces of furniture!" Rosemary shouted, and this was out of character, something she hadn't ever done before. "An object! Just like Alice: stripped down, oiled a bit, polished . . ."

"I do what people want," Dina answered.

"George," Rosemary said, her voice still strained with unfamiliar volume. "Good old George. Why haven't I had a bill?"

Dina put her hand out, as if to shield herself from offensively bright light. Rosemary got up and walked over to her.

"Don't," Dina said.

"Don't what?"

"Don't."

Rosemary put her hand down on Dina's head and felt the dampness of her hair from its fresh combing, smelled the faint odor of sex and furniture oil that clung to her clothes.

"Take those off."

"What?"

"Take those off. They smell of her."

"I'm sorry," Dina said. "I'll change."

"There's no need to," Rosemary said. "I'm spending the night."

"Here?"

"Yes."

"I'm very drunk."

"I know you are," Rosemary said, as she began to unbutton Dina's shirt without any urgency. "I'll put you to bed. And don't tell me you don't sleep in front of people. There'll be no more slogans tonight."

Dina did not feel in control of what was happening. She only knew that Rosemary had seemed very angry and now was not, insistent instead that Dina get out of her clothes and go to bed. Dina wanted to cooperate. She wanted to do anything Rosemary wanted her to, but she couldn't seem to move. She tipped her head against Rosemary and put her hands on those familiar thighs.

"Come on," Rosemary was saying.

She must get out of her clothes. Rosemary didn't like the smell of her clothes.

"That's it. Oh, come on, darling. Come in here."

Dina was in bed now without her clothes and Rosemary was lying next to her, simply lying there. Dina closed her eyes, but the bed was falling like a stone through space. She turned, moaned, found herself in Rosemary's arms, falling, falling, but into a ground swell now, the sickness fading, the rocking nearly pleasant because it was real, but then Rosemary turned onto her.

"No," Dina said.

"Yes."

And Dina received before she closed against the pain of her own desire, shifted, sighed, and slept.

The rain continued for some time to keep Rosemary awake, for whether it was falling on a new grave or a new life she had no way of knowing.

XVII

"Someone should give a party for Peter and Harriet," Amelia said at the dining room table.

"Why?" Cole asked.

"It's done," Amelia answered simply, "and Harriet's mother can't really manage it."

"So you think you should," Agate said.

"I can have it catered."

Agate did not protest as she might have done a month earlier. She was heavily uncomfortable, and her temper, even with Amelia, was often short. There were too many chores for the strength she had and not enough distractions from the anxiety she increasingly felt for herself and the baby she was about to have. Sometimes she wanted to talk with Amelia, confront her with the knotted angers and doubts that Agate couldn't untangle for herself, never before having bothered. But Amelia was too old and too tired, and it was unlikely that she had any of the answers herself. She was really no more interested in analyzing and judging that Agate was. Which was all right on the way to the grave, but on the way to giving birth maybe some things should be understood. Just the other day Agate had been tempted to talk a little with Rosemary Hopwood, but they had established a bantering habit that was hard to break through. Also Agate sensed in Rosemary some trouble or preoccupation of her own, as if somewhere under that easy control she had been badly shaken. And exactly what was there to sort out? The question she really wanted to ask was why she had to go through with it, and who knew why? Maybe it wasn't a question at all but just a protest. Her life in these last months had been full of alternatives, all of them lousy. So much for free will.

"I wonder if we should hire chairs," Amelia was saying. "Our own haven't been out of the shed in five years."

"Let people stand up," Agate said. "They won't stay as long."

"Too many won't be able to stand up at all," Cole answered glumly.

"What are you going to do if it rains? Getting all of you old crocks up the stairs is no joke," Agate said.

"It won't rain," Amelia said. "If it does, the front room is large enough for forty."

"Forty!" Cole repeated.

"You're too young to be getting as antisocial as you are, Cole. Besides, I simply need your help."

"Oh, I'll help," Cole said hastily. "I didn't mean that."

Didn't he? he read in Agate's mocking eyebrows. Well, he knew he had to face Peter sooner or later, and a crowd of forty people was preferable to an hour across from him at the dinner table. With plenty of time to think about it, to plan what he would and what he wouldn't say, he could deal with the brief confrontations of greeting and saying good-bye. Peter himself had instructed Cole in just such formalities. The trick would be not to stammer into phony apologies, for the guiltier Cole felt about avoiding Peter the less he wanted to apologize. If anyone needed to be forgiven . . . but Cole turned away from that idea. The vision of Peter apologizing to him for anything whatever gave Cole hot flashes.

"We're all reluctant," Amelia said. "Peter and Harriet may be, too, but it needs to be done."

"Does it really?" Agate asked.

"Being engaged isn't a private matter," Amelia said, smiling. "Something like having a baby."

"Something."

"Do you always do what's expected?" Agate asked irritably.

"If I can," Amelia said.

"You don't have to be so superior about it," Cole said crossly to Agate. "You work just as hard to do what's unexpected."

"Children, children," Amelia said, knowing it was better for them to bicker through these last hard weeks of Cole's job and Agate's pregnancy than to sulk, but sulking would have been easier on her.

*

It turned out to be an unusually hot day, but in the large, old garden there was shade for twice again the number of people who had been invited. Agate and Cole were stationed at the side path to direct people around the house, through the rose garden, and out onto the lawn, the deepest shade brilliant with begonias.

Ida Setworth and Maud Montgomery were among the first to arrive, never having been able to break themselves of the old-fashioned courtesy of being on time. Peter, Harriet, and Harriet's mother were right behind them, and the cluster of people made it easier than he had anticipated for Cole to greet Peter, but the tic still jumped frantically in his cheek.

"Congratulations," was all he needed to say, and he managed that.

Agate, knowing her size and presence were a scandal to Mrs. Montgomery, went out of her way to be helpful about the uncertain footing for the trifocaled old lady.

"But someone should be looking after *you*," Maud protested.

Agate kept herself from responding by concentrating on the variety of replies that were impossible, the wickedest one of which would have been "How's Arthur?"

What began to look like a pensioners' tea gradually became something more of a community as Harriet's sister and brother arrived with their families, along with several neatly middle-aged women with accustomed husbands, who had probably gone to school with Harriet. Cole, who seemed to know most of them, did the greeting and directing, leaving Agate to observe and occasionally gesture.

Cole, so occupied, did not see Feller and Grace Hill get out of their car, but Grace saw him and stopped in mid-stride.

"I can't," she said to Feller. "I can't go through with it."

"Yes you can," Feller said quietly. "We don't have to stay more than a few minutes."

"I can't."

Agate watched them, not knowing who they were, only seeing

181

the hard distress in a woman who should have been—but somehow was not—attractive, the uncertain concern in her very tired husband. "Cole?" she called quietly. "Cole?"

Cole turned, saw the Hills, and felt both kneecaps dissolve. He wanted to say to Agate just what Grace was saying to Feller, but he couldn't. He had not known they were coming. Unlike his encounter with Peter, which he had had time to plan, he had simply not thought about Grace Hill. But there she was, not fifteen yards away, head sideways like a shying horse. Could he have hit such a woman?

"I'll wait in the car," Grace said. "I'm sorry. I'll just wait in the car."

"All right," Feller said, and he turned back with her.

"What's the matter?" Agate asked Cole.

"Mrs. Hill hasn't been well," he said. "Maybe she . . ."

"Shouldn't you offer to help?"

"I don't know."

"Go on. Don't stand there out to lunch. Maybe she needs a drink of water with her tranquilizer or something."

He didn't want to move. If Grace Hill couldn't face it, why should he? But it must look odd to Agate to have him just standing there doing nothing. Grace Hill was a sick woman. Dina had explained that.

"I'll be right back," he said and walked over to the Hills' car quickly before he could change his mind. "Is there something I can do?"

"My wife doesn't feel very well," Feller said. "She thought she'd better just stay in the car."

"Could I get you something to drink, Mrs. Hill?" Cole asked, forcing himself to look directly at her. "Or would you like to come into the house? It's awfully hot here in the drive."

"No," she said abruptly and turned away.

"There are lots of chairs in the shade," Cole persisted, not knowing why he did.

Grace looked at her husband.

"Don't you want to just try it?"

"Oh, all right! There's no point in making all this fuss."

She got out of the car again, dropping her purse. Cole picked it up and handed it to her. She looked at him for an ironic moment and then said, without rancor, "Thank you."

"It's just around the house here. I'll show you," Cole said, leading the way.

"I haven't been in this garden since I was a kid," Feller said to his wife, partly to distract her but also to ease a bitter nervousness of his own.

As they rounded the house, Grace stopped again but this time simply to admire. "What roses! Look at those trees."

"This garden and the Montgomerys' are about the only ones left," Feller said.

"Cousin A's right over here," Cole said, still directing them.

"Here are Mr. and Mrs. Hill."

Amelia, sitting in one of the old covered swings at the edge of the shade, looked up and smiled. "How good of you both to come. Mrs. Hill, sit here with me and let's get acquainted."

At the front of the house, Agate was greeting Rosemary Hopwood.

"I'm badly late."

"The last of the wheel chairs has been rented," Agate said. "You'll have to get there on your own two feet."

"Shouldn't you be getting off yours?"

"Probably. Cole will be back in a minute, and he can deal with any stragglers. He just had to drag one woman from her car and take her to the garden by force."

"Who?"

"I don't know."

Cole appeared from around the house.

"Who was that woman, Cole?" Agate asked.

"Mrs. Hill."

"Oh," Rosemary said.

"Hello, Miss Hopwood."

"Hello, Cole. Just about everyone here?"

"I think so. Well, I haven't seen Dina."

"She's not coming," Rosemary said.

"Why not?" Cole asked, obviously disappointed.

"She didn't say," Rosemary answered. "You'd better come sit down, Agate."

"Yes, go ahead," Cole said. "I'll just wait a few more minutes and be along."

Ida Setworth, resting a moment from a strained conversation with old Judge Howard, who was deaf, watched Agate and Rosemary come round the house. Anyone next to Agate would fall in the shadow of life. She had the height and carriage to make the size of her belly somehow marvelous, and those golden eyes in her golden face were remarkable. Beside her, Rosemary did not have even an attendant charm. She looked tired, ill, old. Even Harriet, who was walking over to greet them, seemed young and pretty next to Rosemary, though there couldn't be many years' difference.

"Are you being looked after, Miss Setworth?" Peter asked.

"Yes, thank you. I was just thinking how pretty Harriet looks today."

"Yes, doesn't she?" Peter sat down next to Ida, wishing there were something he could say or do, understanding that there was not.

"Was Dina invited?" Ida asked, watching Rosemary.

"Oh yes," Peter said. "She was on everyone's list. I don't see her though. That's odd."

Rosemary was greeting Amelia. "I'm sorry I was late. It's a wonderful thing to see this garden full of people again. Nothing could have made Harriet happier."

"She's a happy sort of person," Amelia said with approval.

Rosemary smiled, but the sweat gathered at her hairline, one drop quickly escaping past her ear. She reached for a handkerchief.

"Just the heat?" Amelia asked, concerned.

"No," Rosemary said with a wry smile.

"I hope you're getting pills then. The blessing nowadays is that you don't have to be that uncomfortable."

Cole came up to Amelia and Rosemary. "I phoned Dina. She's just sitting in the shop. I told her to lock up and come along."

"I hope she said she would," Amelia said.

"She said she'd see."

"Excuse me," Rosemary said. "I must speak to Ida."

Cole glanced at her with alert uncertainty as she left. "Anything wrong?"

"No, dear," Amelia said. "Nothing but change of life."

Cole knew he was blushing and hated it. He was not embarrassed. He was irritated. It seemed to him that women always had some urgently important physiological excuse for everything from sweating to slander. He just had to stand, humiliated, in the tics and twinges of his own system, without periods, pregnancies, changes to excuse his terrors. It wasn't fair.

Across the lawn Peter stood as Rosemary approached, easy in his manners, which was what Cole had first envied and admired in him. A kind invulnerability. Fake. Cole could have forgiven Peter even that. Or thought he could. It was Peter's apparent ability to cover the whole thing up that made Cole angry. He had even somehow been able to influence Feller and Grace Hill so that statements were retracted or at least never made public. And now, to ensure his safety, he was marrying Harriet. Perhaps that was why Dina had not come. She had helped to whitewash him herself, but she obviously couldn't stomach this final step of correction. Cole's indignation only faltered at what should have happened instead. He didn't want Peter humiliated, fired, or jailed. It wasn't that. He wanted only some sign, some gesture ... of guilt? If Peter was guilty, admitted his guilt, the burden of Cole's own fantasy guilts would be more bearable, or at least he thought so. Was that the temptation he had had to read Cousin B's diaries? If even such a woman as that could be shown to have a nervous stomach or secret lust, life might be easier. But Cole didn't want communal shame, even with its comforts. That's what he had struck out against: the unbearable, easy, desired knowledge of Grace Hill's announcement. Still, he hated Peter's way out, and he was ashamed of Dina a little, too. Why did she have to go even so far as to pretend she believed nothing was wrong?

"Cole?"

"Yes, Harriet," he answered out of his distraction, embarrassed again.

"Are you all right?"

"All right? Yes, yes, I'm fine."

"I feel as if I'd lost track of you this summer," Harriet said. Cole, against his resolves, began to stammer the old excuses.

"Yes, I know," Harriet said. "I understand. But it isn't just that, is it? You know, Peter would very much like to talk with you and he simply hasn't had a chance. Don't wait too long to let him, will you? He cares a great deal about you, and he wouldn't want some sort of misunderstanding to settle between you."

"Peter hasn't anything to explain to me," Cole said, in a confused sense of loyalty and fear.

"I think he does. I know he wants to. Sometime give him a chance."

She had to turn away then to speak with Feller and Grace Hill, who were leaving after what Feller considered a decent interval.

He wondered, as he walked back around the house with his wife and Harriet Jameson, if it would be more difficult for him or for Grace to admit that it had been a pleasant hour. They had made such a habit over the years of having no such thing to admit.

Harriet, leading the way, was the first to encounter Dina, standing uncertainly in the front drive in a violet linen dress.

"I'm so glad you're here, Dina," Harriet said. "Do you know the Hills? Of course you do. Everyone knows everyone."

"I didn't know you owned a dress," Grace Hill said.

"We haven't really met," Feller said quickly. "Peter tells me you're as interested as I am in the downtown development plan he's working on."

"Yes," Dina said.

"When it gets to the talking stage, I hope you'll come over to the house one evening. A thing of this sort profits by some off-the-record discussion early on."

"I'd like to."

"Good," Feller said, turning Grace firmly toward their car. "Thank you again, Harriet. You know how pleased we are for you both."

Harriet, embarrassed by Grace Hill, though her own surprise at Dina's dress was acute, waved them off quickly and walked with Dina back into the garden.

"I didn't know you were interested in real estate."

"I have a piece of property next to Mr. Hill's . . . parking lot."

"How interesting."

"It could be," Dina said, her senses suddenly distracted by the roses.

At the edge of the lawn she hesitated, trying to collect the reasons for her so recently changed resolution, for she really had had no intention of being here. What she hadn't realized was that she should then have refused. Cole's phone call was a rebuke which she accepted. She did not want to offend Miss A or Peter Fallidon or Harriet Jameson, no matter how awkward her position would be. So she had put on the dress she had bought so long ago to meet Peter, and here she was, faced with this gathering of friends to celebrate an engagement she did not pretend to understand, and she was simply, genuinely frightened.

"Dina!" Peter called and crossed to her.

Cole saw her at the same moment, and even Peter's intention of greeting her could not postpone his own.

"That woman is Dina Pyros?" Agate asked, near Miss A to see that she was all right and to take some rest herself.

"Yes," Amelia answered.

"I thought she was supposed to be some sort of character in boots and trousers."

"Today she's a guest," Amelia said, not quite taking in the significance of her own remark.

Rosemary, still sitting with Ida, looked down at her own hands.

"It's silly to say I wouldn't have recognized her," Ida said. "Hadn't you better join her? She may need you."

But Dina already had the company of Cole, Peter, and Harriet as she crossed the lawn to greet Miss A. A stranger, observing the party, might even have supposed that this was finally the guest of honor not only from the attention given her but from her own manner, dignified and careful in the unaccustomed clothes, in her fear.

It was Cole who remembered to introduce Agate, out of his guilt at never having taken her to either George's or Nick's. Dina greeted the very pregnant and handsome young Agate with honoring and distant envy which seemed nothing more than kindness to those around them. Agate, who refused to feel awed by anyone, stood for a shy moment and then excused herself to go into the house.

Rosemary, watching Agate leave, saw her own excuse.

"I wonder if she's all right."

Ida no more than nodded to Rosemary's departure. Since it was so rarely possible to care for whom one cared about, it was fortunate that there were always a number of substitutes. Ida did not have to move for anyone. Then she saw that Maud Montgomery was also sitting by herself in the shade. Ida raised herself up and walked over to her old friend.

"Don't you think it's a little peculiar to invite that young woman to a party of this sort?" Maud asked at once.

"Didn't you know she'd bought the three parking lots next to the Hill property?" Ida asked.

"*She* did?"

"Some time ago," Ida said.

"This town is changing out of all recognition," Maud said, looking about the garden, familiar to her since childhood, at faces she had known most of their lives if not of hers. "Some things I find it better simply not to tell Arthur."

"How is Arthur?" Ida asked.

*

"Are you all right, Agate?"

"In great shape," Agate answered, out of the way of the caterers in Amelia's chair in the library, a can of beer beside her.

"It's hot," Rosemary said.

"You want one of these?"

"No, I've had more than enough punch."

"It hasn't anything much in it," Agate said.

They sat in an easy silence for some time, glad of the cool escape, Agate too preoccupied with physical discomfort to care what happened next, but gradually she was aware of Rosemary's own distance.

"Is anything the matter with you?" Agate asked.

"Me? No."

"Who is Dina Pyros anyway?"

"Dina?" Rosemary asked. "What do you mean?"

"I don't know," Agate said. "The way Cole talked about her, I thought she was a sort of a town character, driving around in a beat-up truck."

"Yes, well, she's a furniture dealer . . . antiques."

"She's . . . enviable," Agate said.

"Why do you say that?"

"Oh, I don't know. Imagine pulling off that sort of entrance at such a raggedy little party. And she's got an incredible face. Don't you think so?"

"Yes," Rosemary said. "But so do you."

"Oh well, so do you, if we're handing out morale raisers, and neither one of you is pregnant, which is enviable in itself."

Rosemary didn't answer.

"Social workers aren't supposed to go darkly sensitive all of a sudden."

"Sorry," Rosemary said, getting up.

"Don't dash off," Agate said. "Are you heartbroken over Harriet's carrying off the handsome bank manager . . . or what?"

"In ten years or so I suppose people are going to tell you things like that," Rosemary said, smiling.

"They do now. You're one of the few cool hold-outs."

"A bond between us," Rosemary said.

188

"You can see my big secret before your very eyes," Agate said. "I must go."

Agate watched her from the window. An odd woman whom she'd come to like against her own first judgment, which was that Rosemary Hopwood was cold. Miss A didn't like her. No, that wasn't really true. Rosemary troubled the old lady. Agate didn't know why. They were saying good-bye now, familiarly affectionate. Then, as Rosemary turned to leave, Dina Pyros moved away from the others and spoke to her, standing curiously close for all the space there was. Rosemary listened, then shook her head without looking up, but Dina walked along with her until they got to the roses.

Across the lawn, the old ones were getting ready to leave. Agate couldn't let Maud Montgomery out of the garden without another helping hand. She came down the back steps and out into the group just in time to hear Mrs. Montgomery's parting comment.

"A year ago this wouldn't have been a surprise, but by now we'd just about given up hope."

"Thank you," Harriet said with a smile that was irretrievably sweet.

Cole closed in on Mrs. Montgomery from one side, Agate from the other, and together they jolted her with as much show of accident as they could out of the garden while Amelia and Harriet exchanged amused glances.

"There doesn't have to be any hope for our generation," Ida Setworth said. "It's a good thing there's so much for yours."

Peter leaned over and kissed her on the cheek, realizing that from now on until they died he would be kissing these old ladies good-bye as if he had been born to them.

XVIII

AGATE WOKE ALONE in a dark center of night, thinking at first she
had felt pain. She waited. The child in her was so still it might
no longer even be alive, a thought so suddenly horrifying that
next to it giving birth took on pure value.

"Wake up, little monster," Agate said softly, shifting her weight,
her hands against her belly, and she felt a movement that was not
her own. "That's better."

What had wakened her then? If she was in the beginning of
labor, it might be some time before the next pain, spasm, whatever it was. Better to go back to sleep. But she was anxious and
alert, as if she had been given some warning. Turning on a light,
she sat up awkwardly. Then she waited, as if for some message,
sound, sign. Silly. But she wasn't at all sleepy. Read. There was
nothing to read. She had been so tired in these last weeks that
she had stopped keeping a book beside her bed. Perhaps she
should go downstairs, get a book, or make herself a cup of hot
soup. But she might waken Cole, who slept these days as if he
were on bomb alert. Not for the first time she regretted burning
those last diaries. Just the thing for a time like this: a moth-eaten
scandal or two, a high-minded or seedy little confession. No, she
didn't really regret it. Nobody, dead or alive, should pain the
world with her invented or real motives, judgments, fears. Enough
to have to put up with what people actually did or said. Somebody like Maud Montgomery didn't need a diary. Had Beatrice

Larson, as her sister insisted, been a tactful women? And self-contained? Those mean little diaries used as a harmless dumping ground? Rosemary Hopwood reminded Miss A of Beatrice. Was that why? All that cool good humor being listed like a long, unpaid bill that someone would have to receive in the end. Those were their problems. Agate had her own bill about to come in . . . somebody's anyway. She knew what her mother would say: "This is the price of our permissiveness" . . . no, "trust." Her father? Surely, even without her help, he would have contrived an elaborate way not to know. He didn't believe in creditors, particularly if they were his own children. "The woman pays," Agate said, and snorted. Why think of it like that at all? "Not a debt at all," Rosemary would have said. "Not a punishment. A responsibility" . . . but in her view someone else's, as soon as Agate got on with the job of delivering it. Like milk, or the paper. "I'm the baby girl." Somebody had put an order out in a bottle at the back door. What time was it? Quarter to three. She turned out the light and lay down again, her body as comfortable as she could expect it to be. Why then was she so wide awake and apprehensive?

"You're the diary of my misspent youth," Agate said to her hard house of a belly. "Against the law to get rid of you. Shouldn't have written you in the first place. A couple of bitches, B and me."

A boy or a girl? If she was to give it up—and, with reservations, she had decided to—she was not to think about that. People shouldn't have sex and ego things about their kids anyway, even keeping them.

It wasn't a pain. It was a sound. No sound that indistinct could have wakened her, but why should it even now send a shock of adrenalin through her system? This old house cracked and heaved like a dyspeptic sleeper every night. Was Cole up? She strained in listening and heard nothing. Could she recall it? Something being moved.

Agate got out of bed and started to turn on her light, then decided against it. She wasn't really afraid of burglars, but she was afraid of the sound itself, and, if she was going to locate it, she wanted to be the subject rather than the object of discovery.

In the front upstairs hall there was no sound from Cole's room, his door closed. Miss A's door was open, but she often left it so. Agate did not want to turn on the hall light, though it was difficult to see anything. If she could just look into the room, check Miss A, perhaps that would be all that was necessary. Passing the open bathroom door, Agate nearly tripped on the old slippered foot, extended into the dark hall. A scream died in her chest. Fallen. The old lady had fallen.

"Miss A?" she called softly, as she reached around to turn on the bathroom light.

Amelia Larson, lying on her back, stirred.

"Miss A?"

Her eyes opened, and she said something very softly. Agate knelt down beside her with hardly space for her bulk of body between where Miss A lay and the tub.

"I've fallen," Amelia said again.

"How long have you been here?" Agate asked, a stupid question, which Amelia didn't try to answer. "It's all right. You'll be all right."

Agate wanted to lift Amelia Larson into her arms, but even if she had been able to, she had the sense to know she must not move her. Could she at least put something under Miss A's head? Better not. Cover her. That she could do. Why hadn't Cole awakened?

"Cole! Cole!"

His door opened and he stood blind with sleep, staring at her.

"Miss A's fallen in the bathroom. Call the doctor. Call an ambulance."

He pressed his forehead, brushing the fine hair away, and then simply nodded.

"You can phone from her room," Agate said sharply, as he started down the stairs.

"The numbers are in the library."

"Oh."

Agate went into Miss A's room herself and pulled a blanket off the bed. Back in the bathroom, she covered the old shapeless body, knowing the cold was underneath her, unable to do anything about that.

"How do you feel?"

Again she couldn't hear until she moved down beside Amelia.

"Broken."

"Where?"

"Hip? Leg?"

"Your good one?"

Amelia nodded slightly.

"Have you hurt your head?"

"I don't know," was the soft answer.

"Cole's calling for the doctor now. It won't be long."

Agate pulled the bathmat from the side of the tub and sat down on it right next to Miss A. Then she took the hand that lay quiet on the floor.

"Careful of the baby," Amelia said.

"Sure."

"You're a good child," Amelia said.

"Don't talk. Rest."

Cole came back up the stairs on the run. "The ambulance is on its way," he called and then arrived at the door of the bathroom. There lay Cousin A, under a blanket like a corpse ready to be pitched into the sea, and beside her in a short, transparent nightgown Agate sat, primal, exposed, an arthritic old hand in hers. The sight fixed him in a calm insanity. "I'll stay with her while you get dressed."

Agate looked down at herself. He was right. She couldn't really greet the emergency men like this, but she didn't want to leave Miss A. She didn't want to move.

"Is she ... ?"

"Broken her hip, she thinks," Agate said. "We mustn't move her at all."

"No."

Agate got up clumsily, taking the hand Cole offered. When she had gone, he took her place and the hand she had left.

"Good children," was all Amelia said to him, but even in the faintness of her voice there was a reassuring lucidity.

"They'll be here soon," Cole said.

Soon. There was pain, but it was distant, and her head seemed clear enough though she couldn't remember exactly how she had fallen and didn't know how long she had been lying there. She did not think she had called out to anyone. Then she remembered the word "Sister" and knew she had not spoken it. No use in it, aloud. Still an absolute comfort. She had no hallucination now. She knew first Agate had sat beside her, taking her hand, and now she was clearly aware of Cole, his grasp gentle rather than limp, peculiarly calm. The children. She had had so many of them over the years, wanting them as some people had wanted babies. The children having them, those were hers, and for the last year Cole, who was not all that different from the girls in what he must learn of himself and recognize.

"Now you go change," she heard Agate say. .

"Don't sit on the floor again. It isn't good for you."

The downstairs bell rang, and Agate went to it. Alone for a moment, Amelia felt the fear of being moved. The distant, new pain she hadn't yet really become acquainted with would land and command all the others. She did not want to cry out.

Two men stood above her, perplexed. There was not room to set a stretcher down beside her. There was not even room for gentle purchase. They spoke briefly like movers with an awkward piece of furniture, decided, and began.

Her cry was sharp, involuntary.

"Be gentle with her!" Cole commanded angrily.

"They can't help it," Agate said, a hand on his arm.

With their next maneuver, Amelia was unconscious.

❋

"Maud Montgomery has called the head office, the church, the mayor," Rosemary said tiredly, drinking after-dinner coffee with Cole and Agate in the library. "You can't stay here alone while Amelia's in the hospital."

"It's just plain stupid!" Cole said.

"I agree."

"Somebody's got to look after the house," Agate said. "I can't just go back to the hostel."

"No. I think the solution is to get somebody else to move in," Rosemary said.

"Who?" Cole asked.

"Well, you have a number of volunteers."

"I hope Mrs. Montgomery isn't top of the list," Agate said.

"Fortunately, she has Arthur. Peter would be glad to. Harriet's offered. Dina said she'd come. And I'd be glad to."

"We could have a real house party," Agate said.

"I'm going to leave you two to discuss it," Rosemary said. "Let me know in the morning."

"Look," Cole said, "it would be an awful inconvenience to any of you. Can't you just *say* somebody's here?"

"Amelia's not going to be out of the hospital for months,"

194

Rosemary said. "It might be just as well to have somebody else here for when Agate has the baby."

"Oh Christ!" Agate said.

"We don't need any help with that," Cole said.

"Listen to him! 'We' he says!"

"I just meant I could get you to the hospital."

"Maybe we should all just move to the hospital right now," Agate said.

"I really do think the simplest solution is to let one of us move in for this last couple of weeks. It wouldn't be any problem. Talk about it tonight."

Rosemary got up to leave.

"Would you suggest secret ballots?" Agate asked.

"I'd suggest you decide who would be the least nuisance to you. Good night."

But both Agate and Cole showed Rosemary to the door, and then Cole followed her out to her car.

"I'm sorry, Cole."

"Oh, I know," he said. "It can't be helped. Agate will phone you in the morning."

Cole turned back as tiredly as a husband accustomed to arguments before any decision could be made. Agate could so easily be perverse now, as the old ladies would say, "her time was near." Agate was perverse anyway. But he would not hear of Peter in the house, and, if Harriet came, they couldn't keep Peter away. The choice, therefore, was between Miss Hopwood, "Rosemary" as he was now to call her, and Dina. Wouldn't it be a little difficult to ask anyone but Miss Hopwood since she was there to offer? But Agate might feel pretty strongly about having her social worker hovering over these last couple of weeks. Dina was the only possible solution.

"Let's ask Dina," Cole said, as he came back into the house.

"Dina?" Agate answered in surprise.

"Why not?"

"Well, I don't really know her," Agate said. "I just met her that once at the party. Peter or Harriet . . ."

"I don't want either of them."

"Well, I'm not wild about having a social worker in personal attendance!"

"I knew it! I knew it! Even a simple thing like this, and you've got to make a big thing out of it."

"Who's making a big thing?" Agate demanded. "I'm being sweet reason itself."

"As usual!"

"All right," Agate said quietly. They had both been through more in the last twenty-four hours than they had strength for, and she didn't feel much sorrier for herself than she did for Cole. It was time to try to be sensible. "I know you've got a thing about Peter; so no Peter. But why not Harriet? She knows the house. She's easy to get along with."

"You can't very well tell Peter he can't come to see her."

"Would that be so awful?"

"Yes," Cole said.

"Well, I suppose it has to be Rosemary then."

"What's the matter with Dina?"

"I don't know her," Agate said.

"You'd get to know her. You'd like her. I don't want you to have somebody in the house you don't want to have."

"The person who ought to come, the person Miss A would feel easy about, is Harriet," Agate said. "We wouldn't have to have Peter for dinner. Nobody would expect that anyway."

Cole stared for a moment, not answering.

"Cole?"

"That's true," Cole said finally, sighing.

"And if he tries to rape you, I'll . . ."

"That's not funny!"

"Isn't it? Are you really afraid of him?"

"Of course not," Cole said.

"What is it about him, anyway?"

"It's too dumb to talk about."

"That hasn't stopped you before," Agate said, rude but coaxing.

"I'm afraid he's . . . dishonest."

"Embezzling?" Agate asked with real interest.

Cole shook his head impatiently. "Maybe he isn't really in love with Harriet. Maybe he's marrying her just as a convenience."

"Why do you think that?"

"I don't know," Cole said. "It's probably dumb. Shall I call Harriet?"

"Yes," Agate said. "Then I'll call Rosemary tonight and let her know it's all settled. You don't really mind, do you?"

"No," Cole said. "You're right."

✳

Whether Harriet and Peter were aware of Cole's embarrassment and arranged to see each other away from the house, or whether they simply wanted the privacy, Agate couldn't tell. All she knew was that she did not have to run the interference she had promised herself she would, once Cole had agreed to Harriet. In fact, Agate's role in the house changed markedly with Harriet's arrival. From having free run and almost complete control of the house, she became instead the center of kindly attentions, for Harriet accepted her job less as a chaperone than as some kind of tending mother, not in the wisdom that she thought of as Miss A's province but in the ordinary tasks of the day.

"No more ironing for you now," she would say, moving Agate away from the board, or, "Tonight I'm coming home to cook dinner."

Agate at first tried to protest. She was, she pointed out, being paid to do what she was doing. But her own real fatigue, combined with the obvious pleasure Harriet took in moving about the kitchen or library doing proprietary little jobs, made her give in to Harriet more comfortably than she ever would have to Miss A.

"You love this house, don't you?" Agate said one evening as they sat together with books, free of Cole, who was out at a movie.

"Yes," Harriet said. "I know it's not as practical as some of the new ones, but when Peter and I get around to buying a house, I hope we can find an old one . . . not grand like this, of course, but with space, with high ceilings, with the sense that people have really lived in it before us."

"Does Peter like that sort of thing, too?"

"Yes," Harriet said and smiled. "Isn't that lucky?"

Agate nodded and turned back to her book.

"What kind of a house do you want?" Harriet asked. "I mean . . ."

"When I grow up?"

"It sounded like that, didn't it?" Harriet said apologetically, "I suppose I really just mean I talk too much about Peter and me."

197

"Why not?"

"Happiness can probably be just as much of a bore as ailments and miseries . . . without the excuse."

Agate shook her head. "I like you happy. Not having to work at it. Miss A says, 'Harriet's got a happy disposition.'"

"You sound just like her."

"I've practiced."

"Shall I tell you something dreadful?" Harriet asked. "I used to envy people so who could live here that I used to think I might get pregnant just for the excuse."

"It's a better reason than most people have."

Harriet did not know how to go on, to encourage Agate to talk about herself. Surely she must, in these last days, be frightened. Miss A had said, in the hospital this afternoon, "Do what you can for her. She doesn't really quite want to give the baby up. It's a hard time for her." Harriet, in useless sympathy, had tried to think of something which might really help Agate. Even for a wild hour she had thought of suggesting to Peter that they adopt the baby. The idea wasn't all that far-fetched, but the timing was impossible. They couldn't very well apply for a baby before they were even married, and, because they knew Agate, the authorities wouldn't hear of it anyway. But surely there was something Harriet could do aside from taking some of the work and responsibility away from Agate. If Rosemary had been here, they would probably have had long, useful talks. Harriet didn't have that kind of training, and there was no use pretending she had any compensating experience. She was as hopelessly bookish about unmarried pregnant girls as she was about falling in love and marrying.

"Don't perch," Agate said suddenly.

"Perch?"

"Talk to me about what clothes you're going to buy. What china are all the old gals going to give you? Distract me."

"Do you know, I wish I could wear bright colors the way you do? I'm awfully tired of being drab, but somehow I don't think I could manage them."

"Get Peter the bright colors," Agate said. "What you want to be is subtle. I couldn't ever get away with that."

"But I don't really know how."

When Cole came home, he found the two women busy over sketches Agate was making of Harriet's trousseau. Harriet's light, young laugh seemed to him a little silly, but he was glad that Agate had found something to absorb her attention. The vacancies she had begun to fall into since Cousin A had gone troubled him much more than her edgy temper and rudeness had done.

"Was it a good movie? Should Peter and I go?"

"Just a movie," Cole said. "That's a nice one. I like that one." Agate glanced up at him.

"Can I get anybody else a drink?" he asked.

"Beer," Agate said.

"You shouldn't be drinking so much beer," Cole said.

"He'd make a great male nurse," Agate said.

"Why don't I make us all some tea?" Harriet suggested. "Or better still, Larson hot chocolate."

She was on her feet and gone before either could refuse.

"Everything okay?" Cole asked, putting a hand on Agate's shoulder.

"Did you see her tonight?"

"Yes, for a few minutes."

"How is she?"

Cole shrugged.

"I'm glad you saw her."

"I thought maybe we could go over together tomorrow night," Cole said.

"Well . . ."

"She'd like to see you. Are you afraid to go to the hospital, Agate?"

"Scared shitless," Agate said quietly. "So let's not talk about it. Let's just be good kids and drink our hot chocolate."

XIX

THE SENTENCE, like a fish rising to the bait every time Rosemary did or saw anything to remind her of Dina, came now as she tipped the watering can to the fuchsias: "That is not to be forgiven." Passive, impassive, as without identity as Dina's eyes, waking. That sentence and nothing more. All the rhetoric it might have introduced, Rosemary had to invent for herself afterward, out of scraps of Dina's conversation or out of her own talent to provide herself with something hysterically angry, sometimes calmly detached and technical, but in no matter what mood with no matter what evidence, she finally arrived again at the only thing that had actually been said: "That is not to be forgiven." Until the afternoon of Amelia's party when Rosemary had called by at the shop, as if casually, to see if Dina would come along with her.

"I don't go to things like that," back turned, boots bracing a bottle of beer, boys watching.

Instead of making the scene she had rehearsed in so many styles, Rosemary had walked away, driven away, light-headed with anger, and was angry still when Dina walked into the garden. Then, at the end, Dina had turned to her.

"I didn't realize it was expected of me," she said.

"No," Rosemary agreed.

"I'm sorry."

"For?"

"Would you have supper . . . at Nick's?"

"No," Rosemary said. "I don't go to places like Nick's."

What difference did it make that she had said such a thing? Not to be forgiven offered a certain freedom, surely, a license for some kinds of decorous cruelty. But she did not like the quick glimpse she had had of Dina's face.

"What do you expect?" Rosemary asked quietly of the flowers. "What do you expect?"

There the huge space opened between loving and wanting to love, between fact and fantasy. Rosemary knew perfectly well what Dina expected: a friendship, immune to inconvenience or threat. But that was a fantasy. Dina had to realize also what was expected. She couldn't live out her life in that kind of ignorance. In that kind of brutality. "A Greek, to marry well . . ." "For you it's different. You are a widow." A widow!

"I couldn't have been expected to go on with that," she said. "I simply couldn't."

> Only the dead can be forgiven;
> But when I think of that my tongue's a stone.

A stone.

Sweating. Why hadn't she gone to Nick's? Don't feed the hand . . . All right. Move about. Be amused. Bitter. Beatrice: you survive the grave, unforgiven. And Mother and Father and Jimmy. If another dying made Ida bury them all again, another to love made Rosemary resurrect them all again to marry her failure to their own. There wasn't any way out. A widow? Jane was the widow, along with all the others walking around the world alive.

The doorbell rang. Rosemary turned, tears starting, and ran to open it. There, unprepared for the threat of embrace, was Agate.

"I'm sorry," she said. "You were expecting someone. . . ."

"No . . . no, I wasn't. I'm sorry. Come in," Rosemary said, catching the tears with forefinger and thumb.

"Look, no, I won't," Agate said.

"Please . . ."

It was too awkward not to.

"It was a lousy whim," Agate said, resigned.

"On the contrary," Rosemary said. "As you can see, I need distracting."

"With what, though?"

"Nearly anything would do," Rosemary said. "You're much better than I could have expected."

"A case on a Saturday?" Agate asked. "I came over to find out if you knew any way I could turn my badge in."

"Your badge?"

"Yeah. I just decided this baby's having me, and I'm tired of it. I don't want to go through with it. It's silly."

"Yes," Rosemary said. "I can see that."

"A campy sort of place," Agate said, looking around with mild surprise.

"It belonged to a man who killed himself."

"Oh."

"Actually, I like it."

"Your privilege," Agate said.

"You'd like a beer, I expect."

Agate nodded and followed Rosemary into the kitchen.

"You're nearly through the worst of it," Rosemary said.

"I bet you say that to all the girls."

"The pregnant ones," Rosemary answered with some sharpness.

"It won't take me long to drink this."

"Take your time," Rosemary said.

"I always do. But I'm not going to take much of yours. You don't look enough like a punching bag today, and that's all I wanted, really: that cool, detached character you put on for the public, making speeches about painless, guiltless, trouble-free deliveries. I've already shot the balls off Cole, and I can't really start pounding Harriet—she's read too many books. And the old lady . . ."

"A bad time for that to happen."

"Yeah."

"I don't think she ever says very much," Rosemary said. "It's just that she means it."

Agate shook her head. "She doesn't, you know. She just doesn't bitch about anything."

"Come sit out here. It's cool this time of day."

"No," Agate said. "I'm really not going to stay. I'd be worrying people."

"Just for a minute. I'll drive you back."

"What about the person you're expecting?"

"I'm really not," Rosemary said.

"Gone forever? Never to return?"

"About like that," Rosemary said.

"Well, I hope you're not pregnant."

Rosemary laughed, a breaking melody that startled her and touched Agate.

"So, while you're counting your blessings," Agate said, "why not list some of mine?"

"It really is nearly over," Rosemary said.

"If I had to go on like this forever, lumbered with this four-limbed avenger, I'd make the deal. I don't want to go through with it. I'm terrified."

"Of having the baby?"

"Yes, that. And just of it. Pointing at me in my own private REPENT poster for the rest of my unnatural life. I can't take it. How do I get out of it?"

"It won't be like that," Rosemary said. "For a while, maybe, but you'll forget. You really will. You don't have to feel guilty."

"That's just not true."

"Well, all right," Rosemary admitted. "But you'll go on to feel so many other things more important."

"Like what?"

"Like whether or not you'll pass your exams. Like whether or not you're in love. Like whether or not you really shouldn't sort things out better with your mother or father or sister or brother. Like . . ."

"I don't know. I keep getting this sense that some things, this thing, can't be forgiven. I mean, no matter what I do about it."

Rosemary covered her mouth with her hand and looked away.

"Do you know what I mean?"

"I don't accept it," Rosemary said, "that's all."

"No, I guess I don't either," Agate answered seriously, "except, maybe, I really don't want to join the club. Who needs somebody to forgive you who probably never will, whether it's possible or not?"

"The club?"

"The grown-up club. What else could *you* be crying about?"

"I don't believe in that kind of guilt," Rosemary said.

"I'm not talking about faith," Agate said, impatiently thumping her stomach. "I'm talking about fact."

"You *want* to feel guilty."

"I do not. That's what I'm saying. I want to stand right up there with the rest of them and shout, 'For Christ's sake, it's not rape or murder we're dealing with here. All I'm having is a baby.' "

"Well, go ahead and shout. Feel free."

"Thank you."

"And have another beer."

"What time is it?" Agate asked.

"Nearly five."

"Well, Harriet's cooking."

Rosemary got up and went into the kitchen: "It's not murder or having a baby we're dealing with here. All it is is a minor matter of rape, for God's sake. Join the club." Rosemary reached for the gin, hesitated, and took the ouzo instead.

Agate, in the patio, looked at the fuchsias to walk the child who would soon be restless with her heartburn.

"Thank you," she said. "I feel better."

"Good."

"Have you seen Miss A?"

"Yes."

"I haven't. I couldn't face the hospital," Agate said.

"She knows that."

"Does she?"

"Cole told her."

Agate sighed. It would have been a novelty to end just once in her life with the style of her beginnings, which, however alarming, had flair. Since she knew so well she was a coward about consequences, never could deal with them, perhaps she should learn to stop issuing open invitations. It would be a very dull life, but even that vision had its charms from this angle.

Rosemary drove Agate home, a trip that took longer than they expected because on the hill they found themselves in a line of cars behind Dina's truck, which had obviously failed the first time and was now laboring in reverse.

"In any other place," Rosemary said impatiently, "she'd be arrested."

"Can we pass?" Agate asked. "I'd like to get a look at her."

"Didn't you meet her the other day?"

"In disguise," Agate said. "Or out of disguise. I wondered which."

"She might let us by after the next light."

Dina backed around the corner to get out of the way of the traffic and then follow it up the rest of the gentler slope going forward. As she sat waiting, she saw Rosemary and Agate drive past, Rosemary concentrating on the road, Agate saluting. Dina pumped the ancient, mournful horn.

"What a rig! That's more like it," Agate said, admiring. "Come in for a drink, will you?"

"Yes, thanks, I will."

The "rig," as Rosemary arrived back at her house after a leisurely two drinks at the Larson house, was parked out in front, and Dina was sitting in it, her elbows on the wheel, her chin in her hands. Rosemary took her shaking time to park the car in the garage and comb her hair in the rear-view mirror. The saunter was too slow to accommodate her nerves and turned into a march as she approached the truck. Dina reached over and opened the door on the curb side.

"Get in," she said. "I'm taking you to Nick's for dinner."

"Why?" Rosemary asked. "For revenge?"

"Get in."

Rosemary tried to, but her skirt refused the last four inches. She pulled it impatiently well up her thighs and hoisted herself in beside Dina. They drove with that old, ill-defined silence, in Dina stubbornly bland, in Rosemary hotly embarrassed. The only concession Dina made was to say "Stay there" as she parked. Then she got out and came round to Rosemary's door, opened it and lifted her down onto the street in full view of Feller and Grace Hill, who were just arriving at Nick's for dinner themselves.

"Hello," Feller called. "Will you join us?"

If the idea displeased Dina, she gave no sign of it. And short of simulating a heart attack right there on the street, Rosemary saw no way of avoiding the Hills. The whole circumstance was outrageous, but Dina would discover that Rosemary had one sure talent: she could get through a meal with Grace Hill in a Greek dirty spoon with absolutely impervious good humor, though she would as soon kill the woman as look at her.

"It took Grace years to persuade me to try this place," Feller said. "I was a real local yokel about it, but I really did think it was just for the kids."

Rosemary, who had never been inside Nick's, was surprised at the dining room, not because it was elegant. The decor was what she could have expected, though more shamelessly elaborate, the walls painted periodically with Greek pillars and gods, represented not as they were in myth but as they had come to the Western world out of the ruins, armless, noseless, castrated statues, here offered not in white but in the very persuasive color of flesh. But comfortable in their company, creating a family atmosphere, were a number of people eating what looked like quite good food at clean, pleasantly set tables.

"Let Dina order for us," Grace suggested.

"You want a really Greek meal?" Dina asked.

They all agreed.

"I'll talk to the cook," Dina said, getting up from the table.

Both women watched her cross the room in freshly pressed chinos and an unstained sweat shirt, then turned testing eyes on each other, but Feller distracted them.

"How's Miss Larson?"

Through ouzo and hot cheese puffs, Feller and Rosemary chatted easily about the half a dozen topics the town had given them from their childhood. But by the time the meal began to arrive, Feller and Dina had settled to talk about her parking lots in financial figures which surprised and impressed Rosemary. She had known Dina was interested in real estate, but she had not realized just how involved Dina was with property.

"Feller and Peter and Dina are going to go into some sort of partnership," Grace said. "They don't talk about anything else these days. They think they can make this place possible to live in and make money at it as well."

"And you don't?"

"I wonder," Grace said. "My psychiatrist says only the natives can stand it now, raised crazy and used to it."

Rosemary smiled and saw its easing effect. She could talk with Grace about her psychiatrist, tipping the conversation into her own work if it threatened to get too personal. There was also the periodic distraction of the music, delivered with a waiter through the kitchen door with the plates and plates of very good food being brought to their table.

"Like it?" Dina asked Rosemary once.

"Very much."

"You're a little bit Greek."

"Are you going to dance for us tonight?" Grace asked.

"Yes," Dina said. "I'm going to teach Feller."

He laughed. "I've got two left feet."

"There is a dance for two left feet," Dina said.

In fact, all three got up with Dina's encouragement and in a line learned basic steps with more pleasure than skill, for they had drunk retsina all through the long meal. From other tables, people called to Dina for a solo, and at last she did dance the formal inventions that require strength and control and a sense of spatial isolation. Rosemary admired the performance but saw in it the absolute distance of Dina from anyone who threatened that space. Inviolate dancer against the pink and mutilated gods.

"Has something happened to the Volvo?" Rosemary asked after they had said good-night to the Hills and were walking over to the truck.

"No," Dina said.

"I enjoyed tonight."

Dina accepted that without comment. The stubborn energy of her jealous anger was gone as she drove Rosemary back to the house. Now that the shock of what was expected of her had worn off, the fear and need of it balanced her at dead center. She did not know what to do.

"Are you coming in?" Rosemary asked as Dina stopped the truck in front of the house.

"Shall I?" Dina asked.

"Up to you," Rosemary said, but then she felt Dina's stillness. She could never voluntarily step out of the space she had made for herself. Rosemary reached across and took Dina's hand. "Come on. Come with me."

XX

AGATE'S FIRST PAIN came in the middle of a game of Scrabble, which Harriet had introduced into the household as more challenging than gin rummy, coon hollow, or hearts. Agate saw, with that inspiration, that *o u c* would build nicely down to the *h* of *house,* Harriet's first word. As she set out the letters, both Harriet and Cole turned to her.

"*Ouch,*" Agate said, "All right?"

"Is it a real word?" Cole asked.

" 'Ouch,' " Harriet read from *The Concise Oxford,* " 'a clasp or buckle, often jeweled,' but I'm afraid it's archaic."

"I was thinking actually of an expression of pain," Agate said in academic tones. "You know, *pain*? Like in *labor pain*?"

"This game is supposed to take your mind off things like that," Cole said.

"Apparently the baby isn't sufficiently interested. Poor concentration span maybe, which doesn't bode well for the poor little bastard, does it?"

"You mean . . .?" Harriet began.

"I think I had a pain," Agate admitted, "but after this thoughtful analysis, I'm really not sure. It might have been a clasp or a buckle, jeweled."

"How long ago?" Cole demanded.

"Well . . . two minutes? Three minutes?"

"Okay," Cole said, looking at his wrist watch. "Your turn, Harriet."

"We shouldn't go on playing, should we?" Harriet asked in a tone that suggested it might be sacrilegious as well as impractical.

"It'll probably be hours," Cole said.

"Yes, Harriet, relax," Agate said. "Cole will tell us what to do when it's time."

"There isn't any point . . ." Cole began.

"Let's play Scrabble," Agate said.

The phone rang.

"I'll get it," Harriet said, for she was expecting a call from Peter.

As soon as she had left the room, Cole said, "I'll take you any time you want to go. Only the book says it's better to time them awhile."

"And Miss A says . . .?"

"She told me just not to lose my head. She said pains were sometimes indigestion."

"Did she say anything about *my* head?" Agate asked.

"She said I was to keep that, too," Cole said, grinning.

In the kitchen Harriet was reporting the possibility to Peter in answer to his first question, which was always, "How are things there?" When she had finished, Peter didn't answer at once.

"Peter?"

"I guess we'll all meet at the hospital then," he said. "I'm here now. I dropped in to see Miss Larson."

"I wouldn't wait," Harriet said. "We may be hours."

"The problem is that she's worse. I thought probably Cole . . . but he's got enough on his plate, hasn't he?"

"How much worse?"

"Nobody quite knows," Peter said. "It may be a reaction to some of the drugs; so they've stopped some of them . . . the pain-killers."

"Oh dear," Harriet said.

"Right now she isn't really rational; so there isn't any point in Cole's seeing her. I've gone ahead and asked for private nurses."

"Private nurses?"

"She's being hard to handle."

"Miss A?" Harriet asked, incredulous.

"She isn't herself."

"Poor woman."

"Yes," Peter said, a light quality in his voice that Harriet had learned to recognize as strain.

"But you aren't going to stay, are you?"

"I think somebody should," Peter said.

"Maybe I . . ."

"I don't want the kids to know," Peter said, "not now, and you'd have to tell them if you came down."

"Isn't there someone . . . Miss Setworth?"

"No," Peter said, as if he'd already considered the possibility. "I'll call her later if it seems necessary. It's eight o'clock now. I'll call you at ten . . . or sooner. If you come down with Agate before that, just phone this floor, and I'll come down."

"All right," Harriet said. "But I wish you didn't have to . . ."

"It's time I took a turn," Peter said.

"Is she . . .?"

"She's having a bad time," Peter said.

Harriet wanted to ask specific questions and hear specific answers, but she knew Peter did not want to say more than he had to, out of a negative delicacy in him that he needed to protect.

"Have you something to read?"

"Yes, darling," he answered, and she could hear the smile in his voice.

"Oh, I know, always the librarian: nothing better than a good book. . . ."

"Just don't go far from the phone unless you're on your way down with them, all right? And tell Cole to drive carefully."

"He will. Don't worry about us as well."

"All right," Peter said.

Harriet went back into the library where Agate and Cole were entertaining themselves by exchanging rudenesses.

"It's my turn, isn't it?" she asked.

❋

Apart from her mind, which needed to record rather than order in mortal lunacy, Amelia's body struggled against hell or a vicious mistake. The pain was not like the old companion from which there were a thousand distractions but insisted instead on absolute occupancy. It was taking her to the grave, and she could not go, not if the pain was there, timeless, unendurable. Not possible. A mistake. But no, not a mistake. They were trying to hold her down, trying to make her lie back. She would not. She could not be laid out in this agony, buried in it, a depth of earth against her suffering.

"No! No!"

Accept it, Aunt Setworth said, putrid with horror. Accept it, her father also. The leg, the pain, the hard poem, death. Climb a tree, fly. Not possible.

"I have to!"

The arms of the dead, restraining, pulling her down, down into pain, to bear it, to die with it.

"NO!"

But they were stronger: Father, Mother, Aunt Setworth. She was exhausted. There was no way to give in or to bear it, no self left, simply pain.

"Help me," she whispered. "Sister?"

Sister was a handsome, green-eyed man with brutal hands, crying.

❋

"Give her something strong enough," Peter said to the doctor, standing out in the corridor. "Never mind whether it kills her or not."

"We're doing everything we can," the doctor said.

"You've got to do more."

"She's a very strong-willed old woman," the doctor said.

"She's a human being in pain," Peter said.

"Thresholds are different," the doctor said. "I think she'll rest a bit better now."

Peter turned away and went back into the room where a nurse already stood by the bed. Amelia Larson was for the moment quiet, but she was not resting. She lay rigid with strain, her eyes blind with hostility.

"If only she'd give in to it," the nurse said quietly.

"She can't," Peter said.

Though he knew she must be still, he would almost rather have her struggling than lying like this. Sometimes when he was helping to restrain her, his hands ached with murderous love, and in those moments he knew he could kill her if he had to. Quiet, that insane comfort did not come to him. There was only emasculating pity.

"The doctor did give her something."

Peter nodded.

"You're not her son?"

It was the second time the nurse had asked that question. Peter simply shook his head. He would not say, to explain, that Amelia Larson had been more a mother to him than his own. She had simply trusted and liked him, leaving him no need to wish for any definition of relationship. He was not here now because she had no son. He was not even here because Cole was dealing with Agate. He was here because he loved Amelia Larson as he had not wanted to love anyone.

"She is quieter," the nurse said. "Why don't you get some coffee?"

"Yes, all right."

As Peter stood at the dispenser in the corridor, he looked at his watch. Five minutes to ten. He should call Harriet. Had he another dime?

"There you are," Harriet said, hurrying toward him.

"Have you brought Agate down?"

"Yes," Harriet said. "Cole thought it was too early, but we were all so edgy it seemed better to come along."

"You didn't tell them," Peter said.

"No. How is she?"

"They've just given her something, but I don't know that it's enough."

"You're soaking wet!"

"Yes, well, she's strong."

"Have you had to . . . ?"

"Sometimes."

"Should I go in?"

"Wait a minute," Peter said. "Have some coffee with me first."

They took their paper cups to the waiting room at the end of the corridor.

"Is she dying, Peter?"

"I guess so," Peter said. "The doctor won't commit himself, but he isn't reassuring at all, either."

"Then shouldn't Cole . . . ?"

"I don't know. She isn't recognizing anyone at the moment. He couldn't do anything for her. I don't know."

"Just yesterday, she seemed so . . . steady," Harriet said.

"She's worn out her defenses."

They sat, not saying anything more, until they had finished

their coffee. Then they walked back down the corridor to Amelia's room. She lay, still rigid in the bed, her eyes closed.

"Is she . . . asleep?" Harriet asked softly.

"I don't think so," the nurse said. "But I wouldn't disturb her."

"No," Harriet said.

She stood, looking down at the bloated old face where there was nothing to be read. There never had been, really. You always waited for a gesture or a statement from Amelia Larson, trusting what it would be, from a sure history of experience. Though Harriet understood that she must not call to Miss A, she wanted to. She longed for the ordinary reassurance that had always been there, the easy, accepting love. She moved closer, hoping those eyes would open, would recognize, would understand that she was there, if only for a moment.

"Get out!" Amelia said suddenly, her voice strained but strong.

"Miss A, it's Harriet."

"You got your furniture. Get out!"

Peter took hold of Harriet's shoulders and moved her away from the bed, just as Amelia gestured violently at the space in which Harriet had stood. The nurse moved forward, ready to restrain her, but she did not move or speak again.

"She doesn't know who you are," Peter said quietly. "She doesn't even know that you're here."

"Yes, she does," Harriet said. "She knows."

✳

Cole sat in the maternity waiting room in the chair by the door, waiting to be told that he could go in to see Agate. There were two other men with him who had asked, at once, if this was his first. He shook his head in denial and quickly picked up a magazine. He gathered one was the brother of the other. They could keep each other company. Once Agate was settled, he would stay with her and let Harriet cope with questions less embarrassing to her.

A nurse looked into the room, smiled at Cole, and said, "You can go down to see her now if you'd like."

"Thank you."

It seemed to him extraordinary that only a few months ago, when he drove Kathy to the hospital, he could not have forced himself to take the walk he was now impatient for. But he had not really known Kathy, nor had he known anything about the process of birth, about which he was now so well informed that he irritated Agate with reassuring information. But he did feel confident for her. She was physically strong, and she was built for bearing children. Her fright was like the stage fright of a good actress, real enough before the performance but used up in skill when the time came.

At the door of the labor room Cole hesitated for a moment, unsure of what to do because there were several beds, curtained off. He did not know where Agate was.

"I think you have everything you need," he heard a nurse say behind the nearest curtain.

"Except a bottle of beer."

Cole grinned, stepped forward, and held the curtain back for the nurse who was leaving.

"Hi."

"You've come without a belt," Agate said.

"A belt?" Cole asked, looking down at his waist.

"You're no good to me without a belt. I'm supposed to pull on it. Haven't you read any of the good, old novels?"

The woman in the next bed grunted. Cole forced himself not to swallow. Having a baby was good, hard work, like climbing a mountain. Nobody wanted to vomit at the sound of a grunting mountain climber.

"You don't really think you're going to stay in here," Agate said.

"I don't know why not."

"It's like hiding out in the ladies' toilet. You're past that age."

"It's better than the men's smoker," Cole said cheerfully. "Where's Harriet?"

"Gone to see Cousin A."

"At this time of night?"

"She won't stay," Cole said. "She just wanted to check."

"I guess I wouldn't really rather have a broken hip," Agate decided. "Though I suppose, with luck, I might manage both."

"More likely to break the doctor's," Cole said.

Agate caught her breath sharply and was quiet. Cole reached out for her hand, but she pulled it away. In a moment she relaxed.

"I promise to scream really loud every time," she said. "You'll hear me. You won't miss a thing. Now get out."

"I'd rather . . ."

"Get out," Agate said.

Cole got up. He wanted to make some gesture, lean over and kiss Agate, perhaps. At least take her hand, but she didn't want anything like that.

"I'll check back in a while," he said.

Cole really did not want to go back into the waiting room, but Harriet might be there by now, and, if she was, she'd be some protecting company. Instead of Harriet, Peter Fallidon confronted Cole.

"How is she?" Peter asked at once.

"All right," Cole said. "I think she wants to be on her own to get on with it."

"Why don't we go out for some air then?"

"Where's Harriet?"

"With Miss Larson."

"We'd better wait for her, hadn't we?" Cole asked. The last thing in the world he wanted was a walk with Peter.

"She'll know where we are."

There was an embarrassing silence between them as they rode down together alone in the elevator, but Cole was growing angry as well. Why did he always have to be a victim of other people's suggestions? He didn't want to be this far away from Agate even for a few minutes, and under such circumstances it seemed to him inexcusable of Peter to force him into a private chat. But short of simply refusing to get out of the elevator, he had no choice but to go along.

Out in the parking lot, Peter offered Cole a cigarette.

"No thanks."

"Have you quit?"

"No," Cole said. "I just put one out."

"Cole, this is a tough night to . . ."

"I don't want to hear anything about it," Cole said suddenly. "It's none of my business. I told Harriet you didn't have anything to explain to me, and you don't."

Peter felt his temper flare and fought with it silently.

"I mean it," Cole added weakly.

"No, you don't mean it," Peter said. "You'd rather keep your sordid speculations than have to deal with any sort of truth. But you should have figured out by now that I wasn't going to trouble you. I've been wanting simply to thank you for belting Grace Hill. The thought of it made it easier for me to be nice to her when I had to. It's made it easier for me to be patient with you, too, though you could use a good belt yourself."

"You're not marrying Harriet because you love her," Cole shouted. "You're marrying her . . ."

Peter hit him, then immediately held him by the shoulders and said, "I'm sorry, Cole. I'm sorry."

The boy stood, dazed for a moment. Then he said, "I asked for it. I'm sorry, too," and he turned back toward the hospital, walking first and then beginning to run.

Peter did not try to follow him. His muscles already ached with the strain of holding the old woman, as his hand ached from hitting Cole. He was supposed to have told the boy . . . Peter stopped outside the building and looked up, a child outside his first school, which he'd been terrified to enter, having no idea what he would be asked to learn. He was old now to be walking up the steps of his emotional nursery school, but he did understand what was expected of him, and, tired and ashamed as he was, he was willing to learn.

✳

"They've given her another shot," Harriet explained. "They had to. There's no choice now but to keep her in a light coma."

Peter nodded.

"Did you tell Cole?"

"No, I didn't."

"It's probably better. Why should he have seen her like that?"

Peter wanted to say he had tried to break Cole's jaw instead, but it was not the kind of confession that served any purpose. He knew Cole would not say anything.

"How's Agate?"

"Getting on with it," Peter said.

"Should one of us go down?"

"You go," Peter said. "I'll wait here."

They stood together for a moment, a worn-looking, middle-aged couple, inadequate to the birth and death taking place, not even simply related to it or to each other, there by frail choice.

✳

As Cole ran down the long corridors, dodging nurses and hospital equipment, he felt his jaw begin to ache, but it was relieving a pain so much more serious that he was nearly grateful for it.

216

He passed the maternity waiting room and went on down into the labor room. Agate's bed was empty.

"She's gone in," the nurse said.

"So soon?"

"It won't be long now. She didn't leave much time."

"I wanted to see her. I . . . ."

"She's just fine," the nurse said. "She isn't going to have any trouble at all."

Behind another curtain, Cole heard a nurse say in an impatient voice, "Bear down! Bear down!"

Bear up, surely? Bear with. Cole walked back down to the waiting room to face the brothers.

"She gone in already?" one of them asked.

Cole nodded.

"You're going to be home free tonight."

Cole turned away. It was literally true, for, without Agate there, Harriet had no reason to come back. He did not like the idea of that empty house. He had been alone in it only one other night, the night Kathy had had her baby. Where was Harriet? A long time to be with Cousin A. Probably Peter had gone to be with her.

"Mr. Westaway?"

He turned to the nurse in the doorway.

"The young lady wanted me to tell you, it's a boy."

"Is she all right?"

"Just fine."

"And the baby? Is he . . .?"

"Perfect."

"Can I see her?"

"For a minute."

Agate was being wheeled down to the elevator on a table, but she was propped up on her elbow, and she waved as she saw him.

"Okay?" he called.

"Nothing to it," she called back.

He was walking beside her now, holding her hand, looking down into her sun-yellow eyes, amazed by her happiness, proud of her as she was of herself.

"Go wake up Miss A, will you? Tell her. And tell her the baby's all right."

Cole nodded and smiled.

"And phone Rosemary, too," Agate added, some forced sturdiness coming into her voice.

"I will."

"And come see me once or twice with some beer."

"Sure."

She was wheeled into the elevator, and the doors closed. Somewhere nearby Cole heard the small, outraged cry of a new baby. Agate's? Someone else's. He turned and saw Harriet standing down the corridor waiting for him.

"A boy," Cole said. "They're both fine. You know, we very nearly didn't get her here on time. She wouldn't do anything by the book, would she?"

"Better," Harriet said, smiling.

"She wants me to wake Cousin A, but it's . . ." he looked at his watch, "after eleven. She is asleep by now, isn't she?"

"Cole, she's worse."

Cole looked at Harriet, the strain of sorrow clear on her face, and he wanted to say, "Don't tell me. I don't want to know," but his jaw already smarted with that cowardice.

"Peter's with her now. He's been with her all evening."

"How much worse?"

"She isn't conscious. She's dying."

Cole shook his head.

"I'm so sorry," Harriet said, offering a shy hand to him.

He took it and turned it gracefully into the crook of his arm, to support her and to be reassured that he could take this walk, too, since it was required of him.

Publications of
THE NAIAD PRESS, INC.
P.O. Box 10543 • Tallahassee, Florida 32302
Mail orders welcome. Please include 15% postage.

Daughters of a Coral Dawn by Katherine V. Forrest. Science fiction.
208 pp. ISBN 0-930044-50-9 $7.95

The Price of Salt by Claire Morgan. A novel. 288 pp.
ISBN 0-930044-49-5 $7.95

Against the Season by Jane Rule. A novel. 224 pp.
ISBN 0-930044-48-7 $7.95

Lovers in the Present Afternoon by Kathleen Fleming. A novel. 384 pp.
ISBN 0-930044-46-0 $8.50

Toothpick House by Lee Lynch. A novel. 264 pp.
ISBN 0-930044-45-2 $7.95

Madame Aurora Sarah Aldridge. A novel. 256 pp.
ISBN 0-930044-44-4 $7.95

Curious Wine by Katherine V. Forrest. A novel. 176 pp.
ISBN 0-930044-43-6 $7.50

Black Lesbian in White America. Short stories, essays,
autobiography. 144 pp. ISBN 0-930044-41-X $7.50

Contract with the World by Jane Rule. A novel. 340 pp.
ISBN 0-930044-28-2 $7.95

Yantras of Womanlove by Tee A. Corinne. Photographs. 64 pp.
ISBN 0-930044-30-4 $6.95

Mrs. Porter's Letter by Vicki P. McConnell. A mystery novel.
224 pp. ISBN 0-930044-29-0 $6.95

To the Cleveland Station by Carol Anne Douglas. A novel.
192 pp. ISBN 0-930044-27-4 $6.95

The Nesting Place by Sarah Aldridge. A novel. 224 pp.
ISBN 0-930044-26-6 $6.95

This Is Not for You by Jane Rule. A novel. 284 pp.
ISBN 0-930044-25-8 $7.95

Faultline by Sheila Ortiz Taylor. A novel. 140 pp.
ISBN 0-930044-24-X $6.95

The Lesbian in Literature by Barbara Grier. 3d ed.
Foreword by Maida Tilchen. A comprehensive bibliography.
240 pp. ISBN 0-930044-23-1   ind. $7.95
                                                             inst. $10.00

Anna's Country by Elizabeth Lang. A novel. 208 pp.
ISBN 0-930044-19-3 $6.95

Lesbian Writer: Collected Work of Claudia Scott
edited by Frances Hanckel and Susan Windle. Poetry. 128 pp.
ISBN 0-930044-22-3 $4.50

Prism by Valerie Taylor. A novel. 158 pp.
ISBN 0-930044-18-5 $6.95

Black Lesbians: An Annotated Bibliography compiled by
J.R. Roberts. Foreword by Barbara Smith. 112 pp.
ISBN 0-930044-21-5 ind. $5.95
inst. $8.00

The Marquise and the Novice by Victoria Ramstetter.
A novel. 108 pp. ISBN 0-930044-16-9 $4.95

Labiaflowers by Tee A. Corinne. 40 pp.
ISBN 0-930044-20-7 $3.95

Outlander by Jane Rule. Short stories, essays. 207 pp.
ISBN 0-930044-17-7 $6.95

Sapphistry: The Book of Lesbian Sexuality by Pat Califia.
2nd edition, revised. 195 pp. ISBN 0-930044-47-9 $7.95

The Black and White of It by Ann Allen Shockley.
Short stories. 112 pp. ISBN 0-930044-15-0 $5.95

All True Lovers by Sarah Aldridge. A novel. 292 pp.
ISBN 0-930044-10-X $6.95

The Muse of the Violets by Renee Vivien. Poetry. 84 pp.
ISBN 0-930044-07-X $4.00

A Woman Appeared to Me by Renee Vivien. Translated by
Jeannette H. Foster. A novel. xxxi, 65 pp.
ISBN 0-930044-06-1 $5.00

Cytherea's Breath by Sarah Aldridge. A novel. 240 pp.
ISBN 0-930044-02-9 $6.95

Tottie by Sarah Aldridge. A novel. 181 pp.
ISBN 0-930044-01-0 $5.95

The Latecomer by Sarah Aldridge. A novel. 107 pp.
ISBN 0-930044-00-2 $5.00

VOLUTE BOOKS

Journey to Fulfillment	by Valerie Taylor	$3.95
A World without Men	by Valerie Taylor	$3.95
Return to Lesbos	by Valerie Taylor	$3.95
Desert of the Heart	by Jane Rule	$3.95
Odd Girl Out	by Ann Bannon	$3.95
I Am a Woman	by Ann Bannon	$3.95
Women in the Shadows	by Ann Bannon	$3.95
Journey to a Woman	by Ann Bannon	$3.95
Beebo Brinker	by Ann Bannon	$3.95

Naiad Press, Inc. and its imprint Volute Books (inexpensive mass market paper-backs appear in Volute Books) may always be purchased by mail as well as in your local bookstores.